MARRIAGE AND MODERNIZATION

RELIGION, MARRIAGE, AND FAMILY

Series Editors

Don S. Browning
David Clairmont

MARRIAGE AND MODERNIZATION

*How Globalization Threatens Marriage
and What to Do about It*

Don S. Browning

WILLIAM B. EERDMANS PUBLISHING COMPANY
GRAND RAPIDS, MICHIGAN / CAMBRIDGE, U.K.

Wm. B. Eerdmans Publishing Co.
255 Jefferson Ave. S.E., Grand Rapids, Michigan 49503 /
P.O. Box 163, Cambridge CB3 9PU U.K.

Printed in the United States of America

08 07 06 05 04 03   7 6 5 4 3 2 1

Library of Congress Cataloging-in-Publication Data

Browning, Don S.
Marriage and modernization : How globalization threatens marriage
and what to do about it / Don S. Browning
p.   cm. — (Religion, marriage, and family series)
"The core of this book consists of the Cadbury lectures . . .
at the University of Birmingham, England during the autumn of 1998.
The title of these lectures was 'Globalization and the Family'" — Pref.
Includes bibliographical references and index.
Contents: The world situation of families : marriage reformation
as a cultural work — From West to East : modernization and family
in the U.S. and South Korea — Christianity and the Western family —
Marriage and the male problematic in Aquinas and Luther —
Nature and creation : evolutionary psychology and the family —
A practical theology of families — Feminism, family, and global trends —
Cultural, social, and educational strategies — World Family strategies.
ISBN 0-8028-1112-4 (pbk.: alk. paper)
1. Marriage — Cross-cultural studies. 2. Family — Cross-cultural studies.
3. Civilization, Modern. 4. Globalization — Social aspects. 5. Social change.
6. Family — Religious aspects — Christianity. 7. Family policy. I. Title. II. Series.
HQ728.B747   2003
306.81 — dc21
2003044356

www.eerdmans.com

Contents

Series Foreword

The Religion, Marriage, and Family series evolves out of a research project located at the University of Chicago and financed by a generous grant from the Division of Religion of the Lilly Endowment, Inc. The first phase of the project lasted from 1991 to 1997 and produced eleven books on religion and family. In late 1997, the Lilly Endowment gave the project an additional major grant that supports a second phase of research and publication. The books in the Eerdmans Religion, Marriage, and Family series come directly or indirectly from the initiatives of this second phase.

In some cases, the books will evolve directly out of the University of Chicago project. In other cases, they will be books written in response to that project or in some way stimulated by it. In all cases, they will be books probing the depth of resources in Judaism and Christianity for understanding, renewing, and in some respects redefining current expressions of marriage and family. The series will investigate issues of parenthood and children, work and family, responsible fatherhood, and equality in the family; the responsibility of the major professions in promoting and protecting sound marriages and families; the biblical, theological, philosophical, and legal grounds of Western family systems; selected classics of these traditions; and the respective roles of church, market, and state in supporting marriages, families, parents, and children.

The Religion, Marriage, and Family series intends to go beyond the sentimentality, political manipulation, and ungrounded assertions that characterize so much of the contemporary debate over marriage and family. It plans to develop an intelligent and accessible new literature for colleges and seminaries, churches and other religious institutions, questing individuals and families. Marriage and family issues are not just preoccupations of the United States; they have become worldwide concerns as modernization, globalization, changing values, emerging poverty, and changing gender roles disrupt traditional families and challenge the very idea of marriage throughout the world. It has been predicted that the emerging marriage and family crisis will be the central issue of the twenty-first century. The Religion, Marriage, and Family series hopes to contribute to more balanced and well-informed public debate on this issue, both in the United States and around the globe.

Marriage and Modernization hopes to start a new international dialogue about the meaning of marriage. This may sound strange to the ears of many people. Marriage is not a popular topic. It is often referred to as the "M" word, almost in the same category as other dirty words. Of course, it is not a dirty word, but it is a word that makes people uncomfortable as a topic of serious conversation. Yet it is time to get beyond this sensibility of reluctance.

This book claims that marriage is a big-time issue; it is in the same category as racial injustice, poverty, hunger, AIDS, health, and even war. Why? Because the status, meaning, control, dissolution, and deinstitutionalization of marriage can be strangely associated with all these other problems and issues. This book tries to explain why this is so. It also investigates a variety of solutions to the marriage problem. To save marriage, the meaning and nature of marriage must be reconstructed — reformed. This is a multidimensional task, a complex work of culture.

DON S. BROWNING and DAVID CLAIRMONT
series editors

Preface

The core of this book consists of the Cadbury Lectures that I gave at the University of Birmingham, England, during the autumn of 1998. The title of these lectures was "Globalization and the Family." Because the theme of marriage eventually became so central to these lectures, I finally decided to name this book *Marriage and Modernization.*[1] The immensity of this topic and the emergence of unexpected responsibilities, opportunities, and historical events have conspired to postpone their final revision and publication until now.

The thesis of the Cadbury Lectures, however, is maintained and developed in this book. It goes like this: the processes of modernization and globalization, in spite of their promise for more wealth and health for many people, are also a threat to the institution of marriage. Just as these forces seem to be dividing the world between rich and poor, haves and have nots, they also are separating the world into the married and unmarried, i.e., families that are relatively cohesive and those that are disrupted. Recent research is showing that marital disruption itself contributes to poverty for women and children throughout the world. The growing gap between the rich and poor is due to unequal economic opportunities and unequal distribution of wealth; but independent of these two factors, yet in interaction with them, this divide also is caused by marital and family

---

1. My good friend Adrian Thatcher wrote an important book titled *Marriage after Modernity* (Albany: State University of New York Press, 1999). Although the titles of our books are parallel, the arguments differ considerably, especially with regard to my belief in the reality of the ongoing processes of modernization and the dialectical relation between modernization and globalization.

ix

strains of various kinds.[2] Or, to say it differently, modernization and globalization contribute to this gap in multiple ways, one of which is their disruptive effect on marriage and family. *The cure for this situation, however, does not mean protecting marriage and family at any cost; it entails reforming and reconstructing these institutions while also nurturing a wide range of other social supports and transformations. World marriage revival and reform require a complex cultural work.*

One reason for the delay in the publication of this book was two fruitful trips to South Africa. This experience thrust me more deeply into reflections about families in the sub-Saharan countries of that great continent. Another reason was the unexpected, but important, invitation from the American Assembly of Columbia University to co-author the background book for their late September 2000 assembly, which brought diverse Americans together to create a consensus on major issues facing families in the United States. A third reason was the invitation to spend the 2001-2002 academic year at the Center for the Interdisciplinary Study of Religion in the School of Law at Emory University. There my assignment was to help legal historian John Witte with an ambitious faculty seminar designed to study sex, marriage, and family in the Abrahamic religions — Judaism, Christianity, and Islam. Conversations with scholars of these three religions, as well as with specialists in sociology, the health sciences, law, and the humanities, promised to help me find my way with a bit more security into the challenging subject of this book. I wanted to have this experience before finishing the manuscript.

The book for the American Assembly was written with Gloria Rodriguez and published, along with the consensus statement achieved by nearly sixty Americans invited to the assembly, under the title *Reweaving the Social Tapestry: Toward a Public Philosophy and Policy for Families* (2002).[3] Writing the book for the American Assembly gave me opportunity to think about why marriage and family are not issues solely for the expertise, deliberation, and guidance of the social sciences or government policy wonks. Religious traditions must be involved, even in public philosophy and public-policy decisions. Furthermore, I began to realize that as important as Christianity has been in influencing marriage and family patterns in Western nations, in the future it must cooperate with other religious faiths

2. For documentation of this in the U.S., see James Q. Wilson, *The Marriage Problem* (New York: HarperCollins, 2002). For discussion of this phenomenon in England, see "British society's divide growing," *The New York Times*, May 6, 2002, p. A10.

3. Don Browning and Gloria Rodriguez, *Reweaving the Social Tapestry: Toward a Public Philosophy and Policy for Families* (New York: W. W. Norton, 2002).

in shaping the marriage culture of these societies, and to varying degrees, the marriage cultures of other societies around the world. Muslims, Christians, Jews, American Indians, and professionals from business, social work, law, medicine, psychotherapy, and the military attended a long-weekend assembly held at the Crown Center in Kansas City, Missouri. The political and cultural spectrum, from conservative to liberal, cut through all the groups, parties, and factions participating in this conference. Christians had their opportunity to speak, but it was necessary to moderate what they had to say not only for the wide diversity of Christians there but also for secularists, skeptics, and those from different faith traditions. This experience all the more convinced me that family issues must be addressed through a variety of strategies, not the least of which should be a new look at marriage with the potential contributions in mind of all the major religious faiths. Increasingly, I came to think of the task of reviving and re-forming marriage as a complex cultural work requiring the contributions of many faiths, many philosophies, many disciplines, and many sectors of society. That was the theme of the original Cadbury Lectures and of *Reweaving the Social Tapestry,* and it has been greatly expanded, illustrated, and documented in *Marriage and Modernization.*

My experience at the Center for the Interdisciplinary Study of Religion at Emory University confirmed my confidence in this thesis. My dialogues with this amazing group of scholars deepened my conviction that the reconstruction of marriage is a complex cultural work and one worth pursuing. This goal is indeed idealistic, but ideas and ideals are still what move the world. The book that you are about to read does not accomplish the task of fully outlining what should go into this cultural work. It certainly does not give full attention to all the major religions on marriage and family issues. Its angle of vision is primarily Christian — with the other religions only lightly, but I hope suggestively, brought into the conversation. But it does try to put the programmatic of a grand new interfaith dialogue on marriage and family onto the religious, cultural, and intellectual agenda of thoughtful people. This book is designed to show why such a topic is respectable, possible, and urgent.

But taking on the full subject of marriage in the global context is a very large order, one that goes beyond the competence of any one author. It must be pursued through the contributions of many people in a variety of contexts. It is deflating, I admit, to suggest that this book is primarily an argument about the seriousness of its subject matter. It may be disappointing to hear me say that the topic is too large to be addressed successfully at this early date. It probably seems overly timid simply to invite others to join in its study. However, against the background of the widespread cultural assumption, especially in Western societies, that marriage is no longer important and certainly has little to contribute to the grand topics of inequality, poverty, disease, and ignorance, the simple act of placing marriage on the cultural agenda may not be as weak-kneed and flabby as it might first appear.

Since I first gave the core of this book for the Cadbury Lectures, the events of September 11, 2001, have occurred. These attacks are rightly viewed as acts of political terrorism. Though perpetrated by Islamic fundamentalists, they are correctly seen as deeds completely inconsistent with classic and authentic Islam. The most powerful interpretations of the reasons behind the attacks go something like this: Islam is a religion that believes there should be an organic relation between religion and the state. Although many Islamic countries have secular governments, they also try to be attentive to the directives of the Qur'an in creating the laws that govern their state. Islamic fundamentalists are unhappy with even the slightest separation of the state apparatus from Islamic guidance. In the mind of Islamic fundamentalists it is the United States, with its official separation of church and state, that constitutes the arch example of secularism and godless atheism. It is mainly for this reason that the United States must be attacked, even obliterated, as the world's most dangerous threat to the rule of God (Allah) over the affairs of humans.

As true as this view may be, within and behind this political interpretation of the conflict symbolized by September 11, discord over competing marriage and family customs, patterns, and ethics also is visible. In almost all Islamic states, family law is still under the control of the body of Islamic law called the Shari'a.[4] Shari'a is thought to have its ground in the Qur'an. It is the responsibility of Islamic jurists, not the secular state, to interpret and administer Shari'a. For this reason, the supervision, guidance, and control of marriage and family are thought to be the last bastion of authority for Islam. Give this up and the power of Islamic guidance and control over traditionally Islamic societies may collapse altogether.

The secularizing and modernizing forces emanating from the West, especially countries such as the United States, are thought by many Muslims to threaten even Shari'a family law, this once-secure bastion of Islamic law and rule. Muslim extremists are so alarmed that they believe violence

---

4. For reviews of the relation of Shari'a to family law in most Islamic countries, see Devin J. Stewart, *Islamic Legal Orthodoxy* (Salt Lake City: University of Utah Press, 1998).

against the major source of this threat — the U.S. and other Western societies — is justified. Indeed, the processes of modernization *are* disconcerting forces that eat away at traditional family practices throughout the world. And indeed, Western entanglements with the forces of modernization bring a special twist to modernity's threat to traditional marriage and family patterns. But the United States is only partially implicated in this strange connection between modernization and family disruption. The roots of the problem go much deeper than the short history of this country.

Furthermore, the forces of modernization have been complicated by what many call globalization. However, extremists around the world — who would like to eliminate Western democratic polity and Western patterns of sexuality, marriage, and family — have a faulty view of globalization. The processes of globalization, rather than making the world over into the image of the U.S., may instead be producing a whole new cultural and political world synthesis. Things Western, things Christian, and things democratic may contribute to this synthesis, but they will not be the only voice.

What Christianity might have to contribute to this emerging new dialogue is the more limited subject matter of this book. The questions of this book are twofold: How should Christianity respond to the forces of modernization and globalization as they affect marriage and family issues? And, in addition, how should Christianity begin to relate to other faiths as they respond to these same forces?

Many people are the objects of my gratitude. I must first thank Professor Dennis Turner, who chaired the Department of Religion at the University of Birmingham at the time of my Cadbury Lectures and who graciously hosted my wife and me during the three-week period that we stayed in England. I also wish to thank Professor Emmanuel Lartey, who at that time was Professor of Practical Theology there and who doubtless was instrumental in extending to me the invitation to give these lectures. Since 1991, I have received a variety of grants from the Division of Religion of the Lilly Endowment, Inc. for support of the Religion, Culture, and Family Project that I have directed. I want to thank Craig Dykstra, Vice President of the Endowment, for his wise and helpful support of this project. Everything I have written, edited, or even thought on the subject of religion, family, and marriage for more than a decade is due to the wisdom and generosity of Craig and the Endowment. This includes the present book. These people must not be held responsible for my errors, but they should get credit for the inspiration and resources that made possible the writing of this book.

I must also thank the wonderful staff of the Religion, Culture, and Family Project. Kelly Brotzman was my research assistant during much of the preparation of this manuscript and checked out countless books, articles, and reports that are quoted on these pages. John Wall, David Clairmont, Melanie O'Hara, and Josh Heikkila also helped in various ways and deserve my gratitude. And Christian Green brought her sharp and careful eye to the task of preparing the index. My appreciation goes out to each of you.

The seeds of Chapter Two were originally jointly delivered in 1997 as a lecture in Seoul, Korea, with Professor Bonnie Miller-McLemore of the Divinity School of Vanderbilt University. Since that time, the chapter has gone through several revisions and extensions and changed to the point that it is better to no longer hold her responsible for its present form. I greatly appreciate her kindness in allowing me to publish the amended version in this book.

A very special word of thanks must go to Professor John Witte of the Center for the Interdisciplinary Study of Religion in the School of Law at Emory University. John, who is one of the brightest and best persons I have ever known, also is one of the most generous. He was generous to invite me to be a Woodruff Visiting Professor at the Center for the 2001-2002 academic year. He also was generous in encouraging me, among my other duties, to lay aside time to finish this book. The conversations that occurred at the Center during the fateful autumn of 2001 and the following months provided the best possible context for the first probes into an international discussion about marriage that this book hopes to initiate. Thanks as well should go to the "dream team" of the Center — Eliza Ellison, Amy Wheeler, Anita Mann, and April Bogle — for their unfailing warmth, good cheer, and helpfulness.

And finally, Carol Browning — my wife — could justifiably be listed as co-author. We discuss the ideas in this volume constantly. She dutifully sat through the entire Cadbury Lecture series, giving me feedback at every stage. And she performs the crucial service of providing a news-clipping service that assembles family-related reports from newspapers wherever our travels take us and neatly organizes them in ever-expanding numbers of file-cabinet drawers. Fortunately, she does not do this out of a sense of obligation; she does it because she loves people and the families who nurture them.

Chapter One

The World Situation of Families:
Marriage Reformation as a Cultural Work

Over the last several decades, there has been a momentous debate sweeping across the world over the present health and future prospects of families. This debate has been especially intense in the United States, but during recent trips to Australia, South Korea, England, and South Africa, I learned that these countries have conflicts analogous to those in the United States.

These debates are about real issues. There are powerful trends affecting both advanced and underdeveloped countries that are changing families and undermining their ability to perform customary tasks. These trends are often called the forces of modernization. Of course, theories of modernization are now being extended by theories of globalization. However one refers to them — and they are distinguishable — these processes are having disruptive consequences on families in all corners of the earth. Older industrial countries have the wealth to cushion the blows of this disruption, but family upset throws economically fragile countries deeper into poverty. There are many sources of poverty in the world; family decline is one of them.

Of course, there are other sources of family disruption besides the forces of modernization and globalization. Wars, oppression, racial discrimination, and conflicts between cultures and religions are additional factors. The family disruptions of Bosnia and Afghanistan are fresh on our minds. Before that, there were the sad family tragedies of Vietnam, Cambodia, and apartheid South Africa. But this book is mainly about modernization and globalization as such. From time to time, however, we will see how these forces interact with political oppression, conflicts between racial and ethnic groups, and collisions between alternative cultural and religious ways of life. There is no way to avoid the observation that a significant subtext of the world struggle between Western democracies and the new terrorism is the perceived conflict between modernity and certain family patterns in Islam and other religions that modernization is thought to threaten. This includes traditional privileges of men and women, their roles in and out of the home, their respective responsibilities to children, and the place of children in family and society.

Most social scientists now acknowledge that modernization, independent of factors such as wars and famine, can by itself be disruptive to families in certain ways. But many distinguished sociologists believe there is little that can be done to allay these negative consequences. The social forces producing them, they believe, are simply too deep and powerful to be stopped or changed. I do not share this view. I argue that much can be done, but only if we understand the task as a complex cultural work — one that is like weaving a richly designed tapestry containing many threads. The threads needed for this cultural task are religious, political, legal, economic, and psychological. No one perspective can accomplish alone what needs to be done. In addition, this cultural work must be worldwide in scope. Finally, because there is an inevitable religious dimension to this cultural task, I see it as a work of practical theology conceived as an international ecumenical endeavor. At least from the perspective of what the Christian churches and their theological disciplines can contribute, the field of practical theology may have the most to offer to this complex cultural work.

Central to this practical-theological work is the worldwide revival and reconstruction of marriage. Admittedly, this is a big idea. Some people will call it grandiose, perhaps hallucinatory. And, of course, I do not envision this renewal and reconstruction happening tomorrow. My point, rather, is this: the world disruption of families cannot be addressed solely with policies emphasizing jobs, education, and the economic liberation of women — the favorite strategies of the United Nations, the World Council of Churches, and other international agencies. It is true that such strategies are essential, but more is needed. Without this "more," economic and development strategies can go awry. This additional emphasis should entail a culturally sensitive reconstruction of marriage and the roles that males and females play in this institution. *I am calling for a new international practical-religious dialogue (indeed, practical-theological dialogue) between the major world religions designed to place the matter of marriage before the world community.* Later in this book, I will outline a method for conducting this dialogue in a manner that preserves the core identities of various world traditions yet also effects real reconstruction. This book will not, however, conduct this full practical conversation, but it will investigate and illustrate its possibility. The actual dialogue itself requires other real voices speaking about and for the other religions. I have assigned myself the task of giving voice to the possible contribution of Christianity. Even then, it will be primarily a Christianity viewed from the eye of liberal Protestantism.

A Brief Definition of Practical Theology

Since I am taking a practical-theological perspective on these world family transformations, I need to give some hint as to how I envision that discipline. Practical theology, as I view it, begins theological reflection with concrete questions in social and cultural life — questions that confront both church and society. Practical theology acknowledges that the very task of defining such issues and questions is itself a major intellectual undertaking. To define a major social issue, practical theology first views it from the angle of the grand themes of the Christian faith such as creation, the fall, redemption, and sanctification. But it also should employ the social sciences in a subordinate way to refine its grasp of empirical facts and trends that shape the issue at hand. After a preliminary definition of the issue is achieved through careful description, practical theology should then bring the issue into a more historically critical dialogue with the central themes — the classics, as Hans-Georg Gadamer would call them[1] — of the Christian faith. It tries to retrieve these symbols in search of orientations and answers to the practical issue at hand. The question then becomes: Do we really understand these symbols and what they imply for our preliminary problem? And is what they imply actually true and useful?

This is an exercise in what the philosophers Hans-Georg Gadamer and Paul Ricoeur call understanding or *verstehen* — a concept that I will explain more fully during the course of this book.[2] Let me say this now: the exercise of understanding should be conceived of as practical through and through. As Gadamer has said, a concern with "application" informs

1. Hans-Georg Gadamer, *Truth and Method* (New York: Crossroad, 1982), pp. 173, 331-41.
2. Gadamer, *Truth and Method*, pp. 230-31, 235-45; Paul Ricoeur, *Hermeneutics and the Human Sciences* (Cambridge: Cambridge University Press, 1981).

the understanding process from the beginning and is not something added at the end.[3] Within the context of practical theology, the goal of understanding anything, even the classic religious and philosophical texts of the past, is from the start to create strategies of practical response.

Furthermore, the style of practical theology I practice believes that strategies of action should be critically grounded; that is, those who advance them should be willing to debate, give reasons for their plausibility, and criticize alternative proposals. Practical theology, as viewed in this book, is nurtured by faith and tradition; it is, as is all theology, born out of confession. But it also strives, in both the inner rhythms of ecclesial life and its witness to the public world, for the persuasiveness of good reasons that can be critically defended.[4] In short, my question will be this: Does Christianity have anything to say about modernization and globalization, especially as these forces affect families?

Modernization, Globalization, and the World Situation of Families

Of course, not all changes wrought by modernity are negative to families. In fact, many of them are very positive. Higher incomes for large numbers of families must be seen as a plus. Better health and longer lives for millions are goods that are universally affirmed. But these positive consequences are unevenly distributed; at the same time that modernization pulls many into a better material life, others lose ground. The new educational and economic possibilities for women that often accompany modernity are also promising, but they do not always convert into concrete benefits. Improvements for some women are frequently accompanied by negative consequences such as the mounting impoverishment of millions of mothers and their children due to abandonment, divorce, and nonmarital births; the increased violence of youth; new forms of coerced prostitution; and the growing absence of fathers from their children.[5] This last issue will be a major focus of this book and investigated theologically and philosophically in Chapters Four and Five.

3. Ricoeur, *Hermeneutics and the Human Sciences,* pp. 274, 289.

4. For a fuller discussion of my views on practical theology, see *A Fundamental Practical Theology* (Minneapolis: Fortress Press, 1991), pp. 1-10.

5. For a discussion of Asian and American forms of coerced prostitution, see Rita Nakashima Brock and Susan Thistlethwaite, *Casting Stones: Prostitution and Liberation in Asia and the United States* (Minneapolis: Fortress Press, 1996).

It will be my argument that the usual benefits of modernization in the form of better education and more jobs for both men and women must be supplemented by the worldwide revival and reconstruction of the institution of marriage. Notice that my argument will not pit modernization *against* marriage but will be about having both modernization *and* marriage. Some people will accuse me of wanting it all. Many people say that we cannot have both. It must be one or the other. Such people believe that the world, like some allegedly dull-witted politicians, cannot walk and chew gum at the same time. Marriage, they will insist, belongs to a premodern age. To some extent I agree with these criticisms. Modernization and marriage cannot coexist unless modernity is in some ways curtailed and marriage is in many ways redefined.

Because of the complexity of world family transformations, I will avoid getting lost in the details. I will begin by reviewing the theories of three outstanding sociologists — William Goode, David Popenoe, and Alan Wolfe — who are attempting to describe and assess the worldwide metamorphoses of family life. Although social scientists aspire to objectivity, these three can be distinguished more by their philosophical and ethical assumptions than their empirical facts. Furthermore, in reviewing the thought of these three sociologists, I will not become preoccupied with overly refined distinctions between modernization and globalization. Modernization is generally defined, following Max Weber, as the spread of technical rationality into various domains of life.[6] Some theorists, including Weber, have seen this as a deterministic process that augurs for the triumph of science, the narrow rationalization of all of life (Weber's "iron cage"), and the final defeat of religion. The German social theorist Jürgen Habermas has complicated the theory of modernization; he argues that technical rationality can take the form of either market economics or bureaucratic control.[7] In either case, modernity is generally thought to flow from the West and the North to other countries of the world in the Southern and Eastern parts of the globe.

There is much recent preoccupation in the press and among intellectuals with this first type of globalization — the spread of capitalism in the form of free trade between nations and the unrestricted flow of capital and labor across national boundaries. It is better, I contend, to con-

6. Max Weber, *The Protestant Ethic and the Spirit of Capitalism* (New York: Charles Scribner's Sons, 1958), pp. 181-83.

7. Jürgen Habermas, *Theory of Communicative Action*, vols. 1 and 2 (Boston: Beacon Press, 1984, 1987).

ceive of capitalism, especially in the form of the fashionable neoliberal economics, as just one expression of technical rationality. Bureaucratic rationality, in the form of either welfare policies or harder kinds of socialism and Marxism, is also a form of modernization that can take on global proportions, indeed global ambitions. These two kinds of modernization have technical rationality in common, i.e., the belief that the efficient use of powerful technical means in the form of either business procedures or government bureaucracies can increase our individual and collective satisfactions.

But the inevitability of modernization as the triumph of technical rationality can be overstated. It is certainly not the only form of globalization. And modernization as technical rationality, although real, is not as inevitable and deterministic as some have thought. There is, as Arjun Appadurai has argued, another form of globalization that is aided by but distinguishable from the worldwide spread of technical rationality.[8] This is the move of cultural influences across the world in all directions. Some of these cultural movements, although by no means all, are actually resisting technical rationality even though, to a significant extent, they are communicated by it. Some see this resistance as a kind of "reflexive globalization" that is greatly aided by the rise of modern forms of electronic communication. But whether a form of resistance or a product of spontaneous cultural creativity, these currents are often thought to flow from the West through American movies, television (HBO and MTV), and news media (CNN and Fox). But increasingly the cultural flow is moving from the rest of the world back to the West in the form of art, music, fashions, immigration, and trade.[9] Even as I write, Hamid Karzai, the interim leader of Afghanistan, has recently swept into Washington, D.C., and New York City wearing his green cape and gray fur cap, dazzling alike the media, fashion designers, and their potential patrons. It is just a matter of months, I wager, before men and women in the U.S. will be wearing look-alike capes and hats. Interest among Western women in some modified version of the exotic and mysterious *burkha*, in spite of its association with the oppression of women under the Taliban, is also likely to develop.

8. Arjun Appadurai, *Modernity at Large* (Minneapolis: University of Minnesota Press, 1996); Roland Robertson also has warned against equating globalization with capitalism. See his "Globalization and the Future of 'Traditional Religion,'" in *God and Globalization: Religion and the Powers of the Common Life*, vol. 1 (Harrisburg, Pa.: Trinity Press International, 2000), pp. 53-68.

9. Robertson, "Globalization," p. 27.

This form of globalization is a product of the human imagination rather than the blind forces of technical rationality. It is fed by the images of electronic media (television, movies), but the imagination itself uses them to preserve and recreate identity.[10] The imagination can work to halt or redirect the march of modernity in its more mechanical and rationalistic forms. The imagination creates new centers of locality and solidarity.[11] These new localities are not necessarily territorial; they are more phenomenological products of the imagination that may spread across the boundaries of neighborhoods and nations in all kinds of directions. Appadurai uses the concept of imagination in much the same way that I will use the concept of *phronêsis* or practical reason. It is the human capacity to synthesize received images and present experience with the inherited classics of the past. Imagination and practical reason are reconstructive abilities of humans, not likely to be destroyed by the forces of modernization in the form of spreading technical reason. The imagination, according to Appadurai, can give rise to "micro-narratives" — alternative stories to modernity's dominant narrative about the inevitability of progress wrought by the unfolding victory of what the Greeks called *technē*.[12]

I appreciate Appadurai's more generous view of globalization. But in this book I will employ both views, the narrower view of globalization as the rationalizations of modernity and the fuller view about our imaginative responses to these processes. Although most of the time I will use a nondeterministic version of the first view, there is a sense in which my entire constructive proposal is an illustration of the second. For I will be calling for the revival and the reconstruction of the institution of marriage as a crucial new imaginative response to the forces of technical rationality. I will be calling for the creation of new micro-narratives to counter modernity's dominant message about the inevitable decline of marriage. I will be urging a new conversation between the various micro-narratives about marriage and family that can be found in the world's religions. These religions' stories about marriage have not been micro-narratives in the past, but they appear to many to be small and anemic in the present. This is true because they are not heard well and accurately either by their own adherents or the rest of the world. They are increasingly drowned out by the noisy narrative of technological expansion. But this situation can change.

10. Appadurai, *Modernity at Large*, pp. 3, 15.
11. Appadurai, *Modernity at Large*, pp. 178-80.
12. Appadurai, *Modernity at Large*, p. 10.

William Goode: How Modernization Betrayed Families

William Goode is a leading figure in American sociology. In two massive books written thirty years apart, Goode fearlessly collected huge quantities of data and developed a theory to account for family change in places as diverse as Western Europe, the United States, Asia, and sub-Saharan Africa. In both of these books, he was using the concept of modernity in the first sense described above — modernization as technical reason with its offshoots in industrialization, urbanization, and increased mobility of labor and capital. In 1963, he wrote *World Revolution and Family Patterns,* which demonstrated the global movement away from extended-family patterns toward the convenient fit between industrialization and what he called the "conjugal" or "companionate" family.[13] He thought that the West — especially England and northern Europe — had exported to the world a modernizing trend that joined a conjugal family pattern to a wealth-producing industrialization process. In nearly every country he studied, Goode found trends toward smaller families, more women working in the wage economy, more equality between husband and wife, more mobility, more education for both sexes (especially for women), and less control of extended family over the conjugal couple. This conjugal family pattern, he believed, had helped both to create and then to serve the emerging industrial order. Goode welcomed this new family form even though he acknowledged that there was no clear evidence that it would bring more happiness than older extended and patriarchal patterns. However, he did say,

> I welcome the great changes now taking place, and not because it might be a more efficient instrument of industrialization, for that is irrelevant in my personal scheme. Rather, I see in it and in the industrial system that accompanies it the hope of a greater freedom: from the domination of elders, from caste and racial restrictions, from class rigidities. Freedom is *for* something as well: the unleashing of personal potentials, the right to love, to equality within the family, to the establishment of a new marriage when the old has failed. I see the world revolution in family patterns as part of a still more important revolution that is sweeping the world in our time, the aspiration on the part of billions of people to have the right for the first time *to choose* for themselves

13. William Goode, *World Revolution and Family Patterns* (London: The Free Press of Glencoe, 1964).

— an aspiration that has toppled governments both old and new, and created new societies and social movements.

For me, then, the major and sufficing justification for the newly emerging family patterns is that they offer people at least the potentialities of greater fulfillment, even if most do not seek it or achieve it.[14]

The Disillusionment of Goode

Three decades later, when Goode wrote *World Changes in Divorce Patterns* (1994), his optimism about world trends toward the conjugal model had become tempered for all parts of the globe, including the areas of Northern Europe that gave this pattern its birth. The comfortable fit between this family form and industrialization that he described in 1963 was perceived as breaking down in the 1990s. He now saw industrialization and modernization as playing dirty tricks on the conjugal family, even in the West where their partnership once seemed to thrive. Modernity's speed of change, its capacity to subdue intimate relations to the dictates of rational production, the mobility that it induces, and its tendency to move labor and capital around the world without respect for enduring human relations, have now made this old friend of the conjugal family pattern into a new enemy.

All Western and many non-Western societies are becoming what Goode calls "high-divorce societies."[15] Furthermore, he is aware that cohabitation and out-of-wedlock births have increased dramatically in Western societies and throughout the world. Hand-in-hand with these movements have been the growing poverty and declining well-being of significant percentages of women and children. This "feminization of poverty" has had negative social effects in wealthy countries, but it has had devastating consequences for poor ones.[16] Goode joined Cambridge social historian Peter Laslett in holding that the conjugal family helped create industrialization and modernization and that for at least a couple

14. Goode, *World Revolution and Family Patterns*, p. 380.

15. William Goode, *World Changes in Divorce Patterns* (New Haven: Yale University Press, 1994), p. 336.

16. Goode, *World Changes in Divorce Patterns*, p. 321. For early insights into the feminization of poverty and how family disruption contributes to it, see Lenore Weitzman, *The Divorce Revolution: The Unexpected Social and Economic Consequences for Women and Children in America* (New York: Free Press, 1985).

9

of centuries there had existed a compatible fit between them.[17] Then suddenly, according to Goode, modernization turned and began devouring the conjugal family that helped give it birth. From one perspective, Friedrich Engels seems correct in his prediction that modernization in the form of a market economy would destroy families.[18] Engels did not understand, I might add, that modernization in the form of bureaucratization would have an equally devastating impact, a point I will investigate below.

But, as Goode points out, there is no straight causal connection between modernization and the rise of a high-divorce and family-disruption culture. For instance, as Japan industrialized, divorce rates actually declined and family stability increased. In nineteenth-century Japan, a pattern of early marriage and patrilocality led married couples frequently to divorce, generally due to conflicts between bride and mother-in-law.[19] This practice had few negative social consequences; the bride returned to her parents, generally had not conceived a child, and often got married a second time. But this custom of early marriage and early divorce came to an end due to government pressures. The restoration of the Meiji ruling family brought with it the marriage code of 1898; it discouraged divorce and instituted a patriarchal, samurai, and neo-Confucian marriage pattern.[20] Governmental decree actually stabilized the family for decades during rapid Japanese industrialization, albeit along highly patriarchal lines.

Goode presents other examples of stable high-divorce societies. Most Islamic countries permit men to unilaterally divorce their wives even though the Qur'an actually discourages the practice and Islamic law also exacts financial penalties. In most cases wives will have their dowry returned to their control, and their fathers, brothers, and uncles generally rally to protect and save them from poverty and loneliness. Furthermore, most Islamic countries have been high-remarriage societies because of cultural values that define marriage as the only viable role for women.[21]

Goode nominates Sweden as a third model of a stable high-divorce and family-disruption society. Sweden's extensive system of social sup-

17. Peter Laslett, *Family Life and Illicit Love in Earlier Generations* (Cambridge: Cambridge University Press, 1977), p. 13.

18. Friedrich Engels, *The Origin of the Family, Private Property, and the State* (New York: International Publications, 1972).

19. Goode, *World Changes in Divorce Patterns,* pp. 220-23.

20. Goode, *World Changes in Divorce Patterns,* pp. 224-25.

21. Goode, *World Changes in Divorce Patterns,* pp. 251-57.

ports sustains divorced or never-married mothers, at least financially. It is clear that Goode envisions something like the Swedish stable high family-disruption system for all countries of the world be they rich or poor, East or West, North or South.

Goode's Thesis and the Case of Africa

In Goode's 1963 book, his thesis about the weakening of the extended family pattern appeared to apply even to sub-Saharan Africa. More recent research from South Africa seems to confirm that the conjugal couple has made headway in the southern parts of Africa. Some sociological surveys suggest that even among native Africans, the values of a faithful, monogamous, and gender-equal partnership is the type of marriage more and more being desired.[22] But the forces of modernization may be undermining it even before it can become stabilized. Even in remote tribal areas, traditional agricultural and herding societies have tended to give way to unevenly developing urban and industrial intrusions. Male mobility to urban centers in the pursuit of jobs has weakened the control of the extended family. This has produced more single-mother homes, less supervision of the young, and the decline of authority of the tribal system.[23] When women enter the wage economy, the traditional prerogatives of males are threatened, often evoking both psychological rage and physical retribution on their wives and girlfriends. In a famous incident in Qwaqwa in 1984, four hundred unemployed men raided an industrial park, stoning and chasing away the women employees.[24]

In South Africa, as is the case in many parts of the world, the strains on families caused by industrialization, modernization, and now globalization were further aggravated by racial discrimination, unfair economic practices, and war. The dislocations of modernization and globalization are never completely disconnected from racial and political strife. In fact,

22. Sylvia Viljoen and Anna Steyn, "Values Supporting Quality Family Life: An Exploratory Descriptive Study" (Pretoria: Co-operative Research Programme on Marriage and Family Life, 1997).

23. John Sharp and Andrew Spiegel, "Women and Wages: Gender and the Control of Income in Farm and Bantustan Households," *Journal of Southern African Studies* 16, no. 3 (September 1990): 529-49; C. W. Bester, "The Consequences of Urbanization and Westernization on Black Family Life in South Africa," *Social Work* 30, no. 2 (1994): 101-5.

24. Leslie Bank, "Angry Men and Working Women: Gender, Violence and Economic Change in Qwaqwa in the 1980s," *African Studies* 53, no. 1 (1994): 90.

the two interact and intensify one another. As Henrietta Moore writes, "The history and legacy of apartheid have resulted in a specific configuration of capital, labor supply, sectoral development and economic and political privilege."[25] Moore, in her introduction to a series of articles in the journal *African Studies* (1994), is perfectly aware of the strains that modernization places on kinship patterns. In her remarks about apartheid, she is inviting us to think about both modernization *and* political injustice and how they interact.

Although a professor at the London School of Economics, Moore also points out that the problems of South African families are not just economic. Financial strains raise fundamental cultural questions about the nature of masculinity, the grounds of dignity and self-worth of both men and women, and the nature and value of the institution of marriage itself. With regard to marriage, Moore reports that there is emerging among sub-Saharan women a new reluctance to marry, and this in a society where virtually all women traditionally have wed. This new reluctance by women to marry "seems linked to their inability to control resources within conjugal unions. . . . To a certain extent, in conditions of the kind present in Qwaqwa, marriage undermines women's security rather than improving it. This is the exact opposite of an earlier situation in Africa."[26] Even though the demise of the South African apartheid regime has brought to power a new government that has enacted the principle of universal social security and family benefits, this safety net has not been successful. Small grants, insufficient administrative structures, and a social-support system constrained by national development goals dictated by neoliberal economics have resulted in huge portions of the poor still being excluded.[27] This illustrates the difficulties with Goode's belief that the solution to world family disruption is the extension of the Nordic welfare system to all societies, rich or poor. This might help, if the poor countries of the world could afford it, but it will not be enough. And, for the most part, poor countries cannot afford such a system at the level needed.

Several scholars in addition to Goode have argued that family patterns in southern Africa are distinctive when compared to Europe and Asia. This is part, although not all, of the reason why families there have

25. Henrietta Moore, "Households and Gender in a South African Bantustan: A Comment," *African Studies* 53, no. 1 (1994): 138.

26. Moore, "Households and Gender," p. 141.

27. Jan Vorster and Hester Rossouw, "Transforming State Support for Children and Families in South Africa: Single Mother Households Footing the Bill?," *Social Work* 33, no. 4 (1997): 315-31.

had difficulties with the forces of modernization. In many African groups, bride price traditionally paid by the groom generally went directly to the family of the bride and was seldom held in reserve for her in case of divorce, desertion, or the death of a husband. And the custom of dowry, widely used in other parts of the world to endow the bride, was generally not practiced in southern Africa.[28] These cultural patterns, along with the practice of polygyny, left wives quite vulnerable and often forced them into deep economic need and dependence. This was especially true in agricultural situations where the mother and her children frequently lived separately from the husband and worked her individual plot of land for food.[29]

Polygyny and the absence of bride endowment may have been at one time socially functional, in spite of their difficulties for women. But the twin forces of modernization and urbanization induced huge numbers of husbands to migrate to cities for employment with the expectation that their wife, or wives, would earn most of their living back in the village on their plots of land. Under these circumstances, the influence of the extended family declined.[30] This often led to a rapid increase in both monogamous and polygynous informal unions that were not well supervised by the more cohesive communities that existed in premodernizing sub-Saharan Africa. This contributed to the poverty of women and children and, as is now widely understood, the more recent spread of HIV and AIDS.[31]

28. Goode, *World Revolution and Family Patterns,* p. 171; and Jack Goody, *Production and Reproduction* (Cambridge: Cambridge University Press, 1976), pp. 7, 11; see also Jack Goody, *The Oriental, the Ancient and the Primitive Systems of Marriage and the Family in the Pre-industrial Societies of Eurasia* (Cambridge: Cambridge University Press, 1990), pp. xviii-xix.

29. Goode, *World Revolution in Family Patterns,* pp. 192-93.

30. There is a debate among African social scientists as to whether the extended family has declined in influence or simply now takes a different form, one less intergenerational between grandparents, children, and grandchildren to one more a matter of interdependence between siblings. Isak Neihaus reports, "studies on Southern Africa have recorded intense levels of marital instability and domestic disorganization." He goes on to say that although this is true, it obscures what has taken the place of the conjugal couple. He "suggests that cooperative relations between siblings have become a central principle underlying household formation." I must confess that although it is better to have some form of kinship than little or nothing at all, the sibling pattern is bound to weaken both care for the elderly and care for the very young. It is an admirable strategy for survival but hardly a normative direction for the future. Yet, even as a transient adaptive strategy, it is interesting to note the importance of consanguinity in this pattern, a point that will become more significant as the argument of this book unfolds. See "Disharmonious Spouses and Harmonious Siblings," *African Studies* 53, no. 1 (1994): 116.

31. For discussions of African family patterns, modernization, and the AIDS crisis, see

Part of what accounts for the difference historically between southern African and northern European families in their response to modernization is this: at the same time that the power of the extended family was declining in Europe, a cohesive conjugal couple was gradually taking its place. The rise of the conjugal couple differentiated from extended family also paralleled the emergence of an affluent industrial system that both strained this new family form yet also economically supported it. In Africa, the conjugal couple was less ready and able to fill the gap of the weakened extended family. Furthermore, the stresses of modernization in Africa were mediated by the realities and oppressions of colonization. In 1963, Goode believed that southern Africa would gradually move toward the conjugal pattern. This move, in fact, has been tentative, problematic, and fragile.

David Popenoe and Alan Wolfe

American sociologists David Popenoe and Alan Wolfe have reviewed these same trends. In ways similar to Goode they analyze the forces causing them, but they propose vastly different solutions. Popenoe in his 1988 *Disturbing the Nest: Family Change and Decline in Modern Societies* measured family disruption in the United States and Sweden, with shorter forays into the low-divorce societies of New Zealand and Switzerland.[32] Alan Wolfe in *Whose Keeper? Social Science and Moral Obligation* (1989) compared indices of family disruption in the United States and Sweden.[33]

Here are samples, and something of an updating, of the kinds of sta-

---

Philip and Janet Kilbride, *Changing Family Life in East Africa: Women and Children at Risk* (University Park, Pa.: Pennsylvania State University Press, 1990); Aylward Shorter and Edwin Onyancha, *The Church and AIDS in Africa* (Nairobi: Pauline Publications Africa, 1998); Philip Kilbride, *Plural Marriage for Our Times: A Reinvented Option?* (Westport, Conn.: Bergin and Garvey, 1994). Acknowledging that present disrupted African family and marriage patterns account for some of the contemporary AIDS crisis, the Kilbrides argue for the return to premodernization marriage patterns and to a nomic polygyny that was disrupted by modernity. Shorter and Onyancha recommend reformulating these indigenous patterns, with their high valuation of children and procreation, along the lines of normative Roman Catholic marriage ethics and its analogous high valuation of children. Both tasks would require a huge cultural work. I review both strategies in detail in Chapter Seven.

32. David Popenoe, *Disturbing the Nest: Family Change and Decline in Modern Societies* (New York: Aldine de Gruyter, 1988).

33. Alan Wolfe, *Whose Keeper? Social Science and Moral Obligation* (Berkeley: University of California Press, 1989).

tistics that worry Popenoe and Wolfe. Since the 1960s, the divorce rate has more than doubled in the United Kingdom, the United States, France, and Australia.[34] During this same period, nonmarital births increased from 5 percent to 33 percent in the U.S., from 4 percent to 31 percent in Canada, from 5 to 38 percent in the United Kingdom, and from 6 to 36 percent in France.[35] In the U.S., since 1960 the rate of out-of-wedlock births increased tenfold in the white community to 25 percent and increased three times in the black community, from 22 percent to a rate of 70 percent of all births today.[36] The marriage rate in all advanced countries has declined significantly; there are fewer second marriages and more people live longer periods of their lives in the single state. In the United States, there has been a 30 percent decline in the marriage rate since 1960 and overall, there has been an 11 percent decline in the number of people over age 15 that are married.[37] Much of this can be explained by later marriages and increased longevity. But some of this decline is due to increased lifelong singleness and cohabitation. Since 1960, there has been in the U.S. a drop of over 19 percent for men between ages 35 and 44 who are married and a drop of 16 percent for women between those ages.[38]

The number of couples cohabiting has increased 8 times since 1970 in the U.S.[39] Cohabitation is almost a universal experience in most northern European countries; only 7 percent of Swedes, 24 percent of Norwegians, 12 percent of the French, and 16 percent of the West Germans marry directly without cohabiting first.[40] Studies show that cohabitation is much

34. *Demographic Yearbook* (New York: United Nations).

35. Clarence Page, "When marriage goes out of style," *Chicago Tribune,* February 7, 2001, p. A17. Page is quoting statistics provided by Senator Daniel Moynihan in a September 2001 speech before the American Political Science Association. For more information supporting these trends, see *Eurostat Yearbook* (1995).

36. Tom Smith, "The Emerging 21st Century American Family" (Chicago: National Opinion Research Center, University of Chicago, 1999), p. 3.

37. Barbara Dafoe Whitehead and David Popenoe, "Who Wants to Marry a Soul Mate?: The State of Our Unions 2001" (Rutgers University: The National Marriage Project, 2001), p. 18. The marriage rate is measured by number of marriages per 1,000 unmarried women age 15 and older.

38. Whitehead and Popenoe, "Who Wants to Marry a Soul Mate?," p. 18.

39. Linda Waite, "The Negative Effects of Cohabitation," *The Responsive Community* 10 (Winter 2000): 31. For a comprehensive summary of cohabitation trends in the U.S., see R. Kelly Raley, "Recent Trends and Differential in Marriage and Cohabitation: The United States," *The Ties That Bind: Perspectives on Marriage and Cohabitation,* ed. Linda Waite et al. (New York: Aldine de Gruyter, 2000), pp. 19-39.

40. Kathleen Kiernan, "European Perspectives on Union Formation," *The Ties That Bind,* p. 50.

more unstable than marriage and correlates with higher divorce rates for couples who do go on to marry.[41] Examinations of Swedish cohabiting couples with one child indicate that their dissolution rate is three times as high as it is for legally married couples with a child.[42] Recent research has shown that in the U.S., a significant portion of births out of wedlock actually occur in cohabiting relationships; this suggests that the instability of cohabitation also contributes to the insecurity of the family environment for children.[43] Statistics on divorce and cohabitation for African countries are more difficult to find, but the evidence that exists suggests that there are trends in these parts of the world similar to those of the West, and in some countries they have even more devastating consequences — this independently of the additional ravages of HIV and AIDS.

It is easy to find headlines in newspapers that read like this: "For Europeans, Love, Yes: Marriage, Maybe."[44] "More and more European children are being born out of wedlock into a new social order in which, it seems, few of the old stigmas apply." The nonmarital birthrate is 49 percent in Norway, 62 percent in Iceland, and 31 percent in Catholic Ireland. Although the rate is only 9 percent in Italy, even there we are told that the "old rules are breaking down."[45] It is interesting to see countries flirt with a more traditional pro-marriage policy but then back away. In the autumn of 1998, when I was giving the Cadbury Lectures at the University of Birmingham, the press was full of reports about the Green Paper on the family just released by Tony Blair's Liberal Party government. It contained several pro-marriage proposals, including suggestions that the state might do more with marriage education.[46] The reaction to this initiative ranged from confusion and passivity to outright anger and rejection. Much of the latter came from cabinet members of the Blair government itself, some of whom had their own checkered history of divorce and out-of-

41. David Popenoe and Barbara Dafoe Whitehead, "Should We Live Together? What Young Adults Need to Know about Cohabitation before Marriage: The State of Our Unions 1999" (Rutgers University: The National Marriage Project, 1999).

42. Popenoe, *Disturbing the Nest,* p. 173.

43. Pamela Smock, "Cohabitation in the United States: An Appraisal of Research Themes, Findings, and Implications," *Annual Review of Sociology* 21 (Summer 2000).

44. Sarah Lyall, "For Europeans, Love, Yes; Marriage, Maybe," *New York Times,* March 24, 2002, p. 1.

45. Lyall, "For Europeans, Love, Yes; Marriage, Maybe," p. 8.

46. *Supporting Families* (London: The Stationery Office, 1998). For a summary of the national response to this government position paper that shows the rapid waning of the original emphasis on marriage formation and support, see *Supporting Families: Summary of Responses to the Consultation Document* (London: The Stationery Office, 1999).

wedlock parenthood. Recent reports indicate that, "The British government has all but abandoned that position, acknowledging in a recent position paper that there were many alternatives to the classic family structure."[47]

Increasingly, it appears, that "responsible parenting" is becoming both the cultural norm and the core of government policy in European societies, with less and less interest in whether it takes place within or outside of marriage. According to one news account, some British social scientists are predicting "marriage is doomed and will be virtually extinct within 30 years." Duncan White, head of Relate, an organization of 2000 marriage counselors, believes that within thirty years, only one in five long-term couples will be married in Britain and that legal marriage will be rejected in favor of a "'constellation' of relationships where couples have a series of long-term relationships with children from each.'"[48] Although doubtless an exaggeration, such projections are being heard more frequently and should at least gain our attention.

In the face of such statistics and trends, sociologist Linda Waite and journalist Maggie Gallagher strike a very different tone. They conclude in their recent book *The Case for Marriage* (2000) that a couple's public and legal commitment to the formal institution of marriage appears in itself to contribute to the stability of the union.[49] This point seems, for the most part, to have been lost in public conversations about the significance of marriage, both in the U.S. and in Europe. Furthermore, these authors summarize and extend the mounting evidence indicating that the deinstitutionalization of the family and the decline of marriage have alarming negative consequences for the well-being of women, children, men, and society as a whole. In the 1970s and early 1980s, American sociologists such as Jessie Bernard celebrated the new culture of divorce and nonmarriage as promising a future of creativity, experimentation, and freedom, especially for women.[50] But by the late 1980s, research by feminist scholars Lenore Weitzman and Mary Ann Mason on the negative economic consequences of divorce for women cooled this earlier optimism.[51] By the mid-1990s, reports by demographers such as Sara McLanahan and

---

47. Sarah Lyall, "For Europeans, Love, Yes; Marriage, Maybe," p. 8.

48. Sarah Harris, "Marriage 'will be extinct in 30 years,'" *Daily Mail,* April 20, 2002.

49. Linda Waite and Maggie Gallagher, *The Case for Marriage* (New York: Doubleday, 2000), p. 18.

50. Jessie Bernard, *The Future of Marriage* (New York: World Publishing, 1972).

51. Weitzman, *The Divorce Revolution;* Mary Ann Mason, *The Equality Trap* (New York: Simon & Schuster, 1988).

Gary Sandefur showed that children in the U.S. not living with both biological parents were on average two to three times more likely to have difficulties in school, in finding employment, and in successfully forming families themselves.[52] Income lessens these consequences, but only by 50 percent.

These negative health and economic consequences of family disruption hold, with only minor variations, throughout the world wherever the relevant statistics exist and most likely even in places where the statistics do not exist. *The most interesting base reality of these trends is the increasing distance, if not separation, of fathers from their children.* Divorce, nonmarital births, and teen pregnancies not only correlate with and accentuate poverty, they correlate with a weaker if not completely absent relation with fathers. This means a loss of the financial contributions of the father. It also means a loss of other unique qualities such as conscience formation, the loss of mediation to offspring of the father's "social capital" (the resources of his extended family, his friends, his other social contacts), a decline of trust in the reliability of the world, and even a loss of faith in the dependability of the mother herself.[53] *Fatherless America* (1995) and *Life without Father* (1996), the titles of two flagship books of the 1990s about trends in the U.S., may be aptly pointing as well toward fatherlessness and father absence throughout the world.[54]

Although these are the kinds of facts that worry Popenoe and Wolfe, they interpret them with different theoretical commitments. Popenoe accepts William Goode's theory that modernization weakened first the extended family and then the conjugal family. But he also believes that cultural values such as expressive and utilitarian individualism, independent of the social processes of industrialization, are the main factors fueling family disruption.[55] This leads Popenoe to see the world cure for family disruption in a massive cultural conversion; he envisions the possibility of a worldwide renunciation of overdetermined individualistic aspirations and the birth of a new familism. Handling world family disruptions by imitating Sweden's relatively stable high-divorce society, as William

52. Sara McLanahan and Gary Sandefur, *Growing Up with a Single Parent* (Cambridge, Mass.: Harvard University Press, 1994).

53. For insights into this research, see McLanahan and Sandefur, *Growing Up with a Single Parent*, pp. 3-4, 19-38.

54. David Blankenhorn, *Fatherless America* (New York: Basic Books, 1995); see also David Popenoe, *Life without Father* (New York: Free Press, 1996).

55. Popenoe, *Life without Father*, pp. 46-48; Robert Bellah et al., *Habits of the Heart* (New York: Harper & Row, 1986), pp. 32-35.

Goode would urge, is an option that Popenoe has considered but rejected as both economically unfeasible and culturally destructive.

Alan Wolfe rejects the Swedish alternative as well. He joins Popenoe in seeing the Swedish strategy as culturally destructive; it undermines marriage and family even as it attempts to save them. Wolfe uses the colonization theory of Jürgen Habermas to show how different expressions of modernization are almost identical in their negative effects on families. By coining the intriguing word "colonization," Habermas and Wolfe are employing Max Weber's concept of technical rationality, an idea that was central to Weber's famous theory of modernization.[56] Technical rationality, as I indicated above, is the use of means-end and control-oriented practices to guide the efficient production of wealth. Habermas's metaphor of colonization suggests that all spheres of modern life have become dominated by the spread of technical rationality, even face-to-face interpersonal life in local communities, neighborhoods, and families.

Colonization theory, as I briefly mentioned earlier, teaches that technical rationality enters into daily life from two perspectives — the efficiency goals of the marketplace and the control goals of government bureaucracy. Both disrupt the face-to-face interactions of the "lifeworld" and the intimate spheres of marriage and family. From the market comes the increasing absorption of both men and women into the wage economy and the subsequent erosion of the time for and benefits from parenthood and stable marital relations. From state bureaucracy comes the control of the education of our children, the rise of the welfare state, its preemption of family functions, and its subtle encouragement of the transfer of dependencies from family to the state. Wolfe argues that Sweden is the leading example of colonization of the lifeworld from the perspective of government bureaucracy; the U.S. is the leading example of colonization from the perspective of market rationality.[57] In the end, the results for families of these two forms of colonization are approximately the same — more divorce, more out-of-wedlock births, and the declining well-being of children affected by these trends.

Wolfe joins Popenoe in distrusting Goode's great hope for a stable high-divorce society in the Swedish style for all parts of the world.[58] Popenoe and Wolfe have more faith in the prospects of cultural change

---

56. Jürgen Habermas, *The Theory of Communicative Action*, vol. 2, pp. 333-35; Alan Wolfe, *Whose Keeper?*, p. 20.

57. Wolfe, *Whose Keeper?*, pp. 52-60, 133-42.

58. Popenoe, *Disturbing the Nest*, pp. 243-49.

and reconstruction as the way to address the family issue. On this note, they differ from many family sociologists in the U.S. such as Larry Bumpass, Andrew Cherlin, and Frank Fuerstenberg, who acknowledge the sobering facts about family disruption but believe little can be done about it other than mitigating the pain of its consequences.[59] Indeed, Popenoe and Wolfe advocate a new moral conversation that would lead to a cultural rebirth of marital commitment, one tough enough and realistic enough to deal with the tensions of modernity.

The Neglect of Religion

Popenoe and Wolfe are close to my vision of the need for a new cultural work, initiated principally from the communities of civil society, that would attempt to revive and reconstruct the institution of marriage. Their vision, however, is not fully developed. It does not give voice to the various sectors or spheres of societies that need to be included in this cultural work. And they both neglect the category of religion. This is not surprising. Many sociologists associate Judaism and Christianity with patriarchy and its harmful consequences for women. Or they join Wolfe in believing that secularization has rendered contemporary religious institutions impotent as centers of socially reconstructive moral discourse.[60] Popenoe hopes that religion can help stabilize the postmodern family, but makes little effort to develop a theory of how religious institutions can reconstruct cultural values pertinent to marriage and family. Indeed, it is true that when thinking about marriage from an international and multicultural perspective, the religious factor becomes all the more complex to take into account.

If the family issue is first of all a cultural issue, as Popenoe and his colleagues believe, then religion, as it did in the past, must play a decisive role even today in the reconstruction of marriage and family ideals. This is true as well if one thinks about the reconstruction of marriage, not only in Western societies but wherever modernization has had an impact.

Here are a few generalizations, to be developed in later chapters, about the potential role of Christianity in the world revival and reformation of

59. Larry Bumpass, "What Is Happening to the Family? Interaction Between Demographics and Institutional Change," *Demography* 23 (November 1990): 486, 489, 493; Andrew Cherlin and Frank Furstenberg, *Divided Families* (Cambridge, Mass.: Harvard University Press, 1991).

60. Wolfe, *Whose Keeper?*, p. 6.

marriage.[61] They apply mainly to how Christianity has affected family and marriage theory in Western societies, but they have implications for wherever Christian cultural and legal traditions have spread. These generalizations will show why Christianity, when rightly interpreted, is a major resource for the reconstruction of marriage and family theory for Western societies and, in dialogue with other religions, for other parts of the world as well. My efforts to outline the reconstructive possibilities of Christianity are not to suggest that it is the only religious resource for the modern world. It is, however, a major resource. I believe that parallel efforts to revive and reconstruct the marriage and family traditions of other religions are also possible, although I will not attempt this task in this book. I will, however, make probes that may prove suggestive.

As we will see in Chapter Three, early Christianity, especially pre-Pauline and Pauline Christianity, was a family revolution. It significantly qualified, although it did not completely dismantle, the honor-shame codes that dominated family and marriage in the Greco-Roman world.[62] By honor and shame codes, I mean a family system in which free men gained honor through exhibiting the qualities of dominance and agency and were shamed if they lost these perceived virtues. Women, on the other hand, gained honor by restricting their lives primarily to the domestic sphere and submitting to male protection. They were shamed if they went beyond these boundaries or were violated by the intrusion of other males outside their family and clan. Christianity, we must remember, existed within a cultural context largely formed by a Roman Hellenism that was saturated by these honor-shame codes.

Although early Christianity never completely disconnected from these codes, it qualified them by celebrating male servanthood rather than male dominance, by applying the golden rule and neighbor love to relationships between husband and wife, by requiring males to renounce

61. Information about the Religion, Culture, and Family Project can be found at www2.uchicago.edu/divinity/family. The project has published a series of ten books with Westminster/John Knox and is publishing another series of books with William B. Eerdmans.

62. For review of the application of the insights of cultural anthropology on honor-shame societies to an understanding of the influence of early Christianity on families, see the following: Bruce Malina, *The New Testament World: Insights from Cultural Anthropology* (Louisville: Westminster/John Knox Press, 1993); Carolyn Osiek and David Balch, *Families in the New Testament World* (Louisville: Westminster/John Knox, 1997); Don Browning, Bonnie Miller McLemore, Pamela Couture, Bernie Lyon, and Robert Franklin, *From Culture Wars to Common Ground: Religion and the American Family Debate* (Louisville: Westminster/John Knox, 1997), pp. 129-54.

their sexual privileges with female slaves and young boys, and by elevating the status of women.[63] As the American sociologist Rodney Stark has argued in his *The Rise of Christianity* (1997), pagan women flocked to early Christianity because of its stand against infanticide, its restrictions on divorce (which in antiquity worked to the disadvantage of women), and its demand that men be responsible fathers and faithful husbands.[64] The famous Cambridge anthropologist Jack Goody argues that it was not only the Protestant Reformation that gave birth to the modern conjugal and companionate family, as Harvard historian Steven Ozment has argued.[65] He believes that the seeds of what I will call the equal-regard marriage and family also go back to the value of the individual found in early Christianity and its emphasis on "inter-personal, rather than inter-group, bonds."[66]

This emphasis on the value of the individual influenced eleventh- and twelfth-century Roman Catholic canon law to make mutual consent between bride and groom the decisive factor defining marriage.[67] This move functioned to elevate the status of the conjugal couple over the power, prestige, and control of the extended family. This development limited the power of fathers to arbitrarily give their daughters in marriage for political and economic gain. According to the historian David Herlihy, this emphasis on the integrity and sanctity of the conjugal couple led to the downfall of polygyny and the elevation of monogamy wherever Christianity spread.[68] Although Luther and Calvin rejected the Roman Catholic idea of marriage as a sacrament of grace, they accepted most of the other accomplishments of Roman Catholic canon law on marriage, especially the emphasis on marriage as requiring mutual consent by bride and groom.

But Luther and Calvin added one important element that the societies influenced by the Protestant Reformation may be losing due to the increasing deinstitutionalization of marriage and family. Marriage, ac-

---

63. For amplification of these points, see *From Culture Wars to Common Ground*, pp. 129-56.

64. Rodney Stark, *The Rise of Christianity* (San Francisco: HarperCollins, 1997), pp. 98-118.

65. Steven Ozment, *Protestants: The Birth of a Revolution* (New York: Doubleday, 1992), pp. 151-69.

66. Jack Goody, *The Development of the Family and Marriage in Europe* (Cambridge: Cambridge University Press, 1994), p. 23.

67. John Witte, *From Sacrament to Contract: Marriage, Religion, and Law in the Western Tradition* (1997).

68. David Herlihy, *Medieval Households* (Cambridge, Mass.: Harvard University Press, 1985), pp. 61-62.

cording to the Reformers, was understood as both a public *and* an ecclesial affair. It was for them first of all a natural good and a contribution to secular society and the earthly kingdom. Marriage had to be registered by the state and then could be blessed and sanctified by the church. Marriage for these Reformers arose out of the love and consent of a couple, but it needed completion by both state and church.

The Reformation move to make marriage a public institution requiring state registration gradually brought to an end the phenomena of clandestine or secret marriages. These marriages, although valid before the eyes of the Catholic Church, were unwitnessed by family, priest, or civil magistrate. Their validity rested on their mutual consent — a consent, however, that one member of the couple could later deny without public contradiction. Ever since the Reformation, religion and state in most Western-oriented societies have cooperated to perform a great cultural work in bringing order and coherence to marriage by making it a public institution as well as a personal, consensual, and religious one.

Not only did the Protestant churches develop both an ecclesial and public theology governing marriage, they contributed a rich and complex symbol system that applied to both tasks. The creation story of ancient Judaism is central to Christian marriage theology as well as foundational for much of the Western legal edifice covering marriage. The creation of Adam and Eve as male and female both carrying God's image (Gen. 1:27), their equal responsibility for procreation and "dominion" (Gen. 1:28), God's declaration that it is not good that Adam "should be alone" (Gen. 1:18), the statement that "a man leaves his father and mother and clings to his wife, and they become one flesh" (Gen. 2:24), and the reaffirmation and recontextualization of these classic scriptures within the gospel message of Jesus in Matthew 19:4-6 — these are the scriptures that time and again were interpreted by Catholic and Protestant theologians and even by jurists up into the twentieth century.

It would be wrong to credit these scriptures, and Christian interpretations of them, as the only source of the Western conjugal, public, and companionate marriage and family. To understand the complex synthesis of sources that went into a Christian theology of marriage makes it easier to dialogue with the marriage perspectives of other religious traditions. Christian marriage theology, as Christianity itself, is a complicated mixture of somewhat disparate elements. As we will see in Chapters Four and Five, Christian theology on marriage and family interacted with Aristotle's naturalistic view of family as well as with Roman and German law. Roman Catholic canon law and St. Thomas Aquinas brought these sources together and bequeathed them to the Protestant Reformation, where they were reworked but largely retained. I believe that this is a proud heritage that needs to be critically appreciated by Western societies today. It should also be brought into critical conversation with the other marriage systems of the world.

Notice that I used the adverb "critical" in both contexts. The two efforts of retrieval and dialogue are dialectically related. In order for Christianity to have a world conversation about marriage with other religious traditions, it must go through a critical hermeneutical retrieval of its own complex and multifaceted marriage traditions. With regard to the second task — the task of entering into a world conversation that is both comparative and critical — the goal is not to reduce other systems to distinctively Western and Christian models. The objective is to find points of analogy between diverse systems — points of analogy that can be tested, enhanced, and implemented more effectively as part of the richness of an increasingly diverse cultural and religious environment developing in most modern societies.

I do believe that the Christian perspective on marriage contains the seeds of excellence. Empirically and historically, like everything else in this fallen world, it was often far from excellent in its actual implementation. But in order for it to resist the challenges of modernization discussed by Goode, Popenoe, and Wolfe, the church must be a leader in a new multifaceted cultural work designed to revive and reformulate marriage traditions throughout the world.

Elements in the New Cultural Work

The cultural work needed to revive marriage must have several dimensions to it. No one approach, no one strategy, no one discipline or institution, can accomplish this task alone. There needs to be a new system of voluntary associations, both national and international, that coordinate these complex patterns of dialogue and intervention. These associations must see the reformulation of the ethics of marriage as fundamental to the process of reviving the institution of marriage. They would attempt to devise an interrelated philosophical, religious, economic, legal, educational, and psychological strategy to influence culture, religious institutions, public life, and even the law. They would be based on the best research available in these different disciplines, but the overall task would be practical and hermeneutic, i.e., a matter of understanding, as Hans-

Georg Gadamer would say, for the purposes of *praxis*.[69] It would entail critically understanding not only distinctively Christian traditions but other major religious traditions as well. The various traditions would not be dismantled, but there would be a realistic assessment as to which of their elements can best cope with, restrain, and guide the forces of modernization. Something of a model for this interreligious reconstructive retrieval, with the amendments I would add, can be found in the Religious Consultation on Population, Reproductive Health, and Ethics, a project I review and assess in the last chapter.

Here are some of the elements that would go into this world practical-theological (or better, practical-religious) dialogue.

1. Research and reflection on Western religious heritages would be the first step for the practical theologian. But this research would be both appreciative and critical. It also would show how the various strands of its marriage heritage — Jewish, early Christian, Greek, Roman, Catholic, and Protestant — interacted not only with each other but with other philosophical, legal, and social traditions. Gradually other religions not identified with the Abrahamic traditions would be invited to participate in the dialogue and this task of critical retrieval. The divisive issues of homosexuality and abortion would not be eliminated but would not be center stage. The more tractable issues of fatherlessness, nonmarital births, the declining well-being of children and women, and the deinstitutionalization of marriage and family would be more central.

2. The Western marriage traditions would be not only understood but reconstructed and reformed. Certainly, the most central agendas would be to reconstitute marriage on nonpatriarchal grounds and to address the associated work and family issues that face all modern marriages. This is the intellectual task of creating what my colleagues and I have called a "critical familism" and "critical marriage culture," or what family social scientist William Doherty is presently calling a "critical pro-marriage" philosophy.[70] These ideas refer to a pro-marriage perspective that requires gender equality both within the family and between the family and the public worlds of paid employment and politics. These concepts are elaborated more fully in Chapter Two in my comparison between the U.S. and South Korea and in Chapter Seven in my dialogue with feminism.

---

69. Hans-Georg Gadamer, *Truth and Method*, p. 289.

70. William Doherty and Jason Carroll, "Health and the Ethics of Marital Therapy and Education," *Health, Marriage, and the Professions*, ed. John Wall, Don Browning, William Doherty, and Stephen Post (Grand Rapids: Eerdmans, 2002), p. 216.

It may sound hopelessly utopian to think that either Christianity or other religions can be reconstructed to eliminate or soften patriarchy. For instance, leading feminist political theorist Susan Okin is extremely pessimistic about the potential in this regard of any of the world religions, especially Islam, to contribute to gender equality.[71] But recent research by a variety of scholars demonstrates that almost all of the great religious traditions are complex and contain significant themes emphasizing the equality and dignity of women. The themes are often obscured by the religious and cultural practices of these traditions in particular historic epochs.[72]

3. This practical-theological inquiry can, I believe, provide theological rationales for why marriage must continue to be seen, as it has been for the last four hundred years, as an interest of the state as well as religion. The core of such a public theology can be found in Protestant covenantal theologies where the state is also seen as one of the members of the marital covenant. Catholic subsidiarity theologies also had ways of understanding theologically why the state should be invested in families and marriage. In Chapters Six and Seven, I will define and discuss both covenant and subsidiarity theory as they apply to the institution of marriage. I also will argue that the best public theology for marriage eventually should bring the two models of covenant and subsidiarity together.[73] Marital arrangements need the protections, accountability, and public supports that the state has provided over the last few centuries. Young people should be helped to understand and appropriate why the state can be a friend of marriage, just as it is a friend of the possibility of driving an automobile safely, having clean water to drink, and having good schools to attend. I will contend that marriage is a public institution as well as a deeply meaningful personal and spiritual relationship. In keeping with this, the state should find ways to reward marriage, support the child-

71. Susan Moller Okin, *Is Multiculturalism Bad for Women?*, ed. Joshua Cohen, Matthew Howard, and Martha Nussbaum (Princeton: Princeton University Press, 1999).

72. Keith Soko, "Human Rights and the Poor in the World Religions," *Horizons* 26, no. 1 (1999): 37-39; Peter Donovan, "Do Different Religions Share Moral Common Ground?," *Religious Studies* 22 (September-December 1986): 31-55; Raymond Pannier, "Is the Notion of Human Rights a Western Concept?," *Diagnose* 120 (Winter 1982): 75-102; Abdullahi Ahmed An-Na'im, *Toward an Islamic Reformation: Civil Liberties, Human Rights, and International Law* (Syracuse, N.Y.: Syracuse University Press, 1990).

73. An attempt to bring the two models together can be found in Don Browning et al., *From Culture Wars to Common Ground,* ch. 8; see also D. Browning, "World Family Trends," *The Cambridge Companion to Christian Ethics* (Cambridge: Cambridge University Press, 2001), pp. 243-60.

bearing aspects of marriage with tax breaks, give welfare benefits when needed, and provide state-supported marriage education as now occurs in Australia and the states of Florida and Arizona and as presently advocated by President Bush and debated by the U.S. Congress. State-supported marriage education should supplement, not replace, the marriage preparation of religious institutions and other parts of civil society.

4. Both state and religious institutions must learn to address work and family issues. The way this should occur will take different forms in diverse parts of the world. In the industrial West, market pressures lead couples to delay marriage, absorb more of their time after marriage, and are factors in these societies that contribute to divorce. Married couples in these areas of the world have little time for each other and less time for parenting. New structural accommodations to provide more part-time and flex-time jobs are needed. Furthermore, a family ideal of no more than a combined sixty-hour work week for a couple with children should be encouraged in most of the wealthier modern societies, as my colleagues and I argued in *From Culture Wars to Common Ground: Religion and the American Family Debate* (1997, 2000).[74] To accomplish such an ideal, market and government must work with culture-making institutions such as church, synagogue, and mosque to create a new philosophy of leisure and new restraints on the consumerism that drives our compulsion to constantly earn more money.

Addressing work and family issues in other parts of the world will doubtless take a different form. This will entail providing more jobs; giving women access to employment, savings, and the vote; and providing work that will not entail the migration of family members to distant cities, thereby breaking family and marriage apart. Such recommendations are the standard ones coming from the research groups of the United Nations and other progressive policy centers.[75] As important as these recommendations are, they are often advanced without attention to the larger question of the enhancement and reconstruction of marriage in these parts of the world. More and wider freedoms for women will not lead automatically to the reconstruction of marriage and might unleash another set of difficulties as more and more men and women throughout the

74. Browning et al., *From Culture Wars to Common Ground*, ch. 11.

75. This is the tenor of the proposals advanced by the World Institute of Development Economics Research established by the United Nations and published in Martha Nussbaum and Amartya Sen, eds., *The Quality of Life* (Oxford: Clarendon Press, 1993); Martha Nussbaum and Jonathan Glover, *Women, Culture, and Development: A Study of Human Capabilities* (Oxford: Clarendon Press, 1995).

world pursue their reproductive destinies apart from the supports of marriage. Coping with work and family issues will take vastly different forms in different parts of the world. But in all parts of the globe, work and family issues must be addressed as a key illustration of the challenge to families that comes from what Habermas has called the colonization of the lifeworld by the systems world.

5. In Chapter Eight, I will show why marriage education, as one among a variety of strategies, is a requirement for the development of a critical marriage culture. Marriage education should begin in secondary schools. This is another reason why the state must be a partner in the reformation and revival of marriage. There are new curricula now available that help youth navigate the increasingly hazardous years of searching for an appropriate mate. These curricula also begin preparing young people for the institution of marriage. No one part of society can make such educational programs become fully successful. They must be established on a complex cooperative process supported by church, school, state, and market. They must be informed by critically tested marital ideologies and the best social science research to determine what actually helps. In addition to careful education about the spiritual meaning of marriage, church, synagogue, and mosque must also do their share of education for marriage communication. Knowing how to do marriage communication and use scientifically tested premarital inventories such as PREPARE or FOCCUS should be skills possessed by all ministers, priests, and rabbis and eventually by religious leaders of the other religions throughout the world. At the same time, these materials should be adapted, and in many cases are being adapted, to new cultural and religious contexts. The powerful marriage theologies of the different major religions help ground marital commitment. But amidst the turmoil of modern life, such commitment needs to be buttressed with well-internalized skills in interpersonal relations, conflict management, and what Jürgen Habermas calls "communicative competence."[76] Furthermore, skills and commitment must be reinforced by interacting marriage-supportive institutions.

Chapter Nine will conclude the book with a review and critical analysis of five world strategies for addressing the global crisis of families. The United Nations, the World Council of Churches, the Howard Center, the Roman Catholic Church, and the Religious Consultation on Population, Reproductive Health, and Ethics all have major analyses and solutions for

---

76. Jürgen Habermas, *Communication and the Evolution of Society* (Boston: Beacon Press, 1976), p. 26.

the emerging problems of families in the world. Only two of these global strategies — the Howard Center and the Roman Catholic Church — address the decline of marriage in any significant way or see the renewal of marriage as part of the solution of world family disruption. And neither of these take the reconstruction of marriage and the agenda of "critical familism" with sufficient seriousness.

In conclusion, let me simply repeat my central message. The forces of modernization and globalization are ambiguous for the institutions of marriage and family. They bring benefits, but they also can be destructive. But human beings in their freedom and culture-making capacities have the ability to harness and control these modernizing forces. They have the ability to reform and revive marriage as both a public institution and an intersubjective reality. To do this requires a multidimensional *work of culture* envisioned as an ecumenical, interfaith, intersector, worldwide dialogue. The discipline of practical theology should be a key initiator of this dialogue.

Chapter Two

From West to East: Modernization and Family in the U.S. and South Korea

The phenomena of modernization and globalization have powerful implications for families. As I have indicated, they offer more health, education, and wealth, at least for a portion of the world population. In addition to the goods of education and health, modernization and globalization have led to freer participation by women in the wage economy — goods often denied women in premodernizing countries. From another perspective, however, these forces threaten disruption within families and socio-economic inequality between families on such a scale as to possibly undermine the positive benefits that they promise.

More specifically, modernization and globalization have led to the heightened economic insecurity of many families, the domination of domestic life by the cost-benefit logic of the market, less economic dependency of husband and wife on each other, more divorce, and more non-marital births. Almost everywhere, they have been accompanied by less marriage, less parental time with children, the increased economic liability of children to their parents, increased poverty of single mothers and their children, and a growing absence of large numbers of fathers from the lives of their children. And, as if these were not enough, increased global awareness of the kind Arjun Appadurai discusses creates a heightened sense of relativity and contingency about the family patterns of one's own culture. These forces open new possibilities for family life, but they also sow seeds of uncertainty and confusion about the rightness of inherited family ways. Wealthy countries seem able to soften the economic consequences of these disruptions and confusions. But poor countries find increasing family turmoil a further burden that exacerbates the effects of bad economic conditions, overpopulation, disease, and political unrest. Family disruption is now an object of worldwide concern along with hunger, the population explosion, the pollution of the natural environment, and the AIDS epidemic. Family disruption makes all of these problems even worse.

The Question

What should be the response of Christianity to the consequences for families of the dialectical relation between modernization and globalization, i.e., the spread of technical rationality and the unpredictable new global awareness that goes with it? By asking this question, I am not implying that Christianity should be in the service of technical rationality in either its bureaucratic or market forms. I suggest instead that Christianity must in some manner respond to these trends — trends that Max Weber and others believed Protestant Christianity helped create but that are now autonomous forces with a life of their own. Even if certain forms of Christianity inadvertently helped give birth to these forces, it is now time for churches to recognize, evaluate, and guide this prodigal offspring called modernity. Of all the theological disciplines, practical theology with its concern to describe, critique, and transform human practices should take the lead in this task.

The question of Christianity's response to modernization and globalization is of momentous importance. All parts of the world are now dealing with these phenomena. Many Western intellectuals assume that liberal democratic polity is best suited to help market rationality thrive and, at the same time, best able to control it for the good of all participants. It is also easy for Christians from the United States to presuppose a special affinity between Christianity and liberal democratic social philosophy, therefore assuming that a partnership between them is the best combination to guide modernizing and globalizing forces. But recent trends in Western democracies toward the depleted vitality of civil society, family disruption, high rates of criminality, disappointing health and academic achievement among the young, raises questions as to whether liberal democracy is the only polity compatible with the challenges of modernization and globalization. In fact, as British economist Ralf Dahrendorf has argued, the recent though tentative economic success of certain Asian countries with their neo-Confucian and corporate values has some world leaders wondering whether the days of liberal democracy are numbered and whether globalization guided by the moral values of the East may be the wave of the future.[1] This is another example of the dialectical relation between modernization and globalization. Modernization and liberal democracy may impinge on parts of the East, but the rebound effect of globalization may bring neo-Confucian corporate and family values, as well as values from other parts of the world, back to the West. Indeed, as Hispanic, African, Islamic, and Buddhist groups increase in size in the U.S., their political and cultural voices will become more articulate and possibly influence political and cultural trends. Since September 11, 2001, Islamic voices in the U.S. have become more rather than less articulate, and this is as it should be. It is not clear that the processes of secularization and Americanization will mute these voices; rather, they may instead join other groups in our society to mitigate, or at least redirect, these modernizing forces. How does a Christian practical theology respond to these alternatives?

Christianity, Modernization, and the American Family

I turn now to a consideration of these issues from the perspective of North American experience. During the decade of the 1990s I was the director of the Religion, Culture, and Family Project at the University of Chicago. The first books it produced concentrated on the United States, a large enough field of study in itself. I come to this wider international discussion from the background of this concentration on the American experience. The scholars participating in this large project soon realized that in order to address contemporary family issues in the U.S. — especially the raging debate between conservative and progressive voices — we needed to learn how family philosophy, both religious and secular, emerged in Western and North American history. My colleagues and I tried to gain a more accurate and usable view of this history in *From Culture Wars to Common Ground,* the summary book of the early phases of the project.[2] More specifically, in order to understand contemporary American conflicts over the family, we needed to study how American religious and secular groups responded to the early pressures of modernization before the newer features of globalization as we experience it today emerged.

1. Ralf Dahrendorf, "A Precarious Balance: Economic Opportunity, Civil Society, and Political Liberty," *The Responsive Community* (Summer 1995): 13-38.

2. Don Browning, Bonnie Miller-McLemore, Pamela Couture, Bernie Lyon, and Robert Franklin, *From Culture Wars to Common Ground* (Louisville: Westminster/John Knox, 1997), ch. 3.

The family patterns of any society are deeply rooted in its history. Judaism, early Christianity, Greek and Roman culture, medieval Catholic canon law, and the legal and religious transformations of the Protestant Reformation — in its Lutheran, Calvinist, and Anglican strands — have all influenced the shape of American family life. I will review much of that history in the chapters that follow. Both conservative and progressive voices in the contemporary American family debate have deep roots in competing strands of European and American history. It is sufficient for the purposes of this chapter to begin with eighteenth- and nineteenth-century America.

The earliest decades of America were dominated by two major family patterns, at least for those with European ancestry. In the Northeast, there was the patriarchal "little commonwealth" family with its roots in English Puritanism, Calvinism, and the Protestant Reformation. Although companionate and affectionate in many ways, this model mirrored the hierarchical analogies between the father's authority and that of the minister and king and saw the family as a little school for training children in the virtues of responsible citizenship and free religious piety.[3] In the middle and southern colonies one could find even more patriarchal slave-owning families stemming from the mixture of Protestant and Catholic strands that formed Anglicanism and buttressed its close relation to the English crown.[4] While indigenous Indian families and slave families hovered in the cultural and social background, it was these two dominant white patterns that set the trends; they both ushered in and were the first to cope with the emerging forces of modernization.

These two patterns underwent significant transformations by the time of the Revolutionary War. Armed conflict with England, the beginnings of urban industrialization, the rise of revivalism, and the influence of the English and Scottish Enlightenment (especially the family theory of John Locke) unleashed progressive cultural forces in American life that affected families. These new trends curtailed the power exercised by fathers in the agricultural and craft-based economies of the early colonies.[5]

---

3. For a discussion of the New England Puritan family, see John Demos, *A Little Commonwealth: Family Life in Plymouth Colony* (Oxford: Oxford University Press, 1970); and for the Anglican family of the middle and southern colonies, see Stephanie Coontz, *The Social Origins of Private Life: A History of American Families, 1600-1800* (New York: Verso, 1988), pp. 76-78.

4. Elizabeth Fox-Genovese, *Within the Plantation Household* (Chapel Hill: University of North Carolina Press, 1988).

5. For a discussion of the impact of the Enlightenment on families at the time of the American Revolution, see Linda Kerber, *Women of the Republic: Intellect and Ideology in Revolu-*

Women developed more economic and political power, managed farms when their husbands died or were killed in the Revolutionary War, began to receive inheritances, were exposed to the liberal ideas of Locke, acquired literacy, and read books both to themselves and to their children. Young married couples and their children began to move into the city and participate in the emerging mercantile economy, distancing themselves to a degree from influences and pressures of the extended family.

The developments, however, that created the classic American middle-class family occurred during the early and middle decades of the nineteenth century. This new family was a response, in part, to the early signs of the modernizing process, especially in the form of market rationality. The move from an agrarian and mercantile to an industrial society accelerated the speed with which men left farm and craft and moved into the wage economy. This produced a new pattern of gender relations in marriage. Men earned money rather than growing and harvesting crops on the family farm. Mothers stayed at home, removed themselves from the more domestically centered economic activity of farm and craft, and became dependent on the wages their husbands gained in the competitive world of commerce. These rationalizing trends — this huge shift from farm labor to the wage economy — did much to create the classic nineteenth-century family made up of outside or public breadwinning fathers and domestic and economically dependent mothers.

But these forces were not the only influences on families. These economic trends interacted with the revivalism of the Second Great Awakening. Methodist-style preaching, conversion, and spirituality interacted with this new industrial economy to reinforce, legitimize, and purify this middle-class American family pattern. Mary Ryan in her important book *Cradle of the Middle Class* (1981) tells the story beautifully.[6] Methodist and Presbyterian revivalism, often promoted and organized by mothers and wives, used powerful male speakers to convert the unfaithful — often these same women's own husbands and young sons. In addition to confessing their salvation and allegiance to Christ, these male converts were supposed to be good workers in the new economy, keep from selling their souls to its materialism, refrain from the reckless drinking and fighting associated with the competitive business ethos, and be faithful and de-

tionary America (New York: W. W. Norton, 1980), pp. 13-32; see also Nancy Cott, *Public Vows: A History of Marriage and the Nation* (Cambridge, Mass.: Harvard University Press, 2000), pp. 14-16.

6. Mary Ryan, *The Cradle of the Middle Class: The Family in Oneida County, New York, 1790-1865* (Cambridge: Cambridge University Press, 1981), pp. 60-104.

pendable husbands. In return, wives were to be good housekeepers, competent mothers, faithful and supportive companions, and able teachers of their children. These revivals used the household codes of Ephesians 5:21-33, Colossians 3:18-25, and 1 Peter 3:1-8 (which, in fact, actually had their origins in Aristotle, as we will see below) to endow this family pattern with the aura of sacred legitimation.

The powerful institutionalizing forces of the law also figured in the mix. The relation between law and the dominant religiocultural synthesis was overlapping, if not downright intimate. This helped foster broad cultural agreement on matters pertaining to sex, marriage, and family. It also synthesized economic interests in marriage left over from Europe, the new forces of modernity, and certain images of marriage mistakenly thought to be found in the Bible. At law, the man was defined as the head of the house. The Genesis and Ephesians references[7] to marriage as "one flesh" were construed to mean that the wife's legal identity was absorbed into that of the husband. The one flesh doctrine was also interpreted to mean that the husband had legal, and even coercive, right to ready sexual access to his wife, even against her will.[8] These religious ideas were used to justify coverture, the provision at law that not only collapsed the wife's legal identity into that of the husband but also made her wealth his as well. Powerful and wealthy women sometimes negotiated prenuptial agreements that established exceptions to these rules, but women of average means had no alternatives. The use of the religious concept of one flesh to justify hard and unequal legal contracts had little grounds in scripture as such, a point that we will investigate at length in Chapter Three. But this was before the days of the critical reading of the Bible, a point often lost on contemporary historians who tell this story.[9]

My colleague Pamela Couture has shown that although there were many variations in this middle-class family pattern that was also supported by law, culture, and popular religion, most families — regardless of class, race, or ethnicity — tried to imitate this emerging pattern to differing degrees. Whether one speaks of mid-nineteenth-century southern families, urban black families, westward-migrating pioneer families, or immigrating ethnic Catholic families, they all copied the trappings of this

7. Genesis 2:24 and Ephesians 5:31.

8. Cott, *Public Vows,* pp. 11-12.

9. Cott herself makes no mention of the way scripture was being exploited in the various ways it was used to justify nineteenth-century laws on marriage and nineteenth-century responses to the early phases of modernity. She refers to it as "Christian doctrine" on marriage (p. 11).

emerging middle-class pattern even if they could not always conform to it in reality.[10] Certainly some poor black and white women worked and earned money outside the home, but they often quit at the first opportunity or stayed home as much as possible to support the wage-earning of their young children.

The nineteenth-century middle-class ideal of the family — with its synthesis of commercial, legal, and revivalistic elements — should be seen as a creative if flawed response to modernization in the form of market rationality. On the positive side, this pattern was stable in comparison to late twentieth-century families. Divorce was rare,[11] although many children were deprived of parental direction through the early death of a father or mother.[12] The nineteenth-century middle-class Victorian family was more companionate and child-centered than earlier Puritan families or slave-owning families of the mid-Atlantic or Southeast. This so-called Victorian family freed the domestic mother for volunteer activity in church and society and gave her time for the education of her children and herself.

But this same ideal pattern led to increased economic dependency of wives on wage-earning husbands, decreased and devalued the economic contributions of women, split the public world of paid job and politics from the private world of home and child care, absorbed the wife's legal identity into that of the husband, and maintained the patriarchal authority of husbands and fathers, although now more affectionately expressed. The intimacy of the religious conversion experience became a model for the intimacy of a shared life between husband and wife among many nineteenth-century Christian groups.[13]

Furthermore, in the latter part of the nineteenth century, this family form became hardened by the emerging fundamentalism of parts of evangelical Protestantism. Fundamentalist men began to reassert control of church life after a long drift toward what historian Anne Douglas has called the "feminization of American Christianity."[14] Fundamentalist churches bolstered the weakened patriarchy and separate spheres of the

10. Pamela Couture, "Religion and the Ideal Family: Its Nineteenth-Century Variations," in *From Culture Wars to Common Ground*, ch. 3.

11. Roderick Phillips, *Putting Asunder: A History of Divorce in Western Society* (New York: Cambridge University Press, 1988), p. 463.

12. Stephanie Coontz, *The Way We Never Were* (New York: Basic Books, 1992); see also her "Where Are the Good Old Days?" *Modern Maturity* (May-June, 1996): 38.

13. John Spurlong, *Free Love: Marriage and Middle-Class Radicalism in America, 1825-1860* (New York: New York University Press, 1988), pp. 4-22.

14. Anne Douglas, *The Feminization of American Culture* (New York: Alfred Knopf, 1977).

nineteenth-century family as a way of defending Christianity from the secularizing implications of market rationality and its implicit attacks on the traditional authority of men in home and church. This response by conservative Christian men to the authority-undermining impact of modernity is a phenomenon that began to emerge throughout the world. We have seen particularly disturbing examples of this in Islamic fundamentalism in recent decades, but other examples also abound.[15] In the beginning, this impulse among American evangelical Christian men was laudable; it inspired them to be responsible and do their share in church and home. Gradually, this fundamentalist response to early modernization hardened into a deeper patriarchy and male control of both church and home, all in the name of allegedly Christian values.[16]

These trends put in place the conservative wing of the contemporary American debate over the family. When Republican Ronald Reagan became president in 1980, a grand coalition of conservative political and religious forces began to emerge in American public life. This coalition was dedicated to the defense and preservation of the nineteenth-century middle-class family pattern. This nineteenth-century family pattern was championed by a variety of religiopolitical organizations such as Focus on the Family, the Moral Majority, the Christian Coalition, the Family Research Council, and the Traditional Values Coalition. These groups during the 1990s influenced the voting patterns of approximately one-third of American adults. These pro-family conservative movements tried to preserve and carry forward the nineteenth-century American response to the processes of modernization — processes that took the form of market rationalization in contrast to the bureaucratic rationalization that was developing in the budding new socialist countries of Eastern Europe.

This conservative strategy has its selling points. It accepts modernization in its market forms. In this sense, it is not reactionary. In fact, from one angle of vision, it is extremely pro-modernization. But it believes that the bargain we must strike with modernization is based on preserving a stable family with stable marriages. Furthermore, for the most part, it holds that families and marriages will be most successful if based on the nineteenth-century model, or some close approximation to it. It is as if an unmitigated market economy requires a strong antithesis, i.e., a private

---

15. See the description of machismo as a response to modernization in Elizabeth E. Brusco, *The Reformation of Machismo: Evangelical Conversion and Gender in Colombia* (Austin: University of Texas Press, 1995).

16. Margaret Bendroth, *Fundamentalism and Gender: 1875 to the Present* (New Haven: Yale University Press, 1994).

family with one partner in the work world and the other in the sphere of domesticity functioning as a balance wheel to the dynamism and excesses of market-driven modernity. It should be acknowledged that, when stated in this fashion, the conservative response seems rational. But it also may be unrealistic, unfair to both men and women, and far too optimistic about the power of families to survive the onslaught of market forces. One might say that these conservatives are guilty of wanting their cake and eating it too, i.e., of having and enjoying modernization in the form of a robust market economy but hoping as well that it will not destroy their families.

There are other groups in American life that have taken a very different approach to these same modernizing forces. They have their sources in the more rights-oriented and anti-patriarchal strands of American life, some of which go back, as I suggested above, to the Enlightenment, the Declaration of Independence, and the war with England. The liberal and progressive wings of the Democratic party, liberal social scientists, liberal and progressive feminists, and the liberal wings of mainline Protestant churches have taken a positive attitude to the family changes accompanying market rationalization — changes that have progressed even more rapidly in the twentieth century. These groups have applauded the move of wives and mothers into the wage market and the new economic independence of women. They have been more willing to accept the disruptions that market employment and market-driven consumption have visited on families. They have viewed them as fitting tradeoffs for the increased freedom and autonomy of women.[17] The attitudes of liberal social scientists from 1960 to 1985 were also for the most part positive about family change; they believed that increased divorce, later marriages, more single parenthood, more stepfamilies, and other family experiments were either not harmful or simply inevitable byproducts of a modernizing process that was otherwise benevolent.[18] In fact, the attitudes and values of the social sciences and the liberal churches were mirror images of each other until the early 1990s. While new data available to the social sciences tempered their optimism about recent family changes, the liberal Protestant churches, as revealed in their official statements, seem uninformed by the recent more realistic views.

From 1960 to the 1980s, progressive political and religious voices

---

17. For a more detailed review of the liberal Protestant response to the family crisis, see *From Culture Wars to Common Ground,* pp. 43-48.

18. Jessie Bernard, *The Future of Marriage* (New York: World Publishing, 1972), pp. 283-89.

joined with liberal social scientists to proclaim a new theory of family equality. These groups drew inspiration from the demands for equality of the 1960s black civil-rights movement; they claimed that all family forms were equally good for children, mothers, and men if society could only learn to accept them. If, indeed, there were problems of stress and poverty in some divorced or single-parent homes, modernization in the form of bureaucratic rationality — welfare and other government supports — should help these families survive their momentary disruptions.[19] In light of the prominence of this progressive pole of the family debate, conservative religiopolitical forces should be understood in part as a reaction to a prior, culturally powerful progressive thesis that was highly visible in the 1970s and 80s.[20] They called these progressive strategies the forces of "secular humanism," and felt that they were permeating government, the courts, public education, the professions, and the mass media.[21] Conservatives thought that these progressive forces had a thin theory of human rights that seemed opposed to tradition, at least tradition as the conservatives defined it.

The struggle between these so-called progressive and conservative forces should be seen as two types of positive response to the forces of modernization. Both on the whole are pro-market, and both are positive about the use of science to increase the power of market instrumentalities. Progressives see family disruption as inevitable and want to balance market rationality with bureaucratic rationality in the form of government supports. Conservatives have classically wanted to balance market rationality with a strong family itself, one supported by the institutions of civil society such as church and schools rather than by bureaucratic rationality. Wisdom, I will argue, is somewhere in between.

The conflict between progressive and conservative forces in the struggle over the American family was so intense that in 1991 sociologist James Davison Hunter published a book with the revealing title *Culture Wars: The Struggle to Define America.*[22] At the very moment that this book was published, fresh mediating forces between new groups of neoliberals and

19. For an articulate statement of this view, see Jan Dizard and Howard Gadlin, *The Minimal Family* (Amherst, Mass.: University of Massachusetts Press, 1990).

20. This reaction is nicely chronicled in Lee Rainwater and William Yancey, *The Moynihan Report and the Politics of Controversy* (Cambridge, Mass.: MIT Press, 1967).

21. James Dobson and Gary Bauer, *Children at Risk* (Dallas: Word Publishing, 1990), pp. 21, 24.

22. James Davison Hunter, *Culture Wars: The Struggle to Define America* (New York: Basic Books, 1990), pp. 31-64.

neoconservatives emerged in American cultural life. They were more visible in the halls of the U.S. Congress than they were in churches and synagogues. These individuals and groups were supported by a new generation of social scientists who became concerned about family disruption but did not absolutize the nineteenth-century family ideal. These politicians and social scientists wanted simultaneously to increase the responsibility of men, reduce divorce and out-of-wedlock births, enhance the status of marriage as an institution, and increase family stability, but do all this in such as way as to overcome coverture, avoid oppressive interpretations of one flesh, and enhance the participation of women in public life. They wanted to revise the welfare system to decrease the chronic dependency of recipients on state subsidies while making certain that all needy families received the help they required. They were simultaneously pro-welfare, pro-family, and even pro-marriage, but with a new vision of marriage.

In 1995-96, their cooperative efforts produced a fragile commitment on the part of the U.S. Congress and the Clinton administration to family stability with heightened equality for women and men. But this coalition, at the same time, reformed welfare by putting into law the Temporary Assistance to Needy Families (TANF) program. It gave welfare to the individual states to administer, made it essentially workfare, and limited its duration. Welfare was now being used as a social-systemic and cultural tool to support families by simultaneously reinforcing paid employment, marriage, and the two-parent family.[23] It was hoped that working mothers and fathers gradually would learn once again how to depend on each other rather than depend on government welfare payments. At this writing, there is still no definitive evidence that the coalition of neoliberal and neoconservative political groups that brought this experiment about will hold to assure its refinement and renewal by Congress, or, if this does happen, whether the experiment will work in the long run. Early evidence, it must be admitted, is encouraging; not only is welfare down in most states, but marriage rates and attainment of children have gone up in the states with better medical and child-care supports.[24] One study says there was a 50 percent decline in welfare rolls in the nation between 1996 and

23. Don Browning and Gloria Rodriguez, *Reweaving the Social Tapestry: Toward a Public Philosophy and Policy of Families* (New York: W. W. Norton, 2002), pp. 95-97.

24. The most successful state in implementing the 1996 welfare reforms up to the summer of 2000 was Minnesota. Not only have welfare roles declined, but earnings and marriage rates have increased significantly. See "Reforming Welfare and Rewarding Work: A Summary of the Final Report on Minnesota" (New York: Manpower Demonstration Research Corporation, 2000).

2000; 60 percent of this was due to TANF, with only 20 percent resulting from the improved economy.[25]

TANF should be interpreted, however, as a particular kind of response to the forces of modernization, one that tries to synthesize typically conservative emphases on a strong family with a progressive emphasis on continuing government supports. It may prove to be an effective experiment. But it does little to address the more profound strains between work and family, i.e., the need for more flexible work arrangements, better insurance for part-time employees, and other important supports and adjustments that will make it possible for parents to survive economically, participate in the economy, and yet not be completely inundated by its demands so that parenting and relating to each other are impossible. But I will discuss the work and family issue later in the book.

A Practical-Theological Response
to Modernization as Market Rationality

Market rationality in the U.S. has gone hand in hand with varying forms of cultural individualism. If we follow sociologist Robert Bellah's distinction between expressive individualism that celebrates emotional fulfillment and utilitarian individualism that champions efficient economic production,[26] political liberals have been consistent supporters of the former and conservatives the latter. Individualism is so much a part of American life that we often fail to see it. But when compared with the cultures of Asia and other parts of the world, we are individualistic through and through. We get this individualism partially from the biblical emphasis on the value of each person in the eyes of God, partially from our Enlightenment philosophical emphasis on the freedom and rationality of all persons, partially from the frontier mentality of a newly settled country, and partially from the economic individualism implicit in market economies.

The rapid increase over the last thirty years in the disruption of American families may be in large measure the result of the interaction between expressive and utilitarian individualism. It is good to be reminded, once again, of the marriage and family facts pertaining to the U.S., especially

25. June E. O'Neill and M. Anne Hill, "Gaining Ground? Measuring the Impact of Welfare Reform on Welfare and Work" (New York: Center for Civic Innovation, Manhattan Institute, 2001).

26. Robert Bellah, Richard Madsen, William Sullivan, Ann Swidler, and Steven M. Tipton, *Habits of the Heart* (New York: Harper & Row, 1985), pp. 32-35.

for what they imply for the decline of engaged fatherhood, a central concern of this book. In addition to the nearly 50 percent divorce rate and 33 percent out-of-wedlock birthrate, 44 percent of all children will spend some time under age 18 in a single-parent home, raised generally by the mother and away from the residential presence of the father.[27] Nearly 50 percent of all single mothers and their children are below the poverty level, and divorced mothers and their children suffer a 30 percent loss in income in the years after separation.[28] Although there are important exceptions, fathers on average are not very present emotionally and financially to their children after divorce. Two years after the divorce, only one in six children sees his or her father as often as once a week. Indeed, only one-half have seen their father within the last year.[29] The rates of most childhood health difficulties such as suicide, obesity, and mental illness doubled or tripled from the late 1960s to the late 1990s, with most of these downward trends well advanced before the stagnation of wages began in the 1980s.[30] Very recent statistics show a moderation in these declines in child well-being, but the mental and physical health of our youth is still significantly behind what it was three decades ago. Stagnating wages and global competition exacerbated family problems during this period, but these factors did not initiate the trends. Family difficulties between 1960 and 2000 were primarily a result of our own homegrown mixture of heightened individualism, market pressures, and other changes in cultural values. The trends undercut both families and local communities. Nonetheless, we eagerly export these values and social dynamics to the other countries of the world, some of which are poorly equipped to handle them.

The practical-theological response we argued for in *From Culture Wars to Common Ground* simultaneously affirmed and criticized aspects of both liberal *and* conservative political responses to the North American family crisis. In fact, our book gave something of a theological articulation to aspects of the neoliberal and neoconservative political dialogue that we discussed above. On the one hand, we agreed with liberal political and reli-

---

27. Larry Bumpass and James Sweet, "Children's Experience in Single Parent Families: Implications of Cohabitation and Marital Transitions," *Family Planning Perspectives* 21 (November/December 1989): 256-60.

28. Frank Furstenberg and Andrew Cherlin, *Divided Families* (Cambridge, Mass.: Harvard University Press, 1991), p. 50.

29. Furstenberg and Cherlin, *Divided Families*, p. 35.

30. Victor Fuchs and Diane Reklis, "America's Children: Economic Perspective and Policy Options," *Science* 255 (January 3, 1992): 41-42.

gious responses that want families to be guided by a love ethic of mutuality or equal regard. We thought that the liberal view was consistent in certain respects with early Christianity. It is true: early Christianity, as we will see in more detail later, never fully transcended the patriarchy that dominated the ancient world. But when seen in context, its trajectory was clearly toward extending to families the equal regard implied by the second half of the Great Commandment — "You shall love your neighbor as yourself" (Matt. 22:39). The earliest period of Christianity accomplished several other advances relevant to families. As we will see in more detail in Chapter Three, early Christianity refashioned a new model of manhood based on servant leadership, eliminated unilateral patriarchal divorce, elevated the leadership role of women, and rejected the double standard on sexual behavior that permitted men privileges and license that it denied to women.[31] The directions of early Christian family reform functioned to *fracture*, although never completely undercut, the honor-shame family patterns of the Greco-Roman world. These codes emphasized male dominance and the circumscription of wife, mother, and sister to the rhythms of domestic life. When the gospels, the Pauline epistles, and even the pastoral epistles are interpreted in contrast to these surrounding Greco-Roman family patterns, early Christianity emerges as one of the most egalitarian family movements in the ancient world.[32]

Critical theological reflection on the sources of early Christianity led my colleagues and me to propose for families a version of love as equal regard. This is a term for defining Christian love first introduced by Yale University ethicist Gene Outka.[33] We developed this concept, however, with the help of the neo-Thomistic insights of the Belgian Catholic theologian Louis Janssens.[34] I will say much about what love as equal regard

---

31. For references to the influence of the honor-shame categories of cultural anthropology on New Testament scholarship, see Bruce Malina, *The New Testament World: Insights from Cultural Anthropology* (Louisville: Westminster/John Knox, 1993); Halvor Moxnes, "Honor and Shame," *Biblical Theology Bulletin* 23 (Winter 1993): 167-76.

32. Halvor Moxnes, "Honor and Shame," p. 175.

33. For a classic Kantian-oriented statement on equal regard, see Gene Outka, *Agape: An Ethical Analysis* (New Haven: Yale University Press, 1972). For feminist statements of equal regard, see Christine Gudorf, "Parenting, Mutual Love, and Sacrifice," in *Women's Consciousness and Women's Conscience: A Reader in Feminist Ethics,* ed. Barbara Hilkert Andolsen, Christine E. Gudorf, and Mary D. Pellauer (San Francisco: Harper & Row, 1985), pp. 175-91; and Barbara Hilkert Andolsen, "Agape in Feminist Ethics," *The Journal of Religious Ethics* 9, no. 1 (Spring 1981): 69-81.

34. For a neo-Thomistic version of Outka's more Kantian perspective, see Louis Janssens, "Norms and Priorities of a Love Ethics," *Louvain Studies* (September 1977): 207-37.

means throughout the pages of this book. For now, allow me to say this: this view of love both affirms yet differs from theories of mutual love typical of the liberal-political groups and the liberal wing of the Protestant churches. Although we applied the idea of love as equal regard to marriage and family, we also advanced a *prima facie* theological and cultural case for the centrality of the intact, two-parent family committed to the support of children and the mutual love of husband and wife. We called this a "critical" love ethic of equal regard because of the equality between husband and wife that it first of all should promote and the specific set of secondary goods that it should also aim to enhance and protect. Love as equal regard should first order and help maintain intact families, although of course it can also apply to divorced families, stepfamilies, and single parents and their children. This equal-regard family should function, we argued, within an ecology of communal supports, both religious and secular in kind.

There are several theological sources for this presumption in favor of intact, two-parent families. Classical Lutherans and Calvinists resorted to the orders of creation argument that claimed that God sanctioned and blessed the conjugal couple of "male and female" in the *imago Dei* passage of Genesis 1:26-27 and the "one flesh" passage of Genesis 2:24. We used these testimonies of faith as heuristic guides that, however, must be critically tested and strengthened by arguments drawn from other sources. We found help in Catholic naturalism and contemporary evolutionary psychology's theory of kin altruism. Both of these sources, as we will soon see, give accounts of the natural investments of biologically related parents in their children — an investment that can be dislodged for various reasons but which, on average, is quite intense and therefore should be respected and built upon. We also made use of recent analyses of large demographic surveys by social scientists such as Sara McLanahan and Linda Waite, already discussed in Chapter One, showing the strengths of the two-parent family for both child and parent well-being.

We did not argue for the importance of the intact, mother-father family in ways that disparaged alternatives. We were aware of the overwhelming forces in our society producing family disruption in the form of divorce, single parenthood, and stepfamilies. These families deserve the constructive support of both society and its religious institutions. Nor did we in our book propose a return to the familism of the nineteenth century or the 1950s, with its split between the public breadwinner role of the father and the domestic and caring role of the mother. We argued instead for a "critical" familism and a "critical" marriage culture. By adding the word "critical," we meant to propose an ideal built around the equal-regard marriage that advocated equal respect and equal promotion of goods for both husband and wife, equal access to the privileges and responsibilities of both public and private life, and equal access to a discourse ethic designed to analyze and remove the power relations in families which block the realization of these goals. In addition to building on the neighbor-love ethics of the New Testament and the equal-regard ethics of Outka and Janssens, we also made use of the similar ethical ideals of feminist theologians such as Christine Gudorf and Barbara Andolsen. Our understanding of love as equal regard was also clarified by using Janssens's and Paul Ricoeur's effort to combine Kantian and Aristotelian ethics. They both accomplished this by subordinating Aristotle's view of ethics as promoting the good things of life (commonly called teleological ethics) to Kant's view that ethics deals with principles of universal obligation and mutual respect (commonly called deontological ethics). Furthermore, we placed this combination, as I will soon further explain, within a more encompassing Christian narrative framework.[35]

We argued that Louis Janssens captures the love ethic toward which the New Testament sayings were traveling. A rigorous ethic of equal regard takes with identical seriousness the respect and needs of both self and other, both husband and wife. The core of the New Testament view of love, even marital love, does not justify the legal concept of coverture, i.e., the sacrificial absorption of the wife into the legal oneness of the husband and his arbitrary control over her body. Christian love defined as equal regard does not view self-sacrifice as the end or goal of Christian love in families as do the strong agapic models of love found in Luther and his interpreter Anders Nygren.[36] On the other hand, love as equal regard, as we defined it, does not omit a place for sacrificial love and the cross. It envisions times for wives to sacrifice on behalf of husbands and husbands to sacrifice for their wives. But love as self-sacrifice, according to this view, is a moment within the larger framework of love as equal regard; it is part of the imperative to work hard, perhaps go the second mile, in restoring disrupted family relations once again to mutuality and equal regard. The sacrificial moment in love as equal regard depends, in the New Testament view, on a sense of the supportive grace of God that em-

---

35. Paul Ricoeur, *Oneself as Another* (Chicago: University of Chicago Press, 1992).

36. Martin Luther, *Lectures on Romans,* The Library of Christian Classics, vol. 15 (Philadelphia: Westminster Press, 1953), p. 366; Anders Nygren, *Agape and Eros* (Philadelphia: Westminster Press, 1961), pp. 53-60, 681-721.

powers the couple to deeper communication and forgiveness. Love as equal regard both values and critiques the modern drift toward individualism and self-regard; it balances a legitimate self-regard, which the gospel permits, with equal regard for the other and active work to enhance the good of the other, be this other wife, husband, child, or parent. But love as equal regard expects recognition and regard from the other as well. Love as equal regard is love as mutuality and contains within it the capacity for reversibility between self and other, i.e., the capacity to treat both self and other with equal respect and equal concern.

Implementing an Ethic of Equal Regard for Families

Our task in *From Culture Wars to Common Ground* was not only to conceive of the theological grounds of a new ethic for families but find ways to implement it. In a national survey that we conducted with over 1000 Americans, we found that there has been a colossal cultural shift within a single generation from valuing an ethic of self-sacrifice in marriage and families to an ethic that values mutuality. Fifty-five percent of Americans today believe that a successful marriage correlates with mutuality. Only 38 percent believe it correlates with love as self-sacrifice and 5 percent believe a good marriage correlates with an individualistic love ethic emphasizing self-fulfillment.[37] Women value mutuality even more than men, with 61 percent of female respondents and only 48 percent of males choosing mutuality.

But our respondents believed that their fathers and mothers saw love and family life very differently. Only 29 percent thought their mothers would have correlated a good marriage with mutuality. Fifty-six percent thought that their mothers and 40 percent thought that their fathers would have valued love as self-sacrifice. We do not know if Americans have clear understandings of the meaning of either mutuality or self-sacrifice, but we do know that today's generation of younger couples believe that mutual love is better and that self-sacrifice, standing all by itself, is worse for a good marriage, just the opposite of what they believe their parents thought.

We saw, however, that although Americans are valuing love as mutual-

---

37. *Love and Marriage Survey,* conducted by George H. Gallup International Institute in cooperation with the authors of *From Culture Wars to Common Ground* (Princeton, 1996). This report is on file at the Religion, Culture, and Family Project, Divinity School, University of Chicago.

ity more, they simultaneously are having difficulties manifesting this love
in ways that hold marriages together. Mutuality seems not to be backed
up with enduring commitment. Marital commitment is increasingly devoid of the ability to go the second mile; it seems to be a mutuality without the sacrificial love symbolized for Christians by the figure of Christ
on the cross. The forces of modernization and the cultural impulses of individualism are straining and often breaking even our capacity for mutuality and equal regard. Our emerging fondness for equal regard in marriage does not have the commitment, the tenacity, or the durability that it
needs to handle the hard times and the dynamics of the modernizing process. Family disruption, as the facts show, continues at a rapid pace.

Discourse Ethics and the Ethic of Equal Regard

In our prescriptions for the American family crisis, we emphasized in
From Culture Wars to Common Ground the importance of commitment *derived* from an ethic of equal regard. An ethic of equal regard gains its
meaning in a Christian context from the great symbols and narratives of
that tradition — principally, the concept of covenant and the classic Ephesians analogy between marriage and the sacrificial love of Christ for the
church — "Husbands, love your wives, just as Christ loved the church and
gave himself up for her" (Eph. 5:25). We interpreted this latter analogy to
apply equally to both husband and wife and to refer more to the sacrificial
moment in love as equal regard than to the headship of either husband or
wife over the other. We believed that there were scriptural grounds to do
this.[38] We argued that the religiocultural symbolism of Christian love has
much to offer a new critical familism and critical culture of marriage for
both church and the wider society.

But to be culturally effective, these great symbols must be strategi-
cally articulated in relation to a wide variety of other cultural and social
initiatives. In the last chapter of our book we offered nearly twenty practical suggestions for implementing a love ethic of equal regard. We were surprised, however, by the large role we eventually gave to the new premarital
and marital education movements in the U.S. and other parts of the

---

38. We took Paul's words in 1 Cor. 7:14 seriously when he wrote, "The unbelieving husband can be made holy by the wife." We interpreted that to mean that the Christian wife
could represent Christ to her husband in the way that Jesus represents the love of God to
the church.

world. I will describe this movement in detail in Chapter Eight.[39] It was our view that these programs are basically an implementation between couples and family members of what Jürgen Habermas calls "discourse ethics" and skills in "communicative competence."[40]

In other words, we tried to bring together a theory of discourse ethics, generally applied to solving problems in public life, with the communication needs of marriage and family within the fragmenting forces of modernity. In both politics and family life, there needs to be an ethic governing how we talk to one another — an ethic of conversation and dialogue. And the ethic for these two very different spheres is, strangely enough, more similar than one would think. Both entail an ethics of equal regard, mutual respect, equal right to speak, equal concern with the other's good, and equal obligation to listen and see the other's point of view as nearly as possible.

We took one more step: we synthesized our ethics of dialogue with a theology of covenant. The result was to understand the covenant of marriage as having its foundations in a covenant to dialogue. The marital covenant, we proposed, is a covenant to dialogue not only between husband and wife but also between parents and developing children. It should also be understood as a covenant to dialogue between family, God, church, civil society, and even the state. We followed Calvin in believing that all spheres of society (family, church, government, market) stand in covenant responsibility to God.[41] The history of these covenants in scripture and church history contains degrees of wisdom. But we are obligated to search

39. For the new marriage education programs emphasizing communicative competence, see the following: John Gottman, *What Predicts Divorce* (Hillsdale, N.J.: Lawrence Erlbaum Associates, 1994) and *Why Marriages Succeed or Fail* (New York: Simon & Schuster, 1994); Harville Hendrix, *Getting the Love You Want: A Guide to Couples* (New York: Henry Holt, 1988); and *Keeping the Love You Want* (New York: Simon & Schuster, 1992); Howard Markman, Scott Stanley, and Susan Blumberg, *Fighting for Your Marriage: Positive Steps for Preventing Divorce and Preserving a Lasting Love* (San Francisco: Jossey-Bass, 1994).

40. For a summary of Jürgen Habermas's mature thought on discourse ethics, see his *Moral Consciousness and Communicative Action* (Cambridge, Mass.: MIT Press, 1990). Recognition of the analogies of intersubjectivity in child development and discourse ethics is given by Jessica Benjamin, *The Bonds of Love: Psychoanalysis, Feminism, and the Problem of Domination* (New York: Pantheon Books, 1988), pp. 19-20.

41. See Witte's masterful summary of Calvin's theory of the multiple covenants that order marriage and its relation to witnesses, ecclesia, extended family, and the state in *From Sacrament to Contract*, pp. 94-100. Our emphasis has been to combine covenant theology with Gadamer's theory of interpretation as dialogue and Habermas's theory of discourse ethics. To honor covenants means interpreting covenants in a dialogue with the history of our covenants and with each other.

these sources, interpret them, have dialogue with them, and have dialogue with each other (both within marriage and between families and society) in an effort to discover the right and the good for human life. From the perspective of the family, the covenant to dialogue means the willingness to engage in a critical conversation with tradition, kin, and other spheres of society about the rights and goods associated with marriage and family life. *The great new task of all modern societies in the new global age is to create secular and religious institutions that will educate youth and adults in an ethics of discourse, interpretation, and dialogue as these apply to the family as well as to political life.*

South Korea and Its New Middle-Class Family

In the spring of 1997, Bonnie Miller-McLemore and I lectured on our family research at the meeting of the International Academy of Practical Theology in Seoul, Korea. In preparing for this event, we wondered what the results would be if our love and marriage survey also had been given to citizens of South Korea. Would we also find in this country a move toward valuing love as mutuality more than self-sacrifice? Would older Koreans value love as self-sacrifice more than today's generation? Would younger Korean women value love as mutuality more than men, as in fact younger women do in the United States? Or would images of love be quite different in that distant land? And finally, how are the institutions of marriage and family responding to the processes of modernization and globalization as they have been experienced in this Asian country? We wanted to study the variety of family and religious responses to the process of modernization. Is there a modernization process Korean style? And can the processes of globalization that expand our imagination — that second type of globalization that Appadurai describes — help produce enriched visions of family life for both the U.S. and South Korea by examining each together?

Recent research gives us some answers to these questions. Young middle-class married couples in South Korea have more role flexibility than their parents' generation, and the status of women in some ways has improved.[42] Women participate more in politics and the sphere of paid

---

42. For insights into how gender relations are more equal at the public level, but still less so at group and personal dyadic levels, see Chunghee Sara Soh, "Compartmentalized Gender Schema: A Model of Changing Male-Female Relations in Korean Society," *Korea*

employment, and younger men are somewhat more involved in child care. But in many respects, present family and marriage arrangements mainly reshuffle older patterns.

Discussions of South Korean families in the social-science literature offer the following portrait of that country's past and emerging present. We are told that since the end of World War II and the Japanese occupation, modernization as market rationality has significantly altered the dominant Confucian family pattern made official in Korea for centuries by the Yi dynasty.[43] As recently as the late nineteenth century, the Korean family was predominantly agricultural, and the more prestigious rural families followed the Confucian pattern. In these families, the father was often simultaneously something of a country squire *and* a public servant. His activities were centered "outside" the family, and his honor was based on scholarly learning, Confucian moral rectitude, and ritual enactments on behalf of ancestors. Mothers, on the other hand, were subordinate "inside" people with responsibility for the management of domestic affairs and the support of fathers and children, especially older sons. However, because of the importance of lineage and male sons to its continuation, a mother of a successful son could earn enormous prestige, psychological power, and influence — at least in domestic, familial, and even certain official Confucian circles.[44] Children were trained to honor their parents, especially their fathers, and elder sons were expected to serve and care for parents in their old age in return for the bulk of the inheritance.[45]

Other sectors of society tried to imitate the family patterns of Confucian elites. There were, however, alternative patterns of rather striking variety in rural villages and more remote areas.[46] Although there were, in the nineteenth century, loose parallels between the gender divisions in middle-class families in the U.S. and Confucian patterns in Korea, the reasons for them were quite different. The U.S. pattern was created by the

Journal 33, no. 4 (Winter 1993): 34-47; for the rapid speed of family and gender changes in South Korea, see Cho Uhn, "Compressed Development and Family Culture," *Korea Focus* 5, no. 3 (May-June 1997): 93-102.

43. Kim Doo-bun, "Historical Review of Korean Family Life," *Korea Journal* 3, no. 10 (October 1963): 7-8.

44. Haejoang Cho, "Male Dominance and Mother Power: The Two Sides of Confucian Patriarchy in Korea," *Confucianism and the Family*, ed. Walter Slot and George A. De Vos (Albany: State University of New York Press), pp. 196-98.

45. Eunhee Kim Yi, "From Gentry to the Middle Class: The Transformation of Family, Community and Gender in Korea" (Ph.D. dissertation, University of Chicago, 1993).

46. Hyungsook Yoon, "Rethinking Traditional Marriage in Korea," *Korea Journal* 29, no. 12 (December 1989): 17-27.

pull of men during early modernization into the paid workforce, a process sanctioned and made more responsible by the confluence of Christian revivalism and the family law of that period. In Korea, it came more immediately from the directives of a religiophilosophical ideology, a pattern that had yet to confront modernization.

Summaries of this classic Confucian family are used by some social scientists to show how this pattern is both retained and transformed in present-day, middle-class South Korean families. Some anthropologists refer to the contemporary middle-class Korean family to show that market rationality does not always produce individualism and the related family disruptions that we find in the United States. Anthropologist Eunhee Kim Yi argues that the Confucian high valuation of the father's outside public service to the Emperor has since World War II been transferred into the father's service to the modern corporation and its contribution to national wealth and prestige.[47] In the process, South Korean fathers have become more modernized and urbanized. But they bring a Confucian-like dedication to the companies for which they work that is reminiscent of their fathers' commitment to the imperial bureaucracy.

Wives, in the name of national honor and family success, support their husbands' long workdays and after-hours socialization with coworkers. The mother's primary role is to support the education of her children, especially her sons. Here, more than any other part of South Korean family life, one sees the shadow of the older Confucian family system; education is still the royal road to honor and success, and a mother's honor is significantly associated with the educational attainments of her offspring, especially her male offspring.[48] Although the husband's family line or *chip* is today less powerful than it was in the nineteenth century, it is still highly cohesive in comparison to American extended families.

Middle-class women, we are told, are now educated and frequently work and socialize outside the home. But their paid employment is pursued more for the good of the family and husband's *chip* than as an end in itself or a matter of individual fulfillment. In Korea, some commentators argue, modernization and family solidarity are going hand-in-hand, whereas in other parts of the world, family cohesion is generally sacrificed to these emerging forces. This may be happening because the equal-regard marriage is still not very advanced in that country, if by equal regard one

47. Yi, "From Gentry to the Middle Class," pp. 224-54.
48. Yi, "From Gentry to the Middle Class," pp. 401-9; Byungchui Ahn, "The College Admission and the Family," *Korea Journal* 35, no. 2 (Summer 1995): 82.

includes the idea of equal access by both husband and wife to the responsibilities and privileges of both the public world of work and politics and the private world of child care and domestic duties. Western Christian missionaries to Korea did much to bring their women converts into leadership roles, especially in the field of evangelism. Because of the explosive growth of Christianity and the influence of Christian universities, hospitals, and other institutions, this influence has doubtless mixed with the forces of modernization to enhance the education, power, and status of women in that country.[49] But older patterns are still evident.

Social philosopher Francis Fukuyama believes that as the Protestant ethic gave rise to technical reason and market rationality in the West, the ethos of Confucianism has helped serve and consolidate the market rationality of Korea and other Eastern countries.[50] *But there are important differences between the two ethics. The Protestant ethic has been secularized in the United States and has become a public ethic of "utilitarian individualism," to use the phrase of Robert Bellah and his team.* The Confucian ethic in South Korea has now evolved into a public ethic of "corporate utilitarianism." One Korean commentator calls it an ideology of "efficiency," but with a corporate twist.[51] Dennis Hart says the Korean male is still a kind of Confucian "outside" person but now in the service of corporate industrial goals, not the "social and ethical norms" of the older Confucian order.[52]

In the U.S. culture, the increase of utilitarian values is supposed to enhance the individual; in Korea, utilitarian values enhance the nation, corporation, and *chip*. Although the modernization process is now several decades old in South Korea, its disruption to families has been modest in comparison to most Western societies. For example, its divorce rate moved from 3.1 percent in 1960 to only 16.4 percent in 1995.[53] But the heightened stress on fathers to serve the corporation or, in some cases, the family-based *chaebol*, is enormous. There is equally great pressure on mothers to serve the educational goals of children, to honor the father's

49. Yi Hyo Jae, "Christian Mission and the Liberation of Korean Women," *International Review of Mission* 74, no. 293 (June 1988): 93-102.

50. Francis Fukuyama, *Trust: The Social Virtues and the Creation of Prosperity* (New York: Free Press, 1995), pp. 46-47.

51. Han Wah-Sang, "Korean Society: Population and Development — The Korean System of Values: Centering around the Value System of Expediency," *North Korean Journal* 18, no. 4 (April 1981): 22-29.

52. Dennis Hart, "Class Formation and Industrialization of Culture: The Case of South Korea's Emerging Middle Class," *Korea Journal* 33, no. 2 (Summer 1993): 44.

53. Cho Uhn, "Compressed Development and Family Culture," p. 94.

family, and show ritual respect for his ancestors. And, who knows, fifty years from now, family disruption in Korea may mirror that of the West.

The strategies of both the U.S. and South Korea have been viewed as economically successful responses to the forces of modernity. In addition, they show how religious traditions, customary social patterns, gender relations, and educational values can interact with the dynamism of technical rationality in quite different ways. Both countries have created higher degrees of wealth for the middle and upper classes but probably, as well, greater economic distance between rich and poor. Both strategies — as is the case with all political-economic strategies — contain dangers, excesses, and potential idolatries.

The love ethic of equal regard, as I will interpret it in this book, makes the value of all persons — men, women, and children — the highest end of both domestic and public life. This means that husbands and wives should, in principle, have equal access to the responsibilities and privileges of both public and private life. This requires a reformation, in my view, of each of these spheres of life. Although our interpretation of Christian ethics finds a place for both individual and corporate utility as secondary goods, the manipulation and increase of the goods of wealth and honor — whether for individuals, families, or the state — must always be seen as subordinate to the valuation of persons as ends in themselves and as children of God. Hence, from the perspective of this ethic, neither corporate nor individualistic utilitarianism should ever become ultimate ends ruling a society and its families; neither of these should be permitted to subordinate, dominate, or eclipse persons as ends — as children of God, as *imago Dei,* and as people for whom Christ died. Neither strategy should be permitted to dominate either public life or the life of families. Both societies should take concrete cultural and social action to limit utilitarian expediencies and preoccupations. It is perfectly all right for a society to increase its wealth. Wealth acquisition, however, must be guided, as Habermas argues, by a process of intersubjective dialogue that encourages and respects the selfhood and contributions of all persons affected by the proposed plans, projects, and measures. The ethic of equal regard, as we will see later in some detail, applies to dyads and small groups; it also applies to the processes of social deliberation. It reflects the core of the Christian ethic. It also constitutes a viable social ethic for public affairs.

I have outlined in this chapter how American families have responded to the forces of modernization. I summarized the American debate over the family and suggested what the ethics of equal regard might mean for it. It would be presumptuous for me to become equally concrete about what this ethic might mean for how families should cope with modernization in South Korea or other countries of the East. It safely can be said, however, that wherever Christianity goes, it must struggle to keep in balance the values of family cohesion, equality within the family, the good of children, justice among families, and the proper balance between family needs and the public worlds of politics and paid employment. And it must attempt to subordinate the utilitarian goods of life, whether they take individualistic or corporate expressions, to the kingdom or realm of God.

Chapter Three

Christianity and the Western Family

In Chapter One, I described how modernization was partially produced by the rise of the Western conjugal family with its closer ties between husband and wife, its relatively egalitarian structure, and its high investment in a small number of children. We learned how this family pattern was both exported to the rest of the world through the spread of modernization and why it is now being severely disrupted by the very social processes it helped to create.

We reviewed three responses to this situation now being proffered by social scientists. One view, associated with the work of William Goode, holds that there is little to do to stem the tide of family disruption. Contemporary societies should instead organize themselves to become stable high-divorce societies or, more accurately, stable high family-disruption societies. This can be done by providing a system of social supports — in short, an extensive welfare system. The other view, represented by the thought of David Popenoe and others, insists that in addition to social supports for disrupted families, we must have a cultural rebirth of marital commitment, especially the commitment by men to their spouse and children. Outside of the social sciences, there are the secular and religious groups who promote cultural renewal alone; this position is generally associated with a return to the nineteenth century with its divided spheres, female dependency, and paternal authority. I identify with the middle position but with a much more radical view about the role of civil society in social change, the complex cultural work required to effect such change, and the importance of solving the tensions between work and family life wrought by the forces of modernization.

It is striking, and I believe accurate, to report that in the current international debate over the family, there is no mature and commanding position that has been developed from a Christian theological point of view. The World Council of Churches has made modest efforts toward one. There are more conservative proposals with worldwide implications from Allan Carlson of the Howard Center, and a global interfaith strategy also is being developed by the progressive Religious Consultation on Population, Reproductive Health, and Ethics. Each of these will be reviewed in Chapter Nine. These three religiously informed views, as I will argue, are in their early stages of development and are neither very mature nor very well tested.

The exception to this state of affairs among Christian bodies may be the message and work of the Roman Catholic Church. Some observers believe that the Catholic Church's continued prohibition of divorce, its teachings confining sexual expressions to marriage, its restrictions on artificial birth control and abortion, and its unflinching view of marriage as an unbreakable sacrament are more than just the thoughtless heavy hand of tradition. Some people think these positions reflect an informed analysis of the emerging impact of modernization on the world situation of families. Some commentators hold that such policies are just what are needed if the devastating consequences of these forces are to be averted. Other observers believe the official Catholic position is thoroughly bankrupt and itself further aggravates the world situation of families.

All of the options will be examined. But before I do this, it is best to confront the present and future by taking what Paul Ricoeur calls a "long detour" to the past.

Origins of the Conjugal Family: Preliminary Views

We saw in Chapter One that Goode, Popenoe, and Wolfe all neglect religion. Furthermore, they do little to speculate about the origins of the modern conjugal family. David Popenoe hopes that religion can help stabilize families, but makes little effort to understand its role in creating the modern companionate and conjugal couple. He describes, along with Peter Laslett and his team, some of the demographic family patterns unique to parts of northern Europe.[1] At one point, however, he does report historian Lawrence Stone's hypothesis that the companionate conjugal couple emerged from the Protestant Reformation's higher valuation of the per-

---

1. David Popenoe, *Life without Father* (New York: Free Press, 1996), p. 84.

son, a view derived from the Reformers' belief in the individual's immediate relation to God.[2] Goode goes further and directly credits the Protestant Reformation with creating a family form with the companionate conjugal couple as its core, but he does little to actually demonstrate that this is true.[3] Nonetheless, Goode is firm in his belief that the emergence of the modern conjugal family preceded the industrial revolution. He was aware in the early 1960s that its appearance in England and northern Europe prior to the industrial age could be documented. He observed that conjugal couples in northern Europe from the Reformation on generally lived in abodes separate from their extended families. This slight differentiation from their families of origin gave them the freedom and mobility needed to join the emerging market economy of the eighteenth century.

Goode's 1963 book was published prior to the rise of the scholarly work of Peter Laslett at Cambridge University, done primarily in the 1970s and 1980s. Laslett and his team extensively documented that the nuclear, or better, the conjugal family existed in northern Europe and England for centuries prior to the industrial revolution.[4] The Laslett school rejected the Marxist doctrine that the conjugal couple and their children differentiated from extended family was created by capitalist industrialism. The extensive analysis of church registration and burial records supports the thesis that this pattern of husband and wife close in age, living apart from families of origin, and with few children, existed before industrialization appeared in England. Because of its flexibility and mobility, it may have been an important precondition for the emergence of an industrial market economy.[5] Although the Laslett school is strong in proving that the conjugal family preceded industrialization, it is weak in explaining its ultimate origin and why it was most visible in northern Europe and the British Isles.

Cambridge historian Alan Macfarlane, an associate of the Laslett school, has provided interesting speculations about the origins of the nuclear family and companionate couple. He identifies four interacting forces: (1) the influence of German law, with its strong emphasis on the

2. David Popenoe, *Disturbing the Nest: Family Change and Decline in Modern Societies* (New York: Aldine de Gruyter, 1988), p. 71; Lawrence Stone, *Family, Sex, and Marriage in England 1500-1800*, p. 22.

3. William Goode, *World Revolution and Family Patterns* (London: The Free Press of Glencoe, 1964), p. 23.

4. Peter Laslett, *Family Life and Illicit Love in Earlier Generations* (Cambridge: Cambridge University Press, 1977), p. 13.

5. Laslett, *Family Life*, p. 13.

right of couples to freely consent to marriage without the interference of family, state, or church, (2) the absorption of this principle into Roman Catholic canon law and later embellishment by Protestant individualism, (3) the penetration of German law into England in contrast to the *patria potestas* principle of Roman law which put the power to form marital unions into the hands of fathers, and (4) the emergence in England of a market and private property system as early as the thirteenth century.[6] Law and theology, according to Macfarlane, interacted with emerging economic practices to create the conjugal family. These reasons should be seen as a complex, Weberian-type explanatory model. Ideal factors such as Christian theology and canon law interacted with and mutually reinforced early forms of market and private property to create this family pattern.

These suggestions by Macfarlane are important. His account, however, does not actually explain how Christian theology functioned in this trilogy of religious, legal, and economic causal factors. Macfarlane's account does not deal with the question of whether Christian ideas realized their own intention in history and culture on matters pertaining to marriage. His argument merely suggests how they indirectly and unintentionally liberated the English to pursue a new, individualistic, cost-benefit approach to marriage and family formation — what Macfarlane calls the Malthusian marriage.[7] This is a family in which romance, comfort, sexual satisfaction, and the fulfillment of individual members all get rolled into one. To Macfarlane, this prudential family was the end result of Christian ideas interacting somewhat unpredictably with German law and emergent capitalism.

Macfarlane agrees with William Goode that this new family fit capitalism; together this family model and economic system spread triumphantly to other parts of the world. England, the argument goes, gave the world capitalism and modernization; it also gave it the nuclear and companionate family. But Macfarlane does not discuss the issues that Goode and Popenoe do in their more recent writings, i.e., that the conjugal family once fit modernization but is being destroyed by it. This is an issue that neither Macfarlane nor his colleagues in the Laslett school have attempted to address.

6. Alan Macfarlane, *Marriage and Love in England, 1300-1840* (Oxford: Blackwell, 1986), pp. 335-42.

7. Macfarlane, *Marriage and Love in England,* pp. 35-37, 335-37.

Religion and the Origins of the Conjugal Family

Goode, Popenoe, and Wolfe were vague on the origins of the conjugal family. Only Macfarlane goes back earlier than the sixteenth century in his quest for the origins of the differentiated conjugal couple and their children. They all hint that Reformation Christianity may have had a role in the creation of the modern conjugal and companionate couple, but they never search for sources in early Christianity itself.

The quest for historical causality is generally elusive, even for the trained historian, let alone an amateur. In what follows, I do not attempt to establish clear causal links. Instead, I hope to be suggestive, offering possibilities that need further refinement. I will ask: If early Christianity had the impact on pagan families that recent historical research indicates, what does this mean for why families had the shape they had in the early phases of modernity?

Family Revolutions in Early Christianity

The Subversion of Male Honor-Shame Codes

In *From Culture Wars to Common Ground,* my co-authors and I distilled the best available scholarship on the family in the New Testament world. Here is a summary of the key points.[8] New Testament Christianity continued the high evaluation of the family found in ancient Judaism. This is true even though it also subordinated the family to the kingdom of God, thereby weakening the religiopolitical power over individuals of the ancient patriarchal clan or extended family. Christians were asked to forsake that extended family or clan if necessary in order to be faithful to the demands of the kingdom. In many instances, although certainly not in all, the tension between kingdom and family was resolved by converting the entire extended family, indeed the entire household as was the case with Lydia and her household (Acts 16:15), and incorporating it into the ecclesia or the household of God.

But many scholars today think that the earliest Christian families can be understood best against the background of the Greco-Roman family patterns that dominated urban life in most parts of the Mediterranean

8. Don Browning, Bonnie Miller-McLemore, Pamela Couture, Bernie Lyon, and Robert Franklin, *From Culture Wars to Common Ground: Religion and the American Family Debate* (Louisville: Westminster/John Knox, 1997), pp. 129-56.

world during the first centuries of the common era. This family pattern was characterized by what many anthropologists and New Testament scholars call an "honor-shame" code of ethics. This code celebrated male dominance and courage but also insisted on female submission and the circumscription of their daily activities. Because of the subtle way early Christianity wove together, even for men, an ethic of mutuality with an ethic of self-giving love, it functioned to fracture, although never completely eliminate among first-century Christians, this honor-shame code of the Greco-Roman world. This new Christian ethic emphasized the virtues of male servanthood in place of male dominance. Such words as those found in the famous passage in Ephesians, "Husbands, love your wives, just as Christ loved the church and gave himself up for her," were unthinkable within the strict logic of the honor-shame code. Early Christianity also significantly elevated the status of women, at least when compared to the rest of the ancient world. All of these shifts in family ethics must be understood within the context of the thoroughly patriarchal character of antiquity. Early Christianity never escaped antique patriarchy, but it seriously qualified it.

Rational-Choice Theory and Early Christianity

I will say more at the end of this chapter about the influence of honor-shame perspectives on early Christian families. In the meantime, I want to introduce a slightly different perspective by reviewing the insights into early Christianity and family set forth by Rodney Stark in his controversial *The Rise of Christianity* (1996). Stark is a sociologist of religion and his book is billed as an application of rational-choice theory to the sociology of early Christianity. Rational-choice theory is associated with the classical economic theories of Adam Smith. In recent decades it has been championed triumphantly by my colleagues in the department of economics at the University of Chicago. These more recent versions are called neoclassical economic theories, and they are having considerable impact as well on the disciplines of sociology, psychology, and anthropology. Classical economic theory held that economic activity — indeed, the entire range of human action — is motivated by self-interest. Human motivation works to maximize the satisfaction, within the context of available markets or environments, of a rather narrow range of hardwired human motivations, such as the drives for food, thirst, bodily comfort, pleasure, and procreation.[9]

9. Gary Becker, *The Economic Approach to Human Behavior* (Chicago: University of Chicago Press, 1991), p. 5.

Stark ostensibly relies on this narrow theory of human motivation to explain religion in general and early Christianity in particular. However, he so significantly expands and enriches rational-choice theory that it is better to understand his approach as an explanation of religion informed by a kind of philosophical pragmatism closer to the thought of William James than either the economic theories of Nobel Prize winner Gary Becker or the teachings of the earlier fathers of neoclassical theory such as F. A. Hayek or Milton Friedman. I want to review Stark's understanding of the growth of early Christianity mainly for the light it throws on what happened to the families that entered this religious movement.

Stark makes two very important points for our purposes. First, early Christianity underwent an explosive growth, possibly from as few as 1,000 in 40 A.D. to, as Harnack claimed, the majority of the Roman Empire at the time of Constantine, i.e., perhaps over 33,000,000 or 56 percent of the total population.[10] Constantine made it the official religion, Stark speculates, partially because it in fact had became the dominant religious force of the empire. The question arises, how did Christianity grow so quickly? According to Stark, what Christianity did with families constitutes part of the answer. Stark makes use of social-science research into rapidly growing religious movements such as the Unification Church or the Mormons to make sense of the scattered historical data about early Christianity.

His argument goes like this: early Christianity grew the same way that most rapidly growing religious movements do, i.e., through the conversion of close associates and family members in direct, face-to-face situations where high levels of mutual trust already exist.[11] In fact, the conversion of family members — spouse, children, extended family, and other members of the households such as servants and slaves — was the key to the rapid growth of early Christianity.

Stark's second point centers on how women played a strategic role in this conversion process. How was this so? Stark makes use of the growing body of research that demonstrates why early Christianity, when contrasted with families in the Greco-Roman world, undoubtedly functioned to elevate the status of women. This was true for many reasons, some of which Stark identifies but some of which he actually overlooks. For instance, early Christians prohibited infanticide and abortion. Both prac-

---

10. Rodney Stark, *The Rise of Christianity* (San Francisco: HarperCollins, 1996), p. 12; Adolf Harnack, *The Mission and Expansion of Christianity in the First Three Centuries* (New York: G. P. Putnam's Sons, 1908), vol. 2, p. 29.

11. Stark, *The Rise of Christianity*, pp. 13-21.

tices worked to reduce the number of women in the ancient world. Female infants were often the object of infanticide, and abortion was practiced as a way of limiting female births, especially if the family already had a favorable number of sons. Christians prohibited these practices, and this feature of early Christian communities doubtless attracted many women. It also gave the church other advantages. Stark uses the research of population historian J. C. Russell to estimate that there were between 130 to 140 males to every 100 females in Rome and other parts of Italy and Asia Minor.[12] Stark uses respected social-science theories to show that in groups where women outnumber men, their status rises.[13] Furthermore, women in the ancient world learned that in Christianity, the double standard pertaining to sexual behavior was abolished; men were to behave with the same sexual restraint as wives in the Greco-Roman world were supposed to follow. This also made Christianity attractive to many women. Finally, Christian women were given leadership roles as can be seen in Paul's delegation of missionary duties to Phoebe in Cenchrea and Prisca in Rome. Such roles for women were unusual in the religions of the ancient world, although there was some evidence of the elevation of women in the writings of the Stoic Musonius Rufus,[14] in some so-called mystery religions, and in the ceremonies of some Roman public celebrations.[15]

The key to the rapid growth of early Christianity, according to Stark, was not limited to the conversion of women through networks of female kinfolk or close friends. It resulted as well from the conversion of pagan husbands by their Christian wives. It also came about, according to Stark, because Christians of the second and third centuries cherished marriage and the family more than their pagan neighbors, valued children, refrained from infanticide and abortion, and, to say it bluntly, simply outprocreated their pagan neighbors. Because women were attracted to early Christianity, Christian groups doubtless had more women than men. Hence, Christian women often married exogamously, i.e., chose pagan men outside their Christian communities. Furthermore, since much of pagan religious identity in the ancient world was diffuse, Stark believes it is likely that the firmer identities of Christian wives led to the passive conversion of their pagan husbands, a phenomenon that Stark calls "second-

12. Stark, *The Rise of Christianity*, p. 97.

13. Stark, *The Rise of Christianity*, p. 101; see also Marcia Guttentag and Paul Secord, *Too Many Women? The Sex Ratio Question* (Beverly Hills, Calif.: Sage, 1983).

14. Carolyn Osiek and David Balch, *Families in the New Testament World* (Louisville: Westminster/John Knox, 1997), p. 63.

15. Osiek and Balch, *Families in the New Testament World*, p. 59.

ary conversion."[16] Stark contends that although the status of women was probably higher among those in the Jesus movement than women associated with more orthodox Jewish groups, early Christians otherwise held about the same pro-family and pro-natalist values as Jews. This should not surprise us; early Christians not only used the Hebrew scriptures, but much of their early evangelism was among the Hellenized Jews of the Diaspora.[17] Hence, Hebrew family values shaped much of early Christianity even as these same Christians transformed aspects of Jewish family traditions.

Because of these pro-family and pro-natalist Jewish attitudes, early Christianity grew in part because it simply outproduced pagans in the surrounding society. This hypothesis is all the more plausible in view of the widespread disparagement of marriage and children throughout the Greco-Roman world at that time. Stark writes, "A primary cause of low fertility in the Greco-Roman world was a male culture that held marriage in low esteem."[18] A Roman senator proposed making marriage mandatory as early as A.D. 131, and Augustus and Julius Caesar tried to induce marriage and procreation through various forms of reward. Nothing seemed to work. "Although virginity was demanded of brides, and chastity of wives," Stark uses the research of Pomery and Sandison to assert that the sexual morality of the ancient world was not exemplary. He writes,

> men tended to be quite promiscuous and female prostitutes abounded in Greco-Roman cities — from the twopenny *obalariae* who worked the streets to high-priced, well-bred courtesans. Greco-Roman cities also sustained substantial numbers of male prostitutes, as bisexuality and homosexuality were common.[19]

This is the world into which early Christian family ethics entered and, if we are to believe Stark, this is the world in which it thrived.

There are problems with both Stark's data and his theory. His data neglect important parts of the story, especially ascetic developments in second-century Christianity. The inadequacies of his historical data, however, may not completely destroy his argument. The theoretical limitations of a thoroughgoing rational-choice argument also need to be recog-

16. Stark, *The Rise of Christianity*, p. 111.
17. Stark, *The Rise of Christianity*, pp. 49-71.
18. Stark, *The Rise of Christianity*, p. 117.
19. Stark, *The Rise of Christianity*, p. 117.

nized. However, in spite of the corrections that need to be made, much of Stark's thesis retains the status of a good hypothesis.

First, let's look at the historical facts. Students of early Christianity, especially the second and third century, may be quite surprised to hear Stark say that this fragile movement was pro-natalist. What about the anti-sex and anti-marriage movements in second- and third-century Christianity? These are the themes that run throughout Peter Brown's engaging *Body and Society* (1988). Seen from Brown's perspective, second-century Christianity shifted from its effort to confine sexuality to marriage and to subordinate it to the pursuit of the kingdom of God to a far more skeptical if not an overt rejection of sexuality and marriage. Prophecy inspired by the experience and knowledge of the Holy Spirit became central for such figures as Hermas, Perpetua, and the learned Tertullian. The courage to face persecution and then gradually the capacity for continence, both in and outside of marriage, came to be seen as marks of possessing the Spirit.[20] A more radical renunciation of sexuality and procreation were seen in Marcion and the Encratite Tatian.[21] And the gnostic Valentinus taught not so much a denial of sexuality and marriage as its lesser calling in light of the greater goal of female and male becoming absorbed into the Spirit.

But in nearly all of these cases, these radical teachings occurred within the context of worshiping, multigenerational congregations where many of the followers continued to live conventional married lives. As Brown says, "Married believers were tolerated by the Valentinians" mainly, it seems, because they generated children or souls "which would be gathered, in due time, into the Place of Fullness."[22] This view was shared by the great theologian Tertullian who "thought instinctively in terms of a fixed hierarchy of age groups, and of a church grouped around the Christian household."[23] The renunciations of sex and procreation may have been more counsels for the middle-aged and the elderly; it is not clear that it undercut the channeling of sexuality into marriage and childbirth for the young. Stark could well be right that the residual pro-natalism of early Christian groups and the emerging asceticism of certain elites grew simultaneously and do not, in fact, contradict one another.

However this issue finally may be resolved by historians, at another

20. Peter Brown, *Body and Society: Man, Woman, and Sexual Renunciation in Early Christianity* (New York: Columbia University Press, 1988), pp. 73-77.

21. Brown, *Body and Society*, pp. 89-91.

22. Brown, *Body and Society*, p. 117.

23. Brown, *Body and Society*, p. 80.

more theoretical level, Stark's thoroughgoing rational-choice view of religion and the family is difficult to sustain. Rational-choice as a consistent mode of social-science explanation necessarily minimizes the role of ideas and ideals in shaping human behavior. According to the rational-choice school, humans pursue choices that they find rewarding or satisfying to their basic interests. As an example, rational-choice theorist Gary Becker argues that it was not the ideologies espoused by feminism that opened paid employment to women in the 1960s and 1970s. Rather, it was the reality that employers needed huge numbers of new workers to handle the technology and communication revolutions sweeping through the workplace. Feminist philosophies of equality, he claims, were epiphenomenal to, rather than generative of, the massive movement of women into the wage economy in Western countries during the 1970s.[24]

A close reading of Stark, however, reveals that he provides a greater place for the role of ideas in shaping conduct than the typical rational-choice social scientist. For example, he does not demonstrate that early Christian beliefs prohibiting divorce, infanticide, abortion, and the double-standard sex ethic were themselves produced by rational-choice motivations. Rather, he posits these motivations to show why such beliefs, whatever their origins, were attractive to women and had consequences that caused the Christian movement to grow. Furthermore, Stark does not use economics to explain the origin of Christian ideals that promoted women's greater leadership roles; he simply shows why these ideals might have appealed to the interests of pagan women and thereby attracted them to Christianity. Finally, we do not learn from Stark whether women converted to Christianity in order to improve their social status or whether an improved status was an unintended result of their conversion.

By the end of his book, in the chapter titled "A Brief Reflection on Virtue," rational-choice explanations nearly vanish. With reference to the German historian Adolf Harnack's overemphasis on the role of theology in the spread of Christianity, Stark concedes that one should not go so far as to dismiss "theology as irrelevant." He writes,

> Surely doctrine was central to nursing the sick during times of plague, to the rejection of abortion and infanticide, to fertility, and to organizational vigor. Therefore, as I conclude this study, I find it necessary to confront what appears to me to be *the ultimate factor* in

---

24. Gary Becker, *A Treatise on the Family* (Cambridge, Mass.: Harvard University Press, 1991), p. 356.

the rise of Christianity. . . . Let me state my thesis. *Central doctrines of Christianity prompted, and sustained, attractive, liberating, and effective social relations and organizations.*[25]

This quote is stunning for its ambiguous and inconclusive meaning. One can only assume that Stark is saying that Christianity conquered the ancient world because it had theological ideas that did not have their origin in rational-choice motivations but nonetheless appealed to rational-choice calculations. Christianity, he believes, had many such unique beliefs and teachings. For instance, Stark tells us that the "the simple phrase 'For God so loved the world . . .' would have puzzled an educated pagan." Furthermore, "the notion that the gods care how we treat one another would have been dismissed as patently absurd." Finally, the idea that mercy and pity were virtues of the Christian life and characteristics of God would have seemed equally odd. Stark follows the work of E. A. Judge in saying that ancient philosophy "regarded mercy and pity as pathological emotions — defects of character to be avoided by all rational men."[26] Although this is certainly an overstatement, these qualities may indeed have been rarer in the pagan world.[27] Furthermore, the idea that love, charity, and mercy must go beyond family boundaries was also unique. Strangely, Stark leaves us with the thought that these are the core theological ideas that were attractive to the pagan world and led Christianity to transform family relations in antiquity. As Stark points out, Christianity grew through kinship networks and other intimate associations and spread outward from there to become the majority religion by the middle of the fourth century.

Philosophical Notes on Stark's Argument

Stark's sociological insights into the rise of early Christianity are helpful but not necessarily for the reasons he presents. They enlarge our under-

25. Stark, *The Rise of Christianity,* pp. 210-11.

26. Stark, *The Rise of Christianity,* p. 221; see also E. A. Judge, "The Quest for Mercy in Late Antiquity," in *God Who Is Rich in Mercy,* ed. P. T. O'Brien and D. G. Peterson (Sydney: Macquarie University Press, 1986), pp. 107-21.

27. For an analysis of the Roman concept of *pietas* and how it reveals certain affectional and tender aspects of the Roman father's relation to his children, thus modifying somewhat the extreme heroic image of pagan fatherhood, see Richard Saller, *Patriarchy, Property, and Death in the Roman Family* (Cambridge: Cambridge University Press, 1994).

standing partially because his arguments are, in fact, not strict applications of rational-choice economic theory to the fields of religion and family. In fact, his arguments resonate more with the philosophy of religion of an American pragmatist such as William James than with the theories of neoclassical economists such as Milton Friedman, Gary Becker, and Richard Posner. A careful reading of Stark reveals that he is not the economic reductionist that he seems at first glance to be. He unwittingly does two things to stretch a pure rational-choice perspective into a more generous philosophical pragmatism. First, he unconsciously expands the motivational base that rational-choice theory posits. Not only do humans, according to Stark, desire the various satisfactions of this world, they seek a relation with the divine (even perhaps eternal life in communion with the divine). Humans also want, he seems to assume, a sense of personal validation that is offered by such ideas as the Gospel of John's teaching that God loves every single person.

Second, Stark time and again treats religious ideas as givens; he does not explain their origins. He simply analyzes their consequences. In this, he is like William James in *The Varieties of Religious Experience* (1902) when he repudiates searching for the origins of religious ideas and takes, instead, a phenomenological view of how the objects of religious belief appear to us in our experience and traditions.[28] Indeed, James was interested in the consequences of religious ideas, but he did not reduce religion *to* its consequences. Furthermore, he posited a generous range of human needs which he believed religion addressed. Religion for James not only satisfied our instrumental needs but addressed deeper ones such as our desire for some kind of immortality and an affective relation with the divine.[29] In short, a pragmatic philosophy of religion, of the kind that in part guides this book, acknowledges that the power of religions is based partially on how they satisfy our mundane needs.[30] But religions find their real power in how they address deeper needs of the kind that Stark unconsciously begins to acknowledge toward the end of his provocative book. Finally, we need not be fearful of accounts of how religion, even Christianity, address

28. William James, *The Varieties of Religious Experience* (Cambridge, Mass.: Harvard University Press, 1985), pp. 51-70.

29. William James, *The Will to Believe* and *Human Immortality* (both books bound as one) (New York: Dover Publications, 1956), p. 3 of *Human Immortality*.

30. In fact, the general philosophical position informing this book brings together Jamesian pragmatism and the hermeneutic philosophy of Hans-Georg Gadamer and Paul Ricoeur. Such a synthesis can be found in Richard Bernstein's *Beyond Relativism and Absolutism* (Philadelphia: University of Pennsylvania Press, 1983).

our mundane needs if we are attentive, at the same time, to how it elevates those needs and relativizes them to even deeper religious stirrings.

Early Christianity and Family: Elements Stark Neglected

Although Stark's practice is better than his theory, his lack of a sufficiently rich philosophy of religion blunts his understanding of the full reality of early Christianity's impact on families. Yet, in ways he does not fully comprehend or develop, he introduces an insight worth developing. Stark acknowledges the revolutionary character of early Christianity's view of men. Christianity's reversal of pagan views of men was even more profound than its transformation of pagan ideals of women, although in the end both shifts were dialectically related. He hints at this shift when he observed the centrality in early Christian theology of mercy, pity, and the *generous gift* of God's love ("For God so loved the world") — values that paganism often associated with weakness and cowardice. Stark justifiably could have gone on to say that these virtues were the antithesis of the male virtues of courage, agency, and dominance so celebrated in the Greco-Roman world that surrounded the Jesus movement. Had he done this, he would have opened his argument to some of the crucial insights from cultural anthropology and New Testament studies on the honor-shame cultural background of early Christianity. He also would have been more attentive in early Christianity to what I will later call an "ontology of gift" — a theological idea inspired by Karl Barth but more adequately developed in the philosophy of religion of Paul Ricoeur. This was an insight noticeably absent from the pagan honor-shame cultures over against which early Christianity was struggling to define itself.

In the seminars of the Religion, Culture, and Family Project, New Testament scholar David Balch often said that the early Christian family was "the Greco-Roman family with a twist."[31] This formula meant that in the urban centers of the world of Roman Hellenism, it was Peripatetic or Aristotelian philosophy that shaped popular thinking on the relation of family to the state. Why would this be true? It is so, he would remind us, for one simple reason that we often forget when interpreting the New Testament. Roughly three hundred years before the Christian era, Alexander the Great had conquered the Mediterranean world. Even when Rome ex-

---

31. For the development of this point of view, see Carolyn Osiek and David Balch, *Families in the New Testament World.*

erted its control over this area a few hundred years later, it adopted many of the cultural patterns of Greece. It was Athens, more specifically Aristotle, that provided the so-called *Haustelfen,* or household codes, found in various parts of the New Testament, particularly Matthew 19-20, Colossians 3:18-25, Ephesians 5:20-33, and 1 Peter 3:1-7. Recent research has shown that these codes had their origin in Aristotle's *Politics* and *Nicomachean Ethics.*

Many commentators have noticed the striking similarity between Aristotle and these early Christian texts on the relation of masters to slaves, husbands to wives, and fathers to children.[32] In general, Aristotle taught that there should be a tyrannical relation between master and slave that would serve the good of the master. On the other hand, there should be a constitutional and aristocratic relation between husband and wife; the husband was the superior but had definite obligations to his wife and she, although inferior, still had degrees of authority, responsibility, and privilege. And finally, there should be a monarchical relation between father and child, one that gave the authority to the father but assumed it would be used for the good of his children. In each instance, the relation was defined to support the authority of the male, although husbands and fathers were to use this authority like a wise leader, i.e., for the benefit of the wife and children. The authority of the male was based on the assumed greater rationality of men in contrast to women and children. Aristotle spoke of friendship and equity between husband and wife, but he meant by this a kind of proportional equity whereby the person with the greater honor (in this case the male) would receive the greater goods and rewards.[33]

Aristotle's formulation of these family relations was widely recognized and honored throughout Roman Hellenism and clearly influenced New Testament portrayals of family relations. At first glance, there seems to be a near equivalence between Aristotle and Colossians, Ephesians, and 1 Peter on matters of family patterns and paternal authority. However, a closer look suggests that there are stunning differences — differences, in fact, that are so profound as to make the "twist" that professor Balch said the Jesus movement gave to the Greco-Roman family a very significant twist indeed.

Although early Christianity never completely escaped the patriarchy

32. Aristotle, *Politics,* Bk. 1, ch. 12 and *Nicomachean Ethics,* Bk. 8-9, ch. 10 in *The Basic Writings of Aristotle* (New York: Random House, 1941).

33. Aristotle, *Nicomachean Ethics,* Bk. 8, ch. 3; Bk. 9.

of antiquity, when seen in context it clearly fractured it. A brief comparison of Ephesians and Aristotle helps make the point. First, Ephesians 5:20 asks husbands and wives "to be subject to one another." Aristotle would have found this admonition as an affront to his theory of the superiority of male rationality. It was the task of the wife, according to Aristotle, to be subject to her husband, and it was the task of the husband to be a wise and judicious constitutional ruler of the family. To suggest, however, that this ruler should in some way be "subject" to his wife is a thought far from the core ideas of Aristotle's thinking on these matters. Second, the Greek word for submission is *hypotassomai*, a term taken from the Greek military and often translated as "subordinate." Mutual subordination between husband and wife suggests that Ephesians envisioned a moment during which a husband would be subordinate to his wife, an idea that would have seemed preposterous to Aristotle.

Third, the mutual submission of Ephesians was not based on Aristotle's philosophical assumptions about the superiority of male rationality. It was based, rather, on a common fear or reverence *(phobos)* for Christ that should be exhibited by both Christian man and woman. Both husband and wife were children of God and owed their salvation to the life and ministry of God's Son. Hence, their mutual submission to each other was not based alone on some anthropological capacity that adhered in men and women — something in the nature of the human itself — but on what they each owed to Jesus the Christ. Fourth, a revolutionary idea, when contrasted with the Aristotelian tradition, comes forth when Ephesians tells husbands to love their wives "as Christ loved the church and gave himself up for her" (5:25). This introduces the great theme of *agape* — Christ's sacrificial love for the church — but now applied directly to the behavior of men toward their wives. In doing this, Ephesians reversed the values of dominance and agency associated with Greco-Roman masculinity and replaced them with an image of male servanthood. And finally, Ephesians further assaults the heroic values of pagan antiquity by saying, "Husbands should love their wives as they do their own bodies" (5:29). By saying this, this great passage brings the second half of the Great Commandment, "You shall love your neighbor as yourself," directly into the inner life of marriage and family, further illustrating its meaning with special reference to bodily affections. This suggests an ethic of equal regard that is clearly distinguishable from the ethic of proportional equity carried by the Peripatetic tradition.

Christian Men and the Honor-Shame Code

In short, when Stark hinted that early Christians exhibited an ethic of "mercy and pity" based on the prior gift of God's love and contrasted these values with the heroic virtues of the Greco-Roman world, he was saying more than he realized about the differences between Christianity and paganism in their respective ethics of masculinity. Early Christianity effected not only a revolution for women, it also did so for men in their relation to women and children. Stark caught part of this when he observed that the Jesus movement undercut the double standard that gave men sexual freedoms that were denied to women. But he failed to recognize Christianity's full revolutionary influence on male ideology. This can be seen best when the transformations of early Christianity are placed within the context of the honor-shame ethics that dominated the Greco-Roman world, a topic I already have introduced but which now requires further clarification.

Anthropological research by J. G. Peristiany, Julian Pitt-Rivers, and David Gilmore and biblical studies by Bruce Malina, J. H. Neyrey, and David A. DeSilva have used insights into the honor-shame codes that existed in early twentieth-century Mediterranean communities to go backward in history and understand ancient Greco-Roman culture as well.[34] The patterns in both eras seem remarkably continuous even though they were separated from each other by centuries. The public and political worlds in these two cultures were controlled by free males who, in turn, celebrated the male virtues of dominance, agency, and courage. This is the male honor code. This code signifies an agonistic culture of challenge and riposte; when challenged, a respectable male was to defend his honor with verbal power and, if need be, physical aggression. This code also entailed the male obligation to protect and restrict the mobility of a man's wife, mother, and sisters. To protect them, males for the most part restricted women's movements to the private domain of home, courtyard, family life, and circumscribed ventures to the market. Upper-class women had

---

34. J. G. Peristiany, ed., *Honor and Shame: The Values of Mediterranean Society* (London: Routledge & Kegan Paul, 1965); Julian Pitt-Rivers, *The Face of Shechem* (Cambridge: Cambridge University Press, 1965); David Gilmore, *Manhood in the Making: Cultural Concepts of Masculinity* (New Haven: Yale University Press, 1990); Bruce Malina, *The New Testament World: Insights from Cultural Anthropology* (Louisville: Westminster/John Knox, 1993); J. H. Neyrey, *The Social World of Luke-Acts* (Peabody, Mass.: Hendrickson, 1991); David A. DeSilva, *Honor, Patronage, Kinship, and Purity: Unlocking New Testament Culture* (Downers Grove, Ill.: InterVarsity, 2000)

more prerogatives, especially with regard to matters of legal inheritance.[35] And their homes were often busy places with much penetration to the outside world, even the world of politics.[36]

Although it is not wise to overemphasize the strictures of these honor-shame codes, generally speaking if a woman was in any way insulted, assaulted, or sexually violated, this would cast great shame on the male protectors. On the one hand, for a man to intrude into the private world of another man's wife, mother, or sister and get away with it could in fact add honor to the offending male. Shame for a man meant being rendered passive and submissive, something to be avoided at all costs. On the other hand, a woman according to this code was expected to exhibit shame, meaning that she was willingly to restrict her conduct so as to not constitute a temptation to male intruders from outside her immediate family. Although it would be wrong to believe women had no initiative and power within their own spheres, their movements into the public worlds of trade and politics were limited. On the other hand, the liberty of the free male was expansive; it was both political and public in scope, but it also was sexual with easy access to female slaves, young boys, and prostitutes.

To understand the full meaning of the new Christian ethic of gifted love, mercy, and pity referred to by Stark, it must be placed against the background of the male honor-shame code of the pagan world. This culture of mercy and pity constituted a religiocultural reversal that critiqued and altered men's behavior as they became Christians. It contributed to a new ethic of male responsibility and servanthood. It was an ethic that engendered a direction that never completely overturned patriarchy in its day, even within Christian circles, but did give rise to new trajectories that we still struggle to realize more fully even today.

Honor-Shame in Gospels and Epistles

The fracture of the masculine honor-shame code can be found as well in the gospels and pastoral epistles. Warren Carter in *Households and Discipleship: A Study of Matthew 19–20* (1994) illustrates how the teachings of Jesus subvert the Aristotelian house codes and their embeddedness in the

35. Cynthia Patterson, *The Family in Greek History* (Cambridge, Mass.: Harvard University Press, 1998), p. 93.
36. Patterson, *The Family in Greek History*, pp. 224-25.

honor-shame codes.[37] They seem to fracture and undermine the Peripatetic formulas so pervasive in the ancient Mediterranean world. For example, Matthew 19:6 records Jesus' repudiation of divorce when he said, "For this reason a man shall leave his father and mother and be joined to his wife, and the two shall become one flesh." This breaks one of the key elements in patriarchal rule by the husband — the arbitrary and unilateral divorce of the wife by the husband. Shortly thereafter, we hear Jesus elevating the status of children. He uses children to symbolize discipleship: "for to such," we are told, "belongs the kingdom of heaven" (19:14). Later we hear that the possession of wealth is incompatible with the kingdom of God: "Truly, I say to you, it will be hard for a rich man to enter the kingdom of heaven" (19:23). In chapter 20, we hear the parable of the generous landlord who pays the last workers hired the same as those hired first: "So the last will be first, and the first last" (20:16). And finally, Jesus tells us that discipleship is like being a slave: "whoever would be first among you must be your servant" (20:26).

Carter gives a fresh interpretation of these four scriptures. They assume an audience that has been shaped by the hierarchical Aristotelian family codes that penetrated wherever Roman Hellenism had spread. Jesus' audience knew the customs that sanctioned the male householder's aristocratic rule of wife, royal rule of children, and tyrannical rule of slaves. Carter believes that the teachings and parables in Matthew 19-20 worked to undermine this pagan pattern and promoted a radical equality of discipleship in both household and economic life. He finds this in Jesus' strictures against unilateral patriarchal divorce, his insertion of the principle of neighbor love within the marriage context (19:19), his use of the innocence of children to symbolize life in the kingdom of God, his disassociation of discipleship from the customary honor accorded wealth, and his use of slavery to symbolize discipleship — all of which reversed images of honor associated with male freedom, agency, reputation, and dominance.

Following the anthropological studies of Victor Turner, Carter depicts discipleship in Matthew as a permanent or idealized "liminality." Hierarchy is replaced by a new community of equality between husband and wife, rich and poor, and a new appreciation for the analogies between childhood trust and adult faith.[38] This new liminality was carried into the house churches of the pre-Pauline church. It can be seen in the baptismal

---

37. Warren Carter, *Households and Discipleship: A Study of Matthew 19-20* (Sheffield, U.K.: Sheffield Academic Press, 1994).

38. Carter, *Households and Discipleship*, pp. 31, 41, 49-55.

formula of Galatians 3:28. Scholars believe this announced a new status for those who "have clothed yourselves with Christ": "There is no longer Jew or Greek, there is no longer slave or free, there is no longer male and female: for all of you are one in Christ Jesus." This formula further testifies to the fracture of the household codes of the Greco-Roman world. It reveals how relations between husband and wife, master and slave, Greek and Jew were redefined in these early Christian house churches. Furthermore, as Stephen Barton has suggested, these reoriented relationships probably radiated outward from the gathered *ecclesia* into the private homes of Christians and the wider public world, modeling a new relation between men and women.[39]

It is now time for a fresh understanding of the so-called hard sayings in Matthew and Mark which seem to pit Christianity against families, dividing son from father, mother from daughter, mother-in-law from daughter-in-law (Matt. 1:34-35; Matt. 10:21-23; Mark 13:12-13; Luke 21:12-17). These are not so much anti-family diatribes as critiques of the patriarchal clan family functioning as religiopolitical units that served to block individuals and families from discipleship in the kingdom of God and the ecclesia. They are certainly not attacks on the nuclear family or conjugal couple in our modern and postmodern senses of these terms.

Tension between loyalty to household or clan and loyalty to the kingdom of God has been pervasive throughout Christian history. It was generally resolved by converting entire families to discipleship within the *ecclesia* and then working to reshape the inner life of families to conform to the relational patterns of the house church. When this happened, an amazing interaction occurred between the pattern of life in the *ecclesia* and the symbolism of the family. As Stephen Barton says, family fidelities were maintained but transformed and subordinated to the higher demands of house church and kingdom.[40] At the same time, as the Norwegian New Testament scholar Karl Sandnes points out, the early house church became a new family without dispensing with old families. Furthermore, the church became a social security network of remarkable proportions, undergirding both needy families and individuals when customary supports collapsed.[41]

39. Stephen Barton, "Paul's Sense of Place: An Anthropological Approach to Community Formation in Corinth," *New Testament Studies* 32 (1986): 74.

40. Stephen Barton, *Discipleship and Family Ties in Mark and Matthew* (Cambridge: Cambridge University Press, 1994), pp. 112-20.

41. Karl Sandnes, *A New Family: Conversion and Ecclesiology in the Early Church with Cross-Cultural Comparisons* (New York: Peter Lang, 1994), pp. 56, 62, 177-79.

Here we have gone full circle and returned to the point well stated by Rodney Stark. Early Christianity simultaneously relativized the patriarchal clan family, functioned to differentiate the conjugal couple from its embeddedness in the extended family, affirmed families, converted families to the kingdom, equalized to a degree the balance of power between husband and wife, and supported families within the wider family of God's kingdom. This was its fragile and uneven vision and, as Stark has argued, this vision had consequences, some of which were in fact quite mundane and material.

Crucial to this new perspective was the redefinition of masculinity in early Christianity. As we saw in Chapter One, the great worldwide family transformations wrought by the forces of modernization and globalization have many symptoms and consequences, not the least of which is a new pattern of male detachment from families. Divorce, out-of-wedlock births, the emerging culture of nonmarriage — all of these and more end by removing huge numbers of men from families, their children, and the mothers of their children. Of the transformations brought about by early Christianity, the fracturing of the honor-shame code and the emergence of a new model of male responsibility and servanthood were among the most important. This must be granted even though truth forces us also to acknowledge that this revolution was incomplete. Nonetheless, it gave birth to models of male responsibility that influenced the West. These models were still largely available during the early phases of modernization, at least in the symbols of Christ's love for the church and the husband's love of his wife and children, conveyed by the history of the church. The transformations may have had more to do with shaping the modern, companionate family than Laslett, Macfarlane, Goode, and Popenoe were willing to acknowledge.

Now, these ideals may be collapsing wherever modernization and globalization spread. In some places, modernity's threat to males does more than disconnect procreation from care and male sexuality from long-term commitment to wife and child. Modernity threatens other male prerogatives because it also beckons women into the market and loosens traditional restrictions on their thoughts and actions. Modernity is a threat to men; it makes women a threat as well. Such dynamics are in the background of the great confrontation between religious fundamentalisms of various kinds and the emerging dynamics of modernization and globalization. This conflict, often viewed as one between the United States and Islamic fundamentalists, is more a conflict between modernity and those using religion to form a dogmatic reaction to it. Nonetheless, one of the consequences of modernity has been to aggravate the problem of male responsibility — what I have called the "male problematic."[42] This is the threat of modernity to loosen further the already archaic and fragile tie of males to offspring and their offspring's mothers. This also accounts for the reaction of traditional males to modernity's threats to their customary patterns of responsibility and privilege.

The fundamentalist reaction to modernity's threat to male prerogatives and responsibilities contains a grain of insight. It at least raises a very important question: How can male family involvement be maintained in the face of the challenges of modernity without absolutizing male patriarchy on the one hand or dismantling, in the spirit of an anomic new freedom and equality, male responsibility on the other? The dogmatism of traditional paternalisms may be no worse than the new message being shouted from the rooftops that says both men and women are equally entitled to be self-regarding yet tentative about marital, family, and parental commitment. The fundamentalist reaction intuitively understands the importance of this question even though its solution is unjust to women and children and wrong in its interpretation of both tradition and modernity. Finding a better answer to this question is the single most important task of a Christian response to the world decline of families within the context of modernization and globalization.

---

42. I first discussed the concept of the male problematic in "Biology, Ethics, and Narrative in Christian Family Theory," *Promises to Keep: Decline and Renewal of Marriage in America* (Lanham, Md.: Rowman and Littlefield, 1996), pp. 121-35; see also Browning et al., *From Culture Wars to Common Ground*, pp. 68-69, 113-14, 123-26.

Chapter Four

Marriage and the Male Problematic
in Aquinas and Luther

My question is this: What is a credible response, informed by Christian sensibilities, to the worldwide situation of families in the face of the pressures of modernization and globalization? What should be this response especially in light of the world development of what I have called "the male problematic"? This is the increasing tendency of men, partially due to the pressures of modernity and partially because of archaic evolutionary tendencies, to mate and procreate but live separately from their children and often relinquish their paternal responsibilities?

This chapter does not get to solutions. It addresses the religious and cultural presuppositions behind possible solutions. I will show that one of the accomplishments of the Western religious traditions — and possibly all of the axial religions — was providing a strong religious, even metaphysical, foundation for the integration of fathers into families and the lives of their spouses and children. The point I am preparing to make is this: however we proceed in the future, integrating fathers into families must be part of the program. This is true as a strategy for the Christian churches, but it also should be true for social policy in general. It is not enough to say that things are simply changing and that we just need to get used to what is happening with marriage and family. It is not enough to hold that children need help and that we should therefore intervene directly and meet their needs, although certainly we should take such steps as emergency measures.[1] It is inadequate to say that single mothers need

1. The strategy of meeting the needs of children without also addressing the declining culture of parenting and the capacity of couples through strong marriages to weather the

77

help or that women need education and liberation before their plight can improve. All this is true, but without also addressing the issue of marriage, its reconstruction, and the integration of fathers into this institution on the basis of a new ethic of equal regard, these other steps will have few results of a lasting kind.

The question of modernization, of course, was not an issue at the time of early Christianity. Technical rationality, in its distinctively modern forms, had not been created. *Technē,* however, as the rationality and art of the craftsman as Aristotle and others described it, was both visible and well understood in the ancient world. Efforts to balance *technē,* and make certain that it did not consume all of life were central goals of much of ancient moral philosophy.[2]

On the other hand, it would be wrong to say that there was nothing resembling globalization at the time of early Christianity. Globalization, before the rise of modernization, happened through the processes of war, trade, and the missionary movements of religion. And indeed, these forms of globalization occurred long before television and other electronic media gave global stimulation to our imaginations in the manner described by Arjun Appadurai. (See Chapter One.) War and the march of empires have always served to spread and mix diverse cultures throughout the world, as Alexander the Great did with Greek culture around the Mediterranean and as the Roman Empire did in blending Roman and Greek cultures with a multitude of local customs. Trade, of course, is a tool of globalization as entrepreneurs roam the world looking for markets, goods, and profits. But missionary movements are globalizing forces as well. We saw this in Christianity's spread throughout Asia Minor, Europe, and eventually into Africa, Asia, and the Americas. We saw it in Islam's spread from Mecca and Medina to southern and northern Europe, India, Africa, the U.S., and elsewhere. Globalizing forces may be advanced by powerful ideals, such as the concept of one God who is the author of both creation and salvation for all the world. All of these forms of globalization were present during the early centuries of the Christian movement.[3]

---

stress of modernity is characteristic of laudable organizations such as the Children's Defense Fund. One can hardly criticize the good that it does, but I for one could hope that occasionally the agenda of rebuilding marriage could supplement its social programs that address the well-being of children.

2. Aristotle, *Nicomachean Ethics,* in *The Basic Writings of Aristotle* (New York: Random House, 1941), Bk. 6, chs. 4-5.

3. See Max Stackhouse with Peter Paris, eds., *God and Globalization: Religion and the Powers of the Common Life,* vol. 1 (Harrisburg, Pa.: Trinity Press, 2000), and Max Stackhouse

Globalization can be driven by complex mixtures of forces. At times, globalization and modernization, as we have seen, have gone hand in hand. Furthermore, since the West was the chief source of modernization and since it also has been at times simultaneously Christian, evangelistic, and even militaristic, we can see why modernization, Christianity, and colonization often went together and reinforced each other. Christian family patterns for centuries were associated with the globalizing impulses of Christianity, but it was only in the nineteenth century that modernization was added as a distinctively new element.

A major theme of this book is the situation of men in relation to families within the context of modernization and globalization. Among all the conflicting transformations energized by modernization, the most ominous is the growing alienation of males from families, from the children they have fathered, and from the women who have given birth to their offspring. I have listed some of the reasons why modernization has had this consequence. If this trend is to be allayed, there must be multiple approaches to addressing the problem. Central to any solution must be a strong religiocultural reorientation of the meaning of manhood. We have seen how early Christianity addressed the male problematic through the ideal of male servanthood and the subversion of the honor-shame codes of the Greco-Roman world. In this chapter, I will make some unsystematic observations about how Christianity addressed the male problematic in later centuries, especially in the thought of Aquinas and Luther. We will learn that addressing the male problematic is more central to the genius of Christianity than is often realized.

It was easy for interpreters of the Bible to overlook the subtle ways in which Matthew, Ephesians, and a host of other texts functioned both to enhance male responsibility and moderate male domination. It is clear, however, that a kind of "soft" paternalism reasserted itself in the pastoral epistles. David Balch shows, however, that even in 1 Peter — which contains the notorious sentence, "Wives, in the same way, accept the authority of your husbands" (1 Peter 3:1) — there is a hint that this assertion has apologetic intentions designed to deflect criticism of the increased freedom of women in the early Christian ecclesia.[4] First Peter reveals a certain type of paternalism, but a kinder and gentler one that enhanced a father's

---

with Don Browning, eds., *God and Globalization: The Spirit and the Modern Authorities*, vol. 2 (Harrisburg, Pa.: Trinity Press, 2001).

4. David Balch, *Let Wives Be Submissive: The Domestic Code in 1 Peter* (Atlanta: Scholars Press, 1981).

responsibility for his children and a husband's servant relation to his wife. Primitive Christianity sowed some radical egalitarian seeds, but in the rocky ground of antique patriarchy they did not sprout and grow immediately. But little shoots did appear that have continued to spread throughout the cultural and religious landscape of the societies touched by the symbols of the early Christian story.

Christianity was not the only cultural influence in its day that mitigated the prerogatives, dominance, and arbitrary power of men. Paul Veyne says that in about A.D. 100, a new marriage ethic emerged in Roman societies that replaced an older ethic associated with the days of the Roman Republic. The earlier ethic had emphasized male dominance, *patria potestas*, the father's right to sometimes even commit infanticide, and the husband's freedom to treat his wife as a teenager or servant.[5] None of these prerogatives, as Richard Saller has cogently argued, were exercised as blatantly in practice as some historians have taught.[6] Roman fathers loved their children as fathers have for the most part around the world and throughout the ages. But paternal prerogatives were extensive and this new form of marriage moderated them. This new pattern was idealized among the Roman elite, entailed an unprecedented respect and affection of husband for wife, and a fresh sense of duty for men in the household as well as in politics and public citizenship. What was the source of this new family ethic? Veyne credits Stoicism, not Christianity.

But Veyne overlooks the extent to which Stoicism itself, as Will Deming has shown, influenced Pauline Christianity and how Paul in turn added new elements to Stoicism.[7] When Paul in 1 Corinthians 7 advised couples to exercise abstinence as a defense against lust and also instructed them to render to each other their conjugal rights, he was, to some extent, promoting Stoic values. But, at the same time, Paul placed these Stoic elements within his more encompassing teachings about humans as made in the image of God, his theology of justification by faith, his belief in a God who was also a caring father, and his expectation about the transformation of this world by the coming kingdom of God. Furthermore, if we take Rodney Stark seriously, Veyne may have underestimated in general Christianity's influence on the Roman world. Maybe the male servant-

5. Paul Veyne, "The Roman Empire," in *A History of Private Life,* ed. Philippe Aries and George Duby (Cambridge, Mass.: Harvard University Press, 1987), p. 36.

6. Richard Saller, *Patriarchy, Property, and Death in the Roman Family* (Cambridge: Cambridge University Press, 1994).

7. Will Deming, *Paul on Marriage and Celibacy* (Cambridge: Cambridge University Press, 1995).

hood motifs of Christianity were beginning to radiate to other parts of the Roman world even at that time.

Whatever the sources, Christian or Stoic, it is clear that within Christianity itself, a creative range of forces was coalescing to help fathers become more loving, responsible, and faithful. Indeed, I agree in part with the argument of John Miller in his *Biblical Faith and Fathering* (1989) and *Calling God "Father"* (1999). In these books he claims that the great image in Judaism of God as a caring and loving father was itself a fundamental model for responsible fatherhood among both the Jews and the Jesus movement of the first century.[8] There can be little doubt that when men sincerely believe that it is the basic character of God to be caring and nurturing, it inclines their imagination to be caring fathers themselves. This is doubtless equally true for men in Judaism, Christianity, or Islam; all three religions are based on an image of a creative, generative, and caring God who is the perfect father and the model of all fatherhood.

Where I part company with Miller is his belief that a form of mild patriarchy may be a necessary price to be paid to preserve the image of God as a caring and solicitous father. He is correct in one respect: patriarchy and paternal care can go together, and wherever men care for their children, that must be deemed a cultural accomplishment. As we will see below, Luther, who never completely abandoned a doctrine of male headship, nonetheless thought that a father's care for his children was one of the greatest responsibilities of men before God for one of the greatest of gifts from God. Al-Ghazali, the Islamic philosopher whose thought is full of principled patriarchy, could join Aquinas in saying that "procreation is the prime cause" of marriage and that "on its account marriage was instituted."[9] The belief that procreation was the main reason for marriage was a widespread conviction in the middle ages in Islam, Judaism, and Christianity. But al-Ghazali goes further and affirms paternal care as such. He quotes approvingly the venerable Ibn al-Mubarak who, in the midst of a great war, said that there was one virtue that exceeded fighting a justified battle. His followers asked,

"What is it?" He said, "A virtuous man." He continued, "A virtuous man rose during the night and beheld his sleeping children uncov-

8. For John Miller's argument, see his *Biblical Faith and Fathering* (New York: Paulist Press, 1989); *Calling God "Father"* (Paulist Press, 1999); and Don Browning, "The Idea of God as Father," in *The Faith Factor in Fatherhood: Renewing the Sacred Vocation of Fathering,* ed. Don Eberly (Lanham, Md.: Lexington Books, 1999), pp. 203-18.

9. Al-Ghazali, *Book on the Etiquette of Marriage,* in Madelain Farah, ed., *Marriage and Sexuality in Islam* (Salt Lake City: University of Utah Press, 1984), p. 53.

ered, and so he covered them with his garment. His deed is more virtuous than what we are doing."[10]

There is little doubt that patriarchy and paternal care can go together. It is also possible for equality between husband and wife to be characterized by a profound failure of paternal care and responsibility. In some cases, equality can go hand in hand with a sad neglect of both paternal and maternal care. But in contrast to the perspective of Miller, I claim that the task for our time is to combine a love ethic of equal regard between husband and wife with a powerful ethic of paternal care and responsibility. This, as I have been arguing, is a challenging cultural work.

We can say with confidence that Christian transformations of images of masculinity both built on the monotheism of Judaism and interacted with other movements, particularly Stoicism. But Stoicism was Aristotelian enough to still define the friendship of husband and wife as one of proportionality between a rationally superior husband and a rationally inferior wife. The question is, did the early Christian view of equality of male and female in their baptisms in Christ (Gal. 3:28) and their mutual subjection to one another out of "reverence (or fear) for Christ" (Eph. 5:20) open a deeper level of friendship than is apparent in the new Roman Stoicism?

From the perspective of the liberal gender attitudes of the last several decades, the Stoicism of the Roman Musonius Rufus, about whom I will say more in the next chapter, looks both repressive of natural human sexuality and chauvinistic, in spite of its language of respect and affection for wives.[11] When he said, "But in marriage there must be above all perfect companionship and mutual love of husband and wife," it was still assumed that the husband had the greater authority and that sexual passion was to be kept rigidly under control, even in marriage. His teachings did, however, function in both their philosophical and Christian forms to limit the unmitigated male agency of the honor-shame ethic of Greco-Roman popular culture. Assessed, however, from modern post-Freudian de-repression of sexual pleasure, this Stoic-Christian rapprochement is an easy target for criticism.

When we look at this Stoic-Christian ethic from the perspective of "the male problematic," i.e., the ease with which men fail to bond with

10. Al-Ghazali, *Book on the Etiquette of Marriage*, p. 68.
11. Cora Lutz, ed., *Musonius Rufus: The Roman Socrates* (New Haven: Yale University Press, 1947), p. 89.

wife and children or do so only on the basis of the double standard, it was progressive indeed. When viewed, for example, from the Christian Stoicism of Clement of Alexandria in his effort to find a balance to the sexual asceticism of the desert fathers, the companionate ethic of Stoic Christianity looks even more attractive.[12] Stoicism's narrowing of the purposes of sexual expression to procreation seems excessive today. But it did join forces with Roman law in making procreation one of the defining purposes of marriage. Procreation *(proles)*, along with a few other goods and purposes, was one of the chief goods of marriage that would later be affirmed and carried forth by great Christian theologians such as Augustine, Aquinas, and even Luther and Calvin. Hence, we have in the Stoic-Christian synthesis the mitigation of male agency, a funneling of male sexuality into procreation, an enhanced respect for women, a counting of wives as friends, and a connection of sexuality with having and caring for children. We must not forget Stark's view that the Jewish ethic of sexual restraint had itself contributed to this Stoic-Christian ethic and to the rejection of the Greco-Roman double standard in sexual relations.

As Jewish, Christian, and Stoic traditions interacted with local legal customs, the importance of consent and affection on the part of both husband and wife as conditions for a valid marriage became more firmly established. As this happened, there was a curtailment of the ancient Roman tradition of the right of the father and extended family to give daughters in marriage without their consent. This progressive step occurred in later Roman law, in some manifestations of German law (especially in those areas interacting with Roman law), and later in Catholic canon law.[13] By the tenth and eleventh centuries, this emphasis was so strong in Catholic canon law that the consent of a baptized man and woman in the present, even if unwitnessed or unblessed by priest or parent, was considered a valid, and indeed, a sacramental, marriage.[14]

Whether Roman law, Catholic canon law, or German law was the

12. For a discussion of Clement of Alexandria's synthesis, see Peter Brown, *Body and Society: Man, Woman, and Sexual Renunciation in Early Christianity* (New York: Columbia University Press, 1988), p. 133; see also Clement of Alexandria, "On Marriage," *Miscellanies,* Bk. III, in The Library of Christian Classics, vol. 3, ed. John Alden and Henry Catwalk (Philadelphia: Westminster Press, 1954), pp. 40-92.

13. For the story of the gradual limitation of the principle of *patria potestas,* see Philip Lyndon Reynolds, *Marriage in the Western Church: The Christianization of Marriage During the Patristic and Early Medieval Periods* (Leiden: E. J. Brill, 1994); James Brundage, *Law, Sex, and Christian Society in Medieval Europe* (Chicago: University of Chicago Press, 1987).

14. Brundage, *Law, Sex, and Christian Society in Medieval Europe,* p. 187.

main carrier of the emphasis on consent of both bride and groom is an issue I will not attempt to untangle. I will say, however, that since the interaction of German and Roman law had gone on for centuries, Macfarlane's judgment seems suspect when he claims that free consent by both husband and wife as the crucial component of companionate marriage was primarily a contribution of German law in thirteenth-century England. Nor should we exclude the contribution to the companionate ideal of other layers of history such as the Christian image of male servanthood, the *imago Dei* in both men and women (Gen. 1:27), the one-flesh union of husband and wife (Gen. 2:24), the extension of neighbor love to the marital relation (Eph. 5:28), and the synthesis of these ideas with Aristotelian and Stoic theories of friendship between husband and wife. I make no effort to develop clear causal links between these influences and the creation of the differentiated conjugal couple of the early modern period. I do believe, however, that the interaction of Christian, Stoic, and Roman marriage traditions has been neglected by social historians. Furthermore, the two grand ideas — the mitigation of male agency through male servanthood and the teaching that both male and female have dignity in their reverence for the Lord and their shared *imago Dei* — may have been of key importance for the emergence of the now embattled modern companionate marriage.

Nature, Creation, and the Male Problematic in Aquinas and Luther

It is now time to move toward more systematic considerations. The search for historical causality is important, but at best suggestive. In spite of their consequences on later developments, Christian family ideals must be described and evaluated on their own terms. I know of no better place to begin than with the teachings on marriage and family in Thomas Aquinas. I especially want to investigate the relation between his theology of marriage and family and what I have called the male problematic. The question is, does the Christian view of marriage add an impetus to male commitment which, if removed as a cultural and religious ideal, will weaken male integration with their wives and children?

Throughout these chapters, I have hinted at a plurality of sources that went into the formation of Christian family theory. More directly, I have suggested that Christianity itself cannot alone define for us what marriage and family are. It gives us instead a particular narrative and moral perspective that further qualifies natural tendencies and their institutional embodiment which are not in themselves unique to Christianity. Early Christianity gave special meaning to the interaction between Jewish and Greco-Roman family patterns taking place in the urban centers of the Mediterranean world. Later, it grafted these Christian meanings onto the family theory of Roman and German law. Underneath these non-Christian cultural, legal, and philosophical family theories were certain naturalistic assumptions that were not distinctively Christian. They had to do with how males and females bond, have children, and generally remain together.

I want to illustrate how in the thought of Saint Thomas Aquinas Christian theology built on and redefined generally held cultural assumptions. Even though Aquinas was not attempting to answer the question of family fragmentation in the context of modernization and globalization, when we correctly understand how the ethical and theological levels of his family theory relate to his naturalistic assumptions, we will gain the seeds of answers to several issues I have been addressing. These are the so-called male problematic, the precarious situation of families within the context of modernization, and what religion — more specifically Christianity — can contribute to addressing these issues. But the answers will come slowly, and we must earn them with patience.

Even more to the point, Aquinas will help us understand how religious and cultural symbols build on, redirect, and balance fundamental human inclinations and tendencies. This is what makes such symbols effective and powerful. Judaism, Christianity, and Islam believe that creation is good. The Genesis creation story that feeds each of these traditions depicts God as creating the "swarms of living creatures," "birds," "the great sea monsters," and "everything that creeps upon the ground." After finishing this great and varied work, we are told that "God saw that it was good" (Gen. 1:25). This suggests that all basic human instincts and tendencies were made by God and are good in some very fundamental way. This does not mean that they are always good in the fully moral sense, but they are good in the sense of being useful for living, effective for surviving, or enhancing for human flourishing.

But, as experience testifies, these various natural tendencies and inclinations, good as they are in this premoral sense of goodness, can be distorted by human anxiety, sin, and other forces. They can easily come into conflict. Powerful religious symbols gain their enduring effectiveness, I contend, because they build on these very fundamental inclinations but also redirect and in this sense transform them, rendering them in the process as more compatible with one another and truly enhancing for human life. In more theological terms, it was often said that God's continuing work brings the gift of God's good creation to its ultimate fulfillment.

Aquinas's theory of marriage and family depends significantly on observations that came from the comparative psychobiology of his day, primarily the work of Aristotle and his teacher Albertus Magnus. His psychobiology contained many errors, but, at the same time, contained remarkable insights when compared to recent perspectives developed in the field of evolutionary psychology. I will make some of these comparisons in the next chapter, but for now I will stay with Aquinas. Among his errors was his patriarchal view of women. This view was supported in part by the more dubious parts of his biology. It held that women were weaker both physically and mentally than men and therefore required male guidance in life decisions. Their primary purpose, according to Aquinas, was procreation; in saying this, Aquinas overlooked women's other potentials and capabilities, an issue we will review at length when we discuss the thought of Martha Nussbaum.[15] This view of women is generally referred to as Aquinas's "subordinationism," a feature of his thought that is clearly in error both from the perspective of modern psychobiology and recent biblical and theological research.[16] Nonetheless, there are dimensions of Thomistic naturalism that we should not overlook.

Aquinas gave us insights into some of the basic natural inclinations of life that marriage builds on, redirects, and in this sense completes. And Christian marriage symbolism can be interpreted from the perspective of how this transformational process occurs. Aquinas specified four natural conditions for why humans, in contrast to other animals, form families and develop the attachments that lead to matrimony. These four conditions are very similar, as we will see, to the conditions investigated by contemporary evolutionary biology. All marriage builds on and redirects these tendencies and inclinations, and Christian marriage does this in unique ways. Aquinas starts with the observation that animals procreate. Ulpian, the great Roman jurist, had seen this as a matter of natural law, the *ius naturale*.[17] Humans share this tendency with other animals and in this sense participate in the *ius naturale*. But there is something unique

15. Thomas Aquinas, *Summa Contra Gentiles* (London: Burns, Oates and Washbourne, 1928), vol. 3, ii, p. 115 (hereafter referred to as *SCG*), and *Summa Theologica* (London: R. & T. Washbourne, 1917), vol. 3, q. 92, a.1 (hereafter referred to as *ST*).

16. Kari Borresen, *Subordination and Equivalence* (Washington, D.C.: University Press of America, 1981).

17. Reynolds, *Marriage in the Western Church,* p. 7.

about human procreation. Humans are animals that form more or less enduring families where males join the mother-infant unit and help care for their infants and give aid to their mates. Aquinas asked the question, as does contemporary evolutionary psychology, why do human males bond with their mates and assist in raising their children when very few other mammalian males take on this task?

Here is Aquinas's answer. First, Aquinas believed that although humans share with other animals an inclination to have offspring, human babies are different from most other mammalian infants. They are highly dependent for a very long time on the care of an older parent or adult. For all other mammals and throughout most of human history, this support has come from the mother since she was the source of sustenance for the dependent infant. On the basis of this observation, Aquinas observed that in those species in which the infant is "able to seek food immediately after birth . . . there is no tie between male and female."[18] But when the female needs extra help to keep her highly dependent infant alive and the child needs the care of both parents for a long time, as is the case with human infants, then Aquinas tells us that there is a "very great tie between male and female, to which tie even the generic features of human nature inclines."[19]

But what are some other naturalistic conditions, according to Aquinas, which lead human males to help their mates raise their offspring? The dependency of the infant was not enough in itself to bond males to infant and mother. For instance, Aquinas was fully aware that human males have impulses toward promiscuity and toward the procreation of children with multiple partners. So what balances these male tendencies? Aquinas's answer, and the second major natural condition for matrimony, was this: it came from the recognition and the reasonable certainty that the consort's infant was also actually the male's. Aquinas writes, "Man naturally desires to be assured of his offspring and this assurance would be altogether nullified in the case of promiscuous copulation. Therefore the union of one man with one woman comes from a natural instinct."[20] Of course, when Aquinas said that this union comes from a "natural instinct," he overstated his case. He should have said something like this: among conflicting male tendencies, there are some which, when faced with the dependency of an infant that a human male recognizes as his,

---

18. Aquinas, *ST,* 3, "Supplement," q. 41.1.
19. Aquinas, *ST,* 3, "Supplement," q. 41.1.
20. Aquinas, *SCG,* 3, ii, p. 118.

can be channeled into enduring male-female family arrangements for the purpose of caring for that infant.

Aquinas believed families form for a third natural reason. This is for mutual assistance. As we have seen, Aquinas agreed with Augustine that procreation is the primary purpose of marriage and family, but a closely associated purpose "is the mutual services which married persons render one another in household matters."[21] Mutual assistance works to the benefit of both the male and the female. Just as the male helps his mate with their highly dependent children, the male receives untold help in return. This mutual assistance is clearly one of the natural conditions that function to bring couples together.

Finally, Aquinas acknowledges a modest role for sexual exchange in the creation of marriage and families. Aquinas, as did Paul and Augustine before him, taught that males and females in marriage should pay the "marital debt," that is, meet the sexual needs of their partner in order to avoid the lustful pursuit of nonmarital sex that is so disruptive to family harmony. But Aquinas said something more; he believed that regular sexual exchange was one of the many reasons that lead males to join the infant-mother dyad in the first place.

It is easy to miss the point that Aquinas's flexible natural law argument is not just a theory of family formation; it is more specifically a theory of why males join the mother-infant dyad. This makes his theory all the more interesting and all the more relevant to the global phenomenon that I have called the "male problematic" — the growing worldwide trend for males to drift away from families. The cure for this problem must be found in part in recreating the establishment of these natural conditions that brought about family formation in the first place. Reestablishing these conditions should be viewed as a multidimensional task that will involve economic, political, psychological, and religiocultural perspectives.

I will argue, however, that in spite of the importance of these natural conditions, such arrangements need to be reinforced by highly meaningful religiocultural narratives and symbols. These must be part of the answer as well. They are part of what I mean by the phrase "critical marriage culture." Aquinas's specific theological answer cannot be ours in any simple sense. But he can offer us profound insights into certain essential features of any viable Christian theological response.

Aquinas erected his more specifically ethical and theological understanding of marriage and family on top of this naturalistic base, and we

21. Aquinas, *ST,* 3, q. 41, a.1.

probably need to do something very similar to this today. Furthermore, his religious views take explicit account of both the integrating and disruptive aspects of these natural tendencies. He developed an ethical argument for matrimony before he gave expression to his final theological statement about marriage. It comes in the context of his Christian justification for monogamy.

Let us first examine his ethical argument. He first rejects polyandry — the arrangement whereby many men marry one woman. What is the substance of his negative evaluation of this form of marriage? Aquinas's answer, still primarily at the naturalistic level, is this: "man naturally desires to know his offspring, and this knowledge would be completely destroyed if there were several males for one female."[22] In short, in polyandrous families, men do not know which children born to a common wife are really theirs. Because of this, they are less likely to invest in and care for these children. For these reasons alone, according to Aquinas, such families are less viable arrangements. Here Aquinas is echoing Aristotle in his criticism of Plato's proposal that couples should procreate but allow the state to raise their offspring. In both cases — polyandry and state nurseries — the commitment and attachment of fathers is dampened if not fully undermined.

The problem with polygyny is for Aquinas even more directly ethical. It seems logical to assume that one man mating with several wives whose activity he carefully controlled could assume that the offspring of these unions would be truly his. Therefore, he might be more inclined to invest energy in their care, nurture, and development. But Aquinas, in spite of this reasoning, rejects polygyny as intrinsically unfair to women. In other words, he shifts the logic of his argument from the good coming from the father's investment in the care of his children (which polygyny might discharge with reasonable success) to the issue of the husband's just and equal treatment of the marital partner, his wife. He writes:

> Equality is a condition of friendship . . . were it lawful for a man to have several wives, the friendship of a wife for her husband would not be freely bestowed, but servile as it were. And this argument is confirmed by experience; since where men have several wives, the wives are treated as servants.[23]

22. Aquinas, *SCG*, 3, ii, p. 124.

23. Aquinas, *SCG*, 3, ii, p. 118. Aquinas gets close to stating an extremely important point that contemporary feminist theology is developing. There is cross-cultural anthropological evidence that the high status, equality, and public participation of women in a soci-

Here Aquinas is implicitly invoking the image of God that he believes is found in both male and female, although, it must be acknowledged, he believed it existed less perfectly in women. This image is the foundation for friendship between the sexes. Since this argument against polygyny invoked the doctrine of the *imago Dei* as the ground for friendship between husband and wife, it is also a theological argument based on the doctrine of creation. In short, it was the beginning of a theological-ethical defense of monogamy that held together the good of children, the integration of males into families, and the friendship of husband and wife. Monogamous marriage is required, as the argument goes, in the name of just friendship between husband and wife.

From here Aquinas moves to a more directly theological argument, one based more on the doctrine of salvation than the doctrine of creation. Everything he has said thus far from his standpoint would pertain to all humans, whether Christian or not. What follows in his argument constitutes one of the most authoritative statements supporting the Christian doctrine of marriage that one can find. It is widely known that Roman Catholicism holds that marriage for baptized Christians should be understood as a sacrament, a source of supernatural grace, and for this reason should be unbreakable. It is also widely known that this rules out divorce, although not necessarily annulment understood as an ecclesial judgment that the marriage was invalid from the beginning. But this brief characterization of the Roman Catholic view of marriage overlooks the intricate way in which the naturalistic and ethical levels of Aquinas's argument dialectically interact with his view of the narrative of the Christian faith.

---

ety correlates with the amount of time that husbands and fathers in that society invest in the care of their offspring. Mary Stewart Van Leeuwen has pointed this out in her *My Brother's Keeper: What the Social Sciences Do (and Don't) Tell Us about Masculinity* (Downers Grove, Ill.: InterVarsity, 2002), which just went to press as I was finishing this book. With the help of the anthropological work of Scott Coltrane and others, she argues that fathers' involvement in care of their children is more important for women's equality than other factors such as men's absence in war, relative size of males and females, and whether a particular society is agricultural or made up of hunter-gatherers. See her chapter six. Also see Scott Coltrane, "Father-Child Relationships and the Status of Women: A Cross-Cultural Study," *American Journal of Sociology* 93, no. 5 (March 1988): 1060-95. Aquinas knew that father-involvement in the lives of their children helped produce monogamy and that monogamy was more equal for women. But he missed the point that father-involvement in child care itself directly contributes to the higher status of women.

The Dialectic of Archaeology and Teleology
in Christian Marriage Symbolism

It is easy to miss a very important twist to the Roman Catholic sacramental view of marriage. It is commonly overlooked that it builds on the complex set of naturalistic and ethical arguments that I have just outlined. Furthermore, it is easy to ignore that Aquinas presents his entire sacramental view as an antidote that counterbalances what I have called the "male problematic" — the inclination for males to procreate without bonding to their children and the mothers of their children. This is Aquinas's view of the "archaeology," to use Paul Ricoeur's term, of male embodied subjectivity that the symbolism of Christian marriage organizes and redirects.[24]

A word on Ricoeur's theory of symbolism will help advance this argument. Ricoeur, the great twentieth-century French philosopher of language, has written much about the nature of symbolism. In his *Freud and Philosophy* (1970) and other writings, he argued that in order to interpret a symbol one must understand the unconscious archaeology of desire that is projected into the symbol and, indeed, transformed by the symbol. A symbol, he argued, has a "mixed language" containing a primitive archaeology based on natural inclinations plus a teleology or direction that points toward the person or cultural figure in the external world that has attracted these inclinations or desires. These objects of our love capture our desires and often dialectically redefine and transform them.[25] Ricoeur thought that the language of dreams, interpreted in part by the naturalism of Freud's theory of instinctual energies, was a way of identifying this human archaeology of desire.[26] Although in dreams our desires may only be repressed and disguised, in the symbolism of our mature religious and cultural life these inclinations and desires become refigured and redirected.

Ricoeur developed a theory of the dialectical relation of archaeology and teleology in symbolism, i.e., between the origin of our desires and their future redefinition in our mature religious and cultural narratives, metaphors, and symbols. He did this through a reworking of Freud's theories of identification and sublimation.[27] Desire construes or shapes the object of love through the mechanisms of projection. But Ricoeur uses Hegel's concept of "reduplication of consciousness" to suggest that the

24. Paul Ricoeur, *Freud and Philosophy* (New Haven: Yale University Press, 1970), pp. 12-26.

25. Ricoeur, *Freud and Philosophy,* pp. xii, 65-67, 149-51.

26. Ricoeur, *Freud and Philosophy,* pp. 159-63.

27. Ricoeur, *Freud and Philosophy,* pp. 478-83.

object of desire also shapes in turn the desiring consciousness.[28] To say it simply, we love our parents, but in our effort to maintain our attachment to them, we internalize their images and in the process actually become like them. This process modifies our desires. It is in this way that the objects of our desires, including divine objects, transform our archaeologies of love and carry us beyond our original wishes. The religious symbol, when adequately interpreted, reveals this tension between the archaeology of the original wish and the teleology of the object toward which our desires are transformed. In mature symbols, teleology is dominant over the archaeology of desire; in more regressive symbols and symptoms, the archaeology of the immature wish wins over the teleology of the object.

Ricoeur's theory of the symbol reveals what philosophers of science call a critical realist epistemology. On the one hand, the archaeology of human desire — what Ricoeur sometimes calls the "embodied cogito" — is known only through its inherited language games.[29] From another perspective, Ricoeur retains the naturalism and realism of Freud's rather thin theory of libido. According to Ricoeur, we only know our libidinous desires through the mediations of language, but nonetheless it is precisely these natural strivings that language and symbol in fact reveal, although often in clouded and indirect ways.[30] In what follows, I will retain the outlines of Ricoeur's view of religious symbolism, but I will alter and expand his theory of human desire by employing the following sources: the naturalism of Aquinas, insights into the nature of human desire coming from the new discipline of evolutionary psychology, and resonances to these views that can be found in a variety of ancient texts. I will look at desire, not from the standpoint of Ricoeur's use of Freud, but from the thicker view of desire found in this strange set of bedfellows.

Here is how Aquinas's view of natural desire dialectically interacts with his sacramental theology of marriage. Aquinas's sacramental view of marriage is carried forth by a narrative which sets up an analogy between Christ's love for the church and a husband's and father's love and responsibility to his wife and children. This narrative, when taken seriously, is an illustration of what the great phenomenologist of religion Mircea Eliade has described as fundamental to all experiences of the sacred: the sacred figure becomes a model or paradigm for the mundane life.[31] In the case of

---

28. Ricoeur, *Freud and Philosophy*, p. 461.

29. Ricoeur, *Freud and Philosophy*, pp. 42-47.

30. Ricoeur, *Freud and Philosophy*, pp. 47-54.

31. Mircea Eliade, *The Sacred and the Profane* (New York: Harper & Row, 1961).

the Christian sacred story, Christ's unbreakable sacrificial love for the church is a paradigm or model of a love for wife and children which Christian husbands are to recapitulate and reenact in their own lives. Christian men are to love God and love his son. This means projecting some of their natural desires onto these great religiocultural objects and then having these desires shaped and redirected by these objects in turn.

Christian husbands and fathers are to recapitulate the character of this loved religious figure into their own psyches. Aquinas uses the great passage from Ephesians which I quoted in the second chapter: "Husbands, love your wives, just as Christ loved the church and gave himself up for her" (Eph. 5:25). We already have seen how this passage fractures the hierarchical honor-shame code of the Greco-Roman world even though it did not completely vanquish it. Our purpose now is to view this same passage against the background of Aquinas's archaeology of male inclinations and his wider naturalistic theory of marriage and family formation. *In short, the Ephesians analogy between Christ and church and husband and wife functions to counteract deep male ambivalence about joining the mother-infant family, just as it serves to identify the male with Christ and, indeed, with God.* Note, that for Aquinas, the reinforcement of male inclinations toward family formation includes but surpasses appeals based on individual fulfillment of father, mother, and child; family commitment, especially for males, is also based on their imitation of God as this God, the very foundation of being, is revealed in Christ.

I will argue that Aquinas's mistake was not that he applied this grand analogy to men; in doing so, he addressed and even offered a potent symbolic solution to the male problematic. This was an act of theological genius on the part of Aquinas. *His mistake, however, was that he failed to apply it to women as well.* This was also a shortcoming of the original author of Ephesians but not necessarily of the entire New Testament. My critique of these passages (and critique them we must) does not concentrate on what they did wrong with regard to males but how they failed to include females in the grandness of their vision. Although I have argued that a central goal of marital love is mutuality or equal regard between husband and wife, in order to have and sustain this form of marital love, each member of a marital couple must have capacities for self-sacrificial love, even a sacrificial self-giving of the kind Christ has for the church. Aquinas's analysis of Ephesians, when seen against the background of his archaeology of male and female desire, shows that the sacrifice of each in some sense is compensatory; it serves to balance deep natural, yet ambivalent, inclinations and thereby functions to enhance mutuality. As we have seen already, and will see more deeply as we go along, the symbolism of Christ's sacrificial love compensates for the male inclination not to bond with child and partner. *In the case of the female, it can function to compensate for her tendency to bond with the child at the exclusion of the father.* In the Christian story, a Christian's capacity to build on and redirect these natural inclinations toward sacrificial and enduring love is based on his or her identification with the gift of God in the figure of Jesus. This is an identification that, in the end, should be understood as equally open, and equally required, by both the Christian man and the Christian woman.

The Ephesians analogy should apply to wife and mother just as fully as it does to husband and father. *This is all the more true when we realize that there is a female counterpart to the male problematic. This is the tendency for mothers to reenact the primordial mammalian family, i.e., to have children and raise them by themselves or with the help of a coterie of close female relatives or friends.* Aquinas described this inclination to a degree; he seemed to understand that in most mammals, this is the situation of females. He puzzled, as we have seen, over the conditions that changed this for humans. Can we believe that the worldwide move toward the absence of fathers from homes is without some inclination on the part of mothers to have children with or without the involvement of fathers? Both men and women, in their quest for mutual love, must have the capacity for sacrificial commitment within the context of matrimony.

To reemphasize the importance of a Christian view of marital commitment, however, is not to reduce the family problems created by modernity to a simple matter of building more commitment between husband and wife. More is needed. Stronger supports from civil society, government, and business are required. A new world culture of marriage education is necessary. A new global refocusing of the time available for parenting and spousal relations is needed. But however important these things are, the proper metaphysical ground of marital commitment is crucial to them all.

Luther, Love, and the Male Problematic

I now turn to illustrate the Christian understanding of marriage in Luther from the perspective of the male problematic. It is generally known that Luther helped bring about a monumental revolution in Western family practices. He elevated the vocation of married life over celibacy, encouraged monks and nuns to leave the cloistered life, made marriage a public matter under the control of the state although still blessed by the church, and, in the process, dealt a blow to the medieval practices of secret or clandestine marriage. Secret marriage, as I have mentioned, refers to the rather widespread practice whereby a marriage could be deemed valid with as little as a private exchange of vows between a baptized man and woman, unwitnessed by church, state, parents, or friends.[32] According to the stipulations of canon law, this exchange always had to be stated in the present. It could not be a promise of marriage in the future. But if a Christian man and woman claimed that both of them had stated in the present that they had taken each other as husband and wife, they were deemed by the canon lawyers of the day as married in the eyes of the church — even in the absence of witnesses, the priest, the family, and the congregation. Furthermore, the affirmation alone stated in the present was sufficient to actualize the sacrament of marriage for those who had been duly baptized into the church.[33] Making marriage first of all a public institution, a matter of state registration, and a responsibility of the "earthly kingdom" gradually worked to end secret marriage in Protestant countries.

Luther had his own view of the male problematic and cast his theology of marriage and family partially to overcome it. His view of the male reluctance to become involved in marriage and parenthood was more situationally developed than Aquinas's. Aquinas, as we saw, believed there were deep naturalistic tendencies, aggravated by sin, that led males to be promiscuous and reluctant to bond with spouse and children. Luther, on the other hand, believed that the Roman Catholic prideful and erroneous elevation of celibacy over marriage made huge numbers of males believe that the mundane responsibilities of husband and father were beneath their dignity. Marriage was looked down on and in many ways, women were too. Women were temptresses; their bodies were involved in the natural and messy business of childbirth and menstruation. Men, following the Christian appropriation of Plato and Aristotle, were thought to be more rational, deliberate, spiritual, and godly. The kind of mentality that Luther was opposing can be found in the following quote:

---

32. Steven Ozment, *When Fathers Ruled: Family Life in Reformation Europe* (Cambridge, Mass.: Harvard University Press, 1983), pp. 50-99; *Protestants: The Birth of a Revolution* (New York: Doubleday, 1992), pp. 151-68. For a fresh and positive view of family life in the middle centuries, see Ozment's *Ancestors: The Loving Family in Older Europe* (Cambridge, Mass.: Harvard University Press, 2001).

33. John Witte, *From Sacrament to Contract: Marriage, Religion, and Law in the Western Tradition* (1997), p. 34; Reynolds, *Marriage in the Western Church,* p. 63.

There are many pagan books which treat of nothing but the depravity of woman kind and the unhappiness of the estate of marriage. . . . Every day one encounters parents who forget their former misery because, like the mouse, they have now had their fill. They deter their children from marriage and entice them into priesthood and nunnery, citing the trials and trouble of married life. Thus do they bring their own children home to the devil, as we daily observe. . . . The shameful confusion wrought by the accursed papal law has occasioned so much distress, and the lax authority of both the spiritual and the temporal swords has given rise to so many dreadful abuses and false situations that I would much prefer neither to look into the matter nor to hear of it.[34]

Marriage and women may have been disdained, but sex itself — that was another matter. John Witte aptly describes the situation of sexuality and marriage in Germany during Luther's early career. "Prostitution was rampant. Higher clerics and officials of government regularly kept concubines and visited the numerous brothels of German cities. The small fines incurred for such activity discouraged few. Drunken orgies were commonplace. Women were raped and ravaged, particularly by robber bands and soldiers."[35] In some ways, the male behavior of that day was perfectly consistent with the naturalistic predictions of both Aquinas, and as we will see in the following chapter, the theories of evolutionary psychology. Male sexual expression and procreation went on apace, but now with church doctrine as a defense and excuse not to become attached with and responsible for either mistress or offspring.

Luther heroically countered these ideologies and customs. He invoked the doctrine of creation, specifically the Genesis words that say, "So God created man . . . male and female he created them" (Gen. 1:27). With these words in mind, he argued that maleness and femaleness, the need to unite sexually, and the need to procreate are ordinances of God stamped into the created order. He wrote in "The Estate of Marriage" (1522) the following words: "Therefore just as God does not command anyone to be a man or a woman but creates them the way they have to be, so he does not command them to multiply but creates them so that they have to multiply."[36] Luther, however, resisted Aquinas's naturalistic comparative biol-

---

34. Martin Luther, "On Married Life," *Luther's Works*, vol. 45/II (Philadelphia: Muhlenberg Press, 1955-1986), pp. 36-37.

35. Witte, *From Sacrament to Contract*, p. 47.

36. Martin Luther, "The Estate of Marriage," *Luther's Works*, vol. 45, p. 18.

ogy to make his point; he opted instead for the language of God's will expressed in the orders of creation. Our reality as male or female, our sexual and procreative needs, are not so much commands of God as they are "ordinances" — forms and patterns of our human being that are stamped into the very laws of creation itself. Science may not be able to detect these ordinances, but God's revelation in Genesis through metaphor, symbol, and narrative conveys them to us. Furthermore, the ridiculous behavior that ensues when we try to deny our created natures is further evidence of the reality of these ordinances. If men and women followed God's will as expressed in Genesis, almost every Christian, with the exception of spiritually gifted people specifically called to celibacy, would marry, be faithful, have sex, procreate, and cherish, protect, and educate their children. But instead, they sin, and one of the worst forms of sin was the "popish" idea that it was higher and more sacred to be celibate, thereby teaching educated male priests to look down on the mundane chores of marriage and the family.

To counter this error, Luther made marriage and family matters of divine vocation. Notice the similarity of what Luther says in the quote below to what we observed al-Ghazali communicate in his *Book on the Etiquette of Marriage*. Al-Ghazali wrote, "A virtuous man rose during the night and beheld his sleeping children uncovered, and so he covered them with his garment." Luther once expressed almost identical sentiments when he wrote,

> O God, because I am certain that thou has created me as a man and hast from my body begotten this child, I also know for a certainty that it meets with thy perfect pleasure. I confess to thee that I am not worthy to rock the little babe or wash its diapers, or be entrusted with the care of the child and its mother. How is it that I, without any merit, have come to this distinction of being certain that I am serving thy creature and thy most precious will? O how gladly will I do so, though the duties should be even more insignificant and despised. Neither frost nor heat, neither drudgery nor labor, will distress or dissuade me. For I am certain that it is thus pleasing in thy sight.[37]

Luther, like Aquinas, invoked the Ephesians view of Christ's sacrificial love for the church as a model for a husband's love toward his wife. In his "Order of Marriage for Common Pastors" (1529), he expresses his ap-

---

37. Martin Luther, "The Estate of Marriage," *Luther's Works*, vol. 45, p. 18.

proval of the analogy between Christ and the church and the servant relation of husband to the family. He ends his instructions by prayerfully
thanking God for "the union of the dear Son, the Lord Jesus Christ, and
the Church, his bride."[38] Luther was guilty, as was Aquinas, of retaining
Ephesians' modified patriarchy, even though he was aware of how the passage functioned to balance a particular form of the male problematic.

But Luther, in the end, saw marital love as entailing much more self-
sacrifice than did Aquinas. Luther, in interpreting the love commandment to "Love your neighbor as yourself" (Matt. 19:19), once wrote, "one
can take it to mean that both are commanded: we shall love our neighbor
and ourselves as well." But Luther offers an alternative view: "But another
way to understand it is that it commands us to love only our neighbor
and this according to the sample of our love for ourselves. This is the
better interpretation."[39] Aquinas, as we have seen, believed sacrificial love
between Christ and the church or between husband and wife were not so
much ends in themselves as a transitional ethic designed to restore love as
mutuality, equal regard, or, as he called it, "friendship." I agree with both
Luther and Aquinas. Overcoming the male and female problematics requires love as sacrificial love. But I cast my lot more with Aquinas than
Luther. The love that truly enriches the marital relation is not one that
makes sacrificial love an end in itself. It is a love that celebrates the mutuality of love as equal regard and employs the sacrificial moment as the extra effort, done with the grace and help of God, that is required to restore
strained relations to mutuality once again. Christ gives up his life not as
an end in itself but as a step toward fellowship with the church. Husbands
and wives do not sacrifice for one another as an end in itself but as a step
toward restoring love as mutuality.

For this reason, and for his perceptiveness about the male problematic, Aquinas, more than Luther, should provide a model to be reworked
for a theology of marriage and family for modern times. As I said in the
first chapter, it is my aim in the coming chapters to develop a Protestant
and philosophically pragmatic reworking of certain themes in the marriage and family tradition of the Roman Catholic Church.

38. Martin Luther, "The Order of Marriage for Common Pastors," in *Luther's Works*,
vol. 53 (Philadelphia: Fortress Press, 1965), p. 115.

39. Martin Luther, *Lectures on Romans,* in The Library of Christian Classics, vol. 15 (Philadelphia: Westminster Press, 1961), p. 366.

Chapter Five

Nature and Creation:
Evolutionary Psychology, Marriage, and Family

In the last chapter, we learned that Thomas Aquinas wrote a great deal about human nature, human inclinations, and human instincts, and he did this right at the center of his sacramental theory of marriage and the human family. To say it differently, in the middle of talking about the sacrality of marriage, he spoke about humans as certain kinds of animals that could be compared and contrasted with other animals. Most summaries of Aquinas's theory of marriage emphasize the sacramental aspect but overlook his interest in the kinds of human needs and tendencies that marriage helps to organize. He was quite perceptive, as we will soon learn, in identifying certain fragile but discernible natural tendencies in human males, females, and infants that under average circumstances have led human males to join the primordial mother-infant family. He also was perceptive in understanding that the cultural work of a Christian family theology must build on and order these tendencies.

Aquinas's full theory of the Christian family included much more. As we saw, it entailed an ethical level of argumentation about the moral superiority of monogamy over polygyny and polyandry. And it entailed a more directly theological argument about why Christian marriage requires permanence and hence must be seen as a sacrament that cannot be broken. Throughout his argument, Aquinas shows us how Christian ethics and symbols work to counterbalance certain deep tendencies in males, i.e., their fragile bond with both offspring and mate, their competitiveness with other males in pursuing females, and their concern with securing their immortality through their children. By implication, he was aware that in most mammals, mothers raise infants without the assistance of fathers (the female problematic) and he was aware of the natural conditions that tended to bring fathers into the family at the human level. He also was amazingly perceptive in believing that the primordial human family is the mother-infant dyad, as indeed it is for most species in the mammalian kingdom.

We learned that Aquinas understood that the long period of dependency on the part of human infants was a central reason for why mothers turn to their children's fathers for help and fathers are inclined, often with hesitation, to respond with care and protection, especially when they have a reasonable certainty that the child is biologically theirs. We learned that Aquinas, as did St. Paul and St. Augustine before him, also understood that mutual help and sexual exchange were additional integrating features of family formation.

Preferring Kin Yet Subordinating Them to the Kingdom

Aquinas had a robust theory of kin preference that he located within his Christian theory of the family. He believed that humans tend to treat preferentially those with whom they are biologically related. He saw this as a good, although easily distorted, human inclination, given by God in creation. Furthermore, he believed humans, even Christians, should be morally permitted to follow their natural inclinations and in most instances treat their fathers and mothers, sons and daughters, and brothers and sisters with more consideration than they do those not biologically related to them.

In short, Aquinas was interested in what he called the "order of love." By this he meant a principle by which reason can prioritize and distinguish the various objects that have rightful claims to our affections. God is the first principle of order since God is the source of all goods that we love; for that reason, we must love God most of all.[1] But kin relations constitute another prominent subordinate principle of order. Hence, when Aquinas asks the questions whether we should love those closely connected by blood more than those who are better in virtue, his answer is subtle.

He tells us that we are created to love in different ways, depending on what we are loving. More specifically, he distinguishes between the *intensity* of love and the *object* of love. The intensity of love is measured by the

1. Thomas Aquinas, *ST,* II, 2, q. 26, a.1.

agent — the person loving. From this perspective a "man loves those who are more closely united to him, with more intense affection as to the good he wishes for them, than he loves those who are better" but remote from him in kinship and friendship.[2] But in terms of wishing the spiritual good for others, albeit with less affectional intensity, the Christian should love better the person of greater virtue and, of course, most of all love God who is the greatest good of all. Aquinas goes on to say,

> Accordingly, friendship among blood relations is based upon their connection by natural origin, the friendship of fellow-citizens on their civic fellowship, and the friendship of those who are fighting side by side on the comradeship of battle. Wherefore in matters pertaining to nature we should love our kindred most, in matters concerning relations between citizens, we should prefer our fellow-citizens, and on the battlefield our fellow-soldiers. . . . If however we compare union with union, it is evident that the union arising from natural origin is prior to, and more stable than, all others, because it is something affecting the very substance, whereas other unions supervene and may cease altogether. Therefore the friendship of kindred is more stable, while other friendships may be stronger in respect of that which is proper to each of them.[3]

All of this shows that Aquinas gave a very high preliminary value to kin relationships but also believed that they could be subordinated to other associational values, particularly one's relation to God and the kingdom of God.

What does his position suggest for the so-called hard sayings of Jesus that seem to say that the kingdom of God separates us from our family? In light of Thomas's emphasis on kin relations, how should we interpret such words as, "For I have come to set a man against his father, and a daughter against her mother, and a daughter-in-law against her mother-in-law; and one's foes will be members of one's own household" (Matt. 10:34-36)? Aquinas approaches such passages with a highly nuanced interpretation. He writes, "We are commanded to hate, in our kindred, not their kinship, but only the fact of their being an obstacle between us and God."[4]

---

2. Aquinas, *ST,* II, 2, q. 26, a.7.
3. Aquinas, *ST,* II, 2, q. 26, a.8.
4. Aquinas, *ST,* II, 2, q. 26, a.7.

Did Aquinas Learn Too Much from Aristotle?

We know that Aquinas got much of his psychobiology from Aristotle. Many feminists will tell us that Aquinas made most of his mistakes, especially in his assessment of the rational and moral stature of women, by taking Aristotle too seriously. They are mainly correct in this judgment. Aquinas thought that women were made in the image of God. In believing this, he certainly elevated women to a higher status than Aristotle saw fit to do. But Aquinas also believed that women reflected the divine with less perfection than men. In this, Aquinas continues to cling to Aristotle's belief that women are weaker in their deliberative powers than the male half of the human race.

Aristotle did, however, have considerable insight into what evolutionary psychologists call "kin altruism." This is our tendency to invest ourselves more in those with whom we are biologically related even if, in certain ways, we like or admire other people even more. Aristotle clearly influenced Aquinas, and much of Western thought, on that matter.

Aristotle's pre-scientific theory of kin altruism can be found throughout his writings. In his *Politics,* Aristotle writes, "in common with other animals and with plants, mankind have a natural desire to leave behind them an image of themselves."[5] This simple observation shows the natural law dimensions of Aristotle, i.e., the belief that humans share this impulse with other animals and that for both it constitutes a basic framework within which their behavior proceeds. More specifically, however, this concept sets the stage for his theory of kin preference as the ground of parental investment.

We see the idea of kin altruism once again when he develops his critique of Plato's *Republic.* Plato tells us that Socrates believed that nepotism (the preferential treatment of kin by blood relatives) was the fundamental cause of divisiveness within a city. This factionalism could be decisively lessened, he believed, if the more elite men of the city coupled and had offspring with women who were held in common. These offspring then would be raised by state nurses with neither parents nor children knowing their biological ties with one another. Socrates is quoted by Plato as saying that in such a state everyone will "apply the terms 'mine' and 'not mine' in the same way to the same thing" — especially to children.[6] Hence Plato, the voice behind Socrates, toyed with the idea that the

---

5. Aristotle, *Politics,* Bk. I, ii.
6. Plato, *The Republic,* Bk. V, par. 462.

divisions within a city created by nepotistic and competing clans would be undercut by such a system of procreation and child care.

Aristotle believed that Plato's experiment would fail. In developing his case, we see once again Aristotle's implicit theory of kin altruism. He wrote,

> Whereas in a state having women and children in common, love will be watery; and the father will certainly not say 'my son,' or the son 'my father.' As a little sweet wine mingled with a great deal of water is imperceptible in the mixture, so, in this sort of community, the idea of relationship which is based upon these names will be lost; there is no reason why the so-called father should care about the son, or the son about the father, or brothers about one another. Of the two qualities which chiefly inspire regard and affection — that a thing is your own and that it is your only one — neither can exist in such a state as this.[7]

Aristotle believed that such a society would water down and undermine parental recognition and investment. Furthermore, he believed it would unleash violence. Why? Because the inhibiting factor of consanguinity would be removed. He writes,

> Evils such as assaults, unlawful loves, homicides, will happen more . . . for they will no longer call the members of the class they have left brothers, and children, and fathers, and mothers, and will not, therefore, be afraid of committing any crimes by reason of consanguinity.[8]

It was for these reasons that Aristotle believed that from the perspective of priority in time and basic commitment, the family is more fundamental than the state. On the other hand, from the perspective of concern for the more inclusive good, the state for him was more fundamental than the family.[9] Either way, Aristotle is certainly an early champion of the idea that the family is a basic cell of society and that without the investment between biologically related individuals (and in spite of the perils of nepotism), family love will run thin, violence will rise, and social well-being and cohesion will decline.

This is the part of Aristotle that should be taken seriously; it is a perspective that strongly influenced Aquinas and through him much of

7. Aristotle, *Politics*, Bk. II, iv.
8. Aristotle, *Politics*, Bk. II, iv.
9. Aristotle, *Politics*, Bk. I, ii.

Western religious thought. This part of his psychobiology, I will argue, should be retained. There is much in Aristotle, however, that should be rejected or at least restated, and some of this is found in the family theory of Aquinas.

Much of what is unsatisfactory has to do with Aristotle's view of women. In one place, he defines females as a lack of maleness — a "mutilated male," even though there is controversy about what he meant by this.[10] Males were associated with form and agency; females with matter and passivity. Throughout Aristotle's thought, differences between males and females are communicated by distinctions between superior versus inferior, the ruler versus the ruled, the rational or deliberative versus a deficiency in these capacities.

In "On the Generation of Animals," however, we find his more infamous list of differentiations about the respective role of human male and female in the reproductive process. His views were flawed, but doubtless reflected the cultural attitudes of his times. Aristotle believed that both male and female contributed some kind of semen, but that the male semen "acts and makes, while that which is made and receives the form is the residue of the secretion in the female."[11] "But the female, as female, is passive, and the male, as male, is active, and the principle of movement comes from him." And furthermore, "The male contributes the principle of movement and the female the material."

This is why the female does not produce offspring by herself, but she needs a principle, i.e., something to begin the movement in the embryo and to define the form it is to assume. Male sperm had heat and was assertive; the female contributed to conception only cold and inactive nutrients. Males had spirit and were closer to the divine or metaphysically good; females were material and lower on the metaphysical ladder. Since semen was the efficient cause of the soul, Aristotle could not explain why offspring sometimes favored their mothers.[12] This view was echoed not

10. Michael Nolan, "The Defective Male: What Aquinas Really Said," *New Blackfriars* 75, no. 880 (March 1994): 156-65. This article argues that for both Aristotle and Aquinas, this does not mean that nature was defective or that women were defective. Rather, especially for Aquinas, it meant that the male semen by itself naturally produced a male and that only the wider interaction with other parts of nature brought about a female.

11. Aristotle, "On the Generation of Animals," in *The Basic Writings of Aristotle*, Bk. 21.

12. For a summary of Aristotle's views on women, see Maryanne Cline Horowitz, "Aristotle on Woman," *Journal of the History of Biology* 2 (Fall 1976): 183-213. See also Aristotle, "On Generation and Corruption," pp. 470-534, "The History of Animals," pp. 633-42, "On the Generation of Animals," in *Basic Writings of Aristotle*, pp. 665-88.

only in later Christian medieval writers such as Aquinas; the Islamic philosopher al-Ghazali may also have been influenced by Aristotle when he wrote, "God Almighty has created the pair; He has created the male organ and the two ovaries, as well as the sperm in the sheath; He has prepared for it (the sperm) in the ovaries, arteries and ducts, and created the womb as a depository for the sperm."[13] The idea of the active sperm and the passive womb penetrated the Islamic world as well.

All of this makes Aristotle look like the world's greatest chauvinist and in some ways that is true. Furthermore, many of these thoughts were carried by philosophers for centuries and some were absorbed by Aquinas, although with modification. That makes the Aristotelian influence on Western perceptions of gender quite extensive. And lest you think that Aristotle's view of gender had no influence on anyone except a few elite philosophers and Thomas Aquinas, let me remind you that this perspective on women is a lingering presence in the New Testament household codes, in spite of how they were also, as I have argued, qualified and redefined.

Asymmetrical Reproduction in Aristotle's Biological Psychology

Although most of Aristotle's teachings on the differences between males and females can be rejected, we should be hesitant to dismiss what he taught about the grounds of parental investment. In throwing out the former, we should not be neglectful of the latter. *The most complimentary thing one might say about his view of gender differences is that he may have been fumbling to formulate what contemporary evolutionary psychologists call a theory of the asymmetrical reproductive strategies of human males and females.* In his list of human female characteristics, Aristotle gives us some surprises. For instance, in his "The History of Animals" he writes that females are "more apt in the way of learning" and "more retentive of memory," demonstrating that he was not completely oblivious to female mental powers. More directly pertinent to asymmetrical reproductive patterns, he states that human females are "more attentive to the nurture of the young."[14] Was this Aristotle's way of noting that the human male is less involved in childbirth, less connected with his offspring? Does this mean that his

13. Al-Ghazali, *Book on the Etiquette of Marriage*, in Madelain Farah, ed., *Marriage and Sexuality in Islam* (Salt Lake City: University of Utah Press, 1984), p. 54.

14. Aristotle, "The History of Animals," Bk. 9.

high evaluation of the importance of parental recognition expressed in his criticism of Plato, i.e., his belief that we are more inclined to care for our infants if we know that they are actually ours, has more implications for males than females?

On this last point, Aristotle's theory of the asymmetry of male-female contributions to reproduction may have been onto something. He got this interesting point, however, so mixed with Greek patriarchy, its honor-shame code, its high valuation of male agency, and its distorted view of the disproportionate rationality of men and women, that it ends being fundamentally destructive even if it contained a very small grain of truth.

But in repudiating Aristotle's view of the deliberative inferiority of women and their fundamental passivity, should we overlook his rudimentary theory of the psychobiological grounds of parental investment and his fragile yet discernible theory of the asymmetrical reproductive strategies of males and females? Indeed, should we reject all such theories? For instance, should we reject without examination the powerful new theories found in evolutionary psychology? Should we overlook the analogies between Aristotle and Aquinas and this new discipline? Should we reject Aquinas's view of this matter and his use of these insights in his Christian family theory? Furthermore, should our repudiation of such thinking be so total as to blind us to the subtle differences between Aquinas and Aristotle, differences that show Aquinas in some respects to be closer to contemporary evolutionists than to Aristotle? And should we reject Aristotle's insights into kin altruism and its importance for family formation even though it is contaminated?

I have asked too many questions, but you get my point. I think we should examine the intersection between psychobiology and Christian family theory more carefully than we generally do.

Evolutionary Psychology and the Male and Female Problematics

Evolutionary psychology is a relatively new discipline that uses the concepts of evolutionary theory to order the facts of human psychology. It is variously referred to as evolutionary ecology, behavioral biology, or sociobiology. I prefer the term "evolutionary psychology" because the practitioners of this subspecialty are the least deterministic in their philosophical assumptions and the most open to understanding how cultural patterns influence our evolved biological tendencies.

To understand what evolutionary psychology has to contribute to our concern over the world situation of families, we need to understand the meaning of three concepts: the ideas of kin altruism, the asymmetrical reproductive patterns of mammalian males and females, and the K- versus the R-strategy of procreation and infant rearing. Furthermore, we need to understand what these ideas mean for family formation at the human level. As we will soon see, Aquinas saw the reasons for human family formation in ways quite similar to the views of contemporary evolutionary psychology.

It is easy to observe that humans everywhere tend to give preferential treatment to blood relations. For the early Plato, as we saw, this tendency was seen as the central cause of the divisiveness that riddled ancient societies. In 1964, the geneticist W. D. Hamilton developed a testable theory that explains why kin preference seems to be a central tendency throughout the animal and human world. It comes down to the fact that our natural children, siblings, and parents carry 50 percent of our genes; our nephews, nieces, and grandchildren carry 25 percent; and our first cousins carry 12.5 percent.[15] The theory is that when we care for and enhance the life of those carrying our genes, we contribute to our own "inclusive fitness," i.e., the continuation of our own genes down through the generations.

Early evolutionary theory held that the unit of evolutionary selection was the individual, indeed, the individual gene. This gave rise to the theory of the selfish gene — the idea that evolution is powered by the struggle of the individual gene, not even the human person as such, to survive and sexually transmit itself to future generations. Since Hamilton, however, it has been held by evolutionary theorists that behavior is driven not only for the survival of the individual (or individual gene) but also by its replication in the survival and enhancement of close kin. This is called the theory of inclusive fitness; it means that our concern for our individual fitness is likely, under certain circumstances, to include a concern for others who share and can help preserve our genes. One does not need to hold that this is the only or master motivation of humans in order to grant that it is a central one — one that also shapes a wide variety of lesser tendencies. Aristotle, as we saw above, seemed to understand this drive when he wrote: "mankind have a natural desire to leave behind them an image of themselves."

15. W. D. Hamilton, "The Genetical Evolution of Social Behavior, II," *Journal of Theoretical Biology* 7 (1994): 17-52.

In this individualistic age in which fewer people have children or have fewer children when they do have them, it is easy to believe that deep tendencies toward inclusive fitness have little hold on modern persons. Yet, in spite of the fact that having children in most modern nations no longer pays economically, couples still procreate with astonishing regularity and feel pangs of emptiness and regret when they have no offspring whatsoever. The theory of inclusive fitness predicts that parents, especially in the early phases of their children's lives, will sometimes sacrifice for their welfare at considerable, and sometimes even ultimate, cost to themselves — partially because their progeny are veritable continuations of themselves.

Pierre van den Berghe describes with considerable flourish how humans, along with a few other mammals, have gravitated toward the K- in contrast to the R-strategy in their reproductive behavior. The R-strategy produces a large number of offspring (in the manner of rabbits and tadpoles) with the hope that a few will survive. The K-strategy invests great energy, care, and sacrifice in a relatively few offspring with the hope that a much higher percentage will survive.[16] Ever since our hominid forefathers left the trees and vines of the forest and began searching for berries and game on the grassy plains of Africa, *homo sapiens* have followed the K-strategy and worked out their kin altruism and inclusive fitness by having a relatively small number of offspring.

Humans are even more unusual with respect to one additional feature. For the most part, *homo sapiens* males have been unique among mammalian males in becoming involved in the care of their children. Mammals by definition are species in which the females are the first and primary source of nourishment for their infants. Mammalian mothers, including human mothers, have been largely sufficient unto themselves for the feeding of their infants. This has meant, for the most part, that mammalian mothers, even among higher primates, have raised their infants without help from their male consorts, depending instead on assistance from their female relatives and friends — allomothers, as evolutionary anthropologist Sarah Blaffer Hrdy calls them.[17]

But something happened in the course of human evolution. Human males joined the primordial family (the mother-infant dyad) and began to provide food for their consorts and offspring, to protect them, and to assist in various ways in the raising of their children. How this happened is a

16. Pierre van den Berghe, *Human Family Systems* (New York: Elsevier, 1979), pp. 25-26.
17. Sara Blaffer Hrdy, *Mother Nature: A History of Mothers, Infants, and Natural Selection* (New York: Pantheon Books, 1999), pp. 90-92.

great mystery and one of the central questions debated by physical anthropologists and evolutionary psychologists.

To understand why this is such a challenging puzzle, I must explain
one more concept central to evolutionary psychology. This is the idea of
the asymmetrical reproductive patterns between mammalian males and
females.[18] This asymmetry is especially acute at the human level and
comes down to this: males have an unlimited capacity to father children
and can do so with little physical cost or expenditure of time and energy.
On the other hand, females can only bear a limited number of children
and give birth to their infants with great expenditures of time, energy, and
physical pain to themselves.

This asymmetry of low investment on the part of males and high investment on the part of females leaves the latter, especially at the human
level, very vulnerable. It leaves human males with few reasons to become
attached to a single female and their jointly produced children. So why, in
the course of human evolution, did males become attached to their female consorts and invested in their children? And as we puzzle about how
it came about, we should also ask, *is there worldwide evidence that this unique
human phenomenon is coming undone? Could it happen that for a significant part
of the population, procreation could become uncoupled from long-term mother-
father bonding? And if so, are we losing something in the process?*

The discipline of evolutionary psychology has identified several conditions that worked to bring about long-term male investment in their
children and mates. They have striking similarity to the four reasons
which, in the last chapter, we found in Aquinas and on top of which he developed his ethical and sacramental views of marriage. In his terms, these
had to do with (1) human infant dependency, (2) a male's recognition and
certainty that an infant is his, (3) sexual exchange as payment of the marital debt, and (4) mutual helpfulness. Of course these conditions were for
Aquinas based on naturalistic observations available to humans prior to
the rise of modern gene theory and therefore were completely devoid of
the models and tests that inform contemporary evolutionary psychology.
They were also, fortunately, without the reductionistic metaphysics that
generally accompanies the modern discipline.

Let us listen to the statement of these same four reasons for family
formation from the voice of the new discipline of evolutionary psychology. With regard to the first point about infant dependency, biologist

18. Martin Daly and Margo Wilson, *Sex, Evolution, and Behavior* (Belmont, Calif.:
Wadsworth Publishing Co., 1983), pp. 77-100.

Donald Symons points out that, because of their enormous heads, human infants must be born before they become too large to slide down the birth canal. Hence, they are born virtually helpless. Human infant development is slow and the burden of this dependency lasts for a long time. It requires enormous energy to raise such a creature. This dependency and the energy it drains, Symons argues, stimulated human females to turn to their male consorts for assistance, thus setting the stage for some degree of bonding between male and female.[19]

This dependency of the newly born human baby, the argument goes, was a necessary but insufficient condition for male bonding with the mother-infant dyad. Rutgers University evolutionary theorist Robert Trivers in a series of papers written in the 1970s argued that paternal certainty and paternal recognition were additional needed conditions.[20] Paternal certainty refers to the male's sense that an infant is most probably his and not another male's. Paternal recognition points to the evolutionary-psychological principle that a male is more likely to bond with and care for an infant if he judges it actually to be his child. The counterpoint to these concepts is the fact that females, because they carry the infant and expend energy on it for months before its birth, always have known that the baby was theirs, whereas males never know with absolute certainty that a child born to their partner is actually theirs. The reality of kin altruism, however, stands in the background of the point being made. Trivers presents elaborate demonstrations showing that a male's dim awareness that an infant is his — is, in that sense, part him — increases his willingness to invest in the care of his infant. Such attention and care (such investment) is an extension of his inclusive fitness.[21]

The third reason, also paralleling Aquinas, that evolutionary psychologists give for why males at the human level became family men goes like this. Males are reinforced in their investment in their offspring and mate through sexual exchange with their consort. Males found sex a unitive experience, developed regard and solicitude for the mate who provided it, and were lured into giving up their promiscuous ways and R-strategies in procreation for regular sexual relations with a single consort.

19. Donald Symons, *The Evolution of Human Sexuality* (Oxford: Oxford University Press, 1979), p. 31.

20. Robert Trivers, "Parental Investment and Sexual Selection," in *Sexual Selection and the Descent of Man*, ed. B. Campbell (Chicago: Aldine Publishing Co., 1972), pp. 139-41.

21. S. Gaulin and A. Schlegel, "Paternal Confidence and Paternal Investment: A Cross-Cultural Test of a Sociobiological Hypothesis," *Ethology and Sociobiology* 1, no. 4 (December 1980): 301-9.

The fourth condition given by the evolutionary theorists broadens the idea of exchange to a wider set of values. It resonates with the last point put forth by Aquinas. Males joined the mother-infant primordial family as a part of what evolutionary psychologists call reciprocal altruism. Parents care for their children out of motivations stemming from kin altruism, but males and females become bonded partially through reciprocal altruism. Reciprocal altruism is a complex pattern of mutual assistance that emerges between them. With the introduction of these last two points, Trivers's early theory about the importance of kin altruism and paternal certainty for inducing male involvement in families is now seen as insufficient. Sexual exchange and reciprocal helpfulness are also necessary. At least, these are also necessary to complete the naturalistic story.

Homicide and the Restraints of Kin Altruism

In very different languages and with different sets of explanations, Aquinas and modern evolutionary psychology pretty much agree on the naturalistic conditions bringing human males into the mother-infant dyad. *But Aquinas, as we saw, added much more to his theory of matrimony, and this is terribly important to understand.* He developed an ethical theory showing why monogamy realizes a higher degree of friendship between husband and wife than either polygyny or polyandry. And he developed a sacramental theory of marital permanence designed to stabilize male tentativeness about marital commitment. Furthermore, in ways that Aquinas did not fully realize, it is just as important to children's well-being for the mother to become attached to the father as it is for the father to become attached to the mother and child. Since for millions of years the successful mammalian family was the mother-infant dyad, there is reason to believe that if human males are not genuinely helpful and human mothers can find alternative means of support, the latter will work out their inclusive fitness (and inclinations to have and care for children) without the aid of a man.

This disconnection of men from marriage, children, and families may be happening throughout the world. This is the fear that compelled Senator Daniel Patrick Moynihan to once lament in the halls of the Senate in the early 1990s, almost with a note of hysteria, that there might soon be a 40 percent out-of-wedlock birthrate in the U.S.[22] At the time of this writing, we

22. Carol Jouzzitus, "Welfare Debate Begins with 'I told you so,'" *New York Times,* August 8, 1995.

have not quite reached this level, but we are moving steadily toward it. Moynihan feared that this meant a great increase in the number of fatherless children. It was, to him, almost a turning point in the history of the human species, a reversal, if you will, in the long course of human progress where one of the great accomplishments was to bring males at the human level into contact and care for spouse and offspring. Now, he speculated, this accomplishment may be in the process of being undone. Furthermore, if evolutionary psychology is correct, this unraveling may be due to deep ambivalences and asymmetries in both males and females, even at the human level. Hence, we must conclude that there is not only a male problematic; there is, as well, *a female problematic*.

The coincidence of evolutionary psychology and Aquinas's naturalism may be interesting, but is there evidence that male involvement in families is really necessary for children? The answer is "yes," and we saw some of the evidence already in Chapter One. But one bit of additional evidence also should be introduced. This has to do with the increased violence toward children in families where they live with a single parent or stepparent.

An outstanding book by Martin Daly and Margo Wilson titled *Homicide* (1988) shows how little violence there is among blood relatives. It surprises people to hear this because we read so much about domestic violence. But domestic violence is not always violence between blood kin. It is often between lovers, spouses, stepfathers and stepmothers, and acquaintances. It is an omnibus term that covers a wide variety of domestic living arrangements. Violence between actual kin is surprisingly low. We need to understand this. A study of 508 solved homicides in Detroit in 1972 showed that 243 (48 percent) were committed by unrelated acquaintances, 138 (27 percent) by strangers, and 127 (25 percent) by relatives. Of the 127 homicides committed by relatives, only 32 (6.8 percent) of the 508 solved homicides were committed by consanguine relatives. Of the remaining 95, 80 were spouses — 36 women were killed by their husbands and 44 men were killed by their wives. Although most studies of urban homicides have not distinguished between those who were or were not related by blood, homicide statistics from Miami by William Wilbanks and Philadelphia by Marvin Wolfgang came up with similar percentages.[23]

A deeper analysis of the Detroit data has demonstrated that people living together who are not blood related are "eleven times as likely to be

23. Martin Daly and Margo Wilson, *Homicide* (New York: Aldine de Gruyter, 1988), pp. 19-20.

murdered" as cohabitants who are blood related.[24] This explains why spouses kill each other more than parents murder their children or children their parents. Homicide and physical abuse are not only higher among nonkin spouses or intimate partners, they also correlate with higher levels of child abuse. One study in Hamilton, Ontario, found that children under age five living with one biological parent and one stepparent were forty times more likely to be abused than were children living with both biological parents.[25]

One alert is in order. Assertions of the kind found in Daly and Wilson are not arguments for monogamy as such; they are arguments for the importance on average of consanguinity in the reduction of violence. They can just as easily explain why polygynous fathers can be invested in their children although, perhaps, far less so in their several wives. Such evidence gives support for Aristotle's prediction that if natural parent-child ties are suppressed, as suggested in Plato's *Republic*, "violence" will multiply and affections will become "watery."

Nature and Creation in Catholicism and the Reformation

The point of this excursion into evolutionary biology is to suggest that there are analogies, but not necessarily identities, between the psychobiology of Aristotle and Aquinas and contemporary evolutionary psychology. These diverse sources have similar insights into the nature of kin altruism and asymmetrical male-female reproductive patterns and how under certain conditions these somewhat contradictory natural tendencies function to create families that endure over time. Understanding these natural conditions, however, helps make intelligible how such long-term bonding can become either monogamous or polygynous and how fathers can become invested in their offspring within either of these two classic systems. *But the evolutionary-psychological model also shows that natural tendencies are ambivalent, even asymmetrical, and that their higher moral ordering requires cultural — possibly even religiocultural — guidance, sanction, and reinforcement.*

This psychobiological analysis, whether accomplished through Aquinas or contemporary evolutionary psychology, only helps specify what moral philosophers call the *premoral* values that form the basement — the

24. Daly and Wilson, *Homicide*, p. 23.
25. Daly and Wilson, *Homicide*, p. 89.

archaeology or foundational natural values — that get organized, and indeed reorganized, in the human institution of matrimony. By premoral values, I mean the peculiar compromise of natural needs and inclinations that are satisfied, suppressed, redirected, and given moral form by more fully human principles, rules, and institutions. When these natural needs and goods are actualized and organized within institutional patterns that enhance the wider human good, these institutional forms are given moral and, quite often, sacred legitimation. Premoral goods can contribute to the moral good, but without higher-level ordering, they are not themselves strictly moral.

Notice how important the human capacities for recognition and awareness are to the stabilization of these conflicting natural tendencies. It is not only the premoral brute fact that the son or daughter contains 50 percent of the genes of both mother and father that contributes to parental investment; it is the additional fact that both mother and father recognize this to be so — indeed, have some *self-awareness that this is so and take steps to further protect and enhance this premoral attachment in the form of active care for the child.* This awareness is more certain for the mother and more a matter of probability for the father. As we know, this is an awareness and knowledge that children wish to satisfy as well. "Who are my parents?" they ask. They seek to know, "Who is my father or my mother?" The lasting bond between a man and a woman who conceive, or wish to conceive, a child is not a mechanical inevitability. Awareness of the natural realities — plus cultural factors such as higher levels of commitment, promise, covenant, and sacrament — direct and stabilize these inclinations. *The point is, however, that these additional cultural factors build on and guide these natural tendencies.* We ignore these natural factors at the peril of the stability of our families, both in Western postindustrial societies and throughout the world.

But notice my argument; I am not saying that in all instances natural parents constitute the best parents. There are obviously incompetent, insensitive, cruel, and overtly destructive natural parents. There are criminal, alcoholic, and drug-crazed natural parents who are so encumbered by their burdens and difficulties that they are unable to care or, even worse, uninterested in caring for their offspring. Nor am I saying that there is not a place for the adoption of children within a Christian perspective. Aquinas's two reasons for loving children make this systematically clear. We love our children because they are partially us, but also because God loves all children and therefore we should as well. This last reason is sufficient to inspire and warrant extending love, care, and yes adoption to all needy children. *My argument is, instead, that the natural inclinations of kin al-truism should constitute a prima facie case for their institutional and cultural en-couragement, proper channeling, and moral sanctioning.* These inclinations pro-vide premoral foundations for more morally defensible patterns and institutional expressions. Exceptions to these general inclinations will be found and must be recognized. Adoption is an important and powerful human institution and one recognized and honored in many traditions, certainly in Christianity.

Let us return to our theological discussion. Aquinas believed that the will of God for marriage and family was revealed in the Genesis creation stories. Although matrimony was for him a sacramental reality of the New Law revealed by Christ, it also had been willed by God from the foun-dations of creation, even before the advent of sin which the sacrament of marriage was designed to cure. He called marriage in this primordial form an "office of nature." At this level it could be illuminated by the natural law, especially that aspect of natural law that identifies those natural in-clinations that are, however, further guided by interventions of "the free will" and "acts of virtue."[26] But marriage was also a reality revealed in scripture, specifically the Genesis account of creation. To prove this, he quotes in the Supplement to the *Summa Theologia* Matthew 29:4, "Have ye not read that He Who made man from the beginning 'made them male and female,'" a verse that itself refers back to Genesis 1:27. Nearby he refers to Genesis 2:21 and claims that before sin and from the foundations of cre-ation, God "fashioned a help-mate for man out of his rib."[27] This implies what the full Genesis passage makes explicit, "It is not good that the man should be alone; I will make a helper as his partner" (Gen. 2:18).

But Aquinas believed that the creation story on the origins of mar-riage corresponded to and completed the inclinations of nature as known by natural reason. Luther, as is widely known, rejected this easy congru-ence between the revelation of the creation story and the direct testimony of nature known by reason. To understand God's will for how humans should live, Luther thought that divine mandates expressed through cre-ation as revealed in Genesis, not nature apprehended by fallen reason, were the more reliable source. In the beginning of his famous essay titled "The Estate of Marriage," Luther presents the classic Genesis scriptures that say God made us male and female (Gen. 1:27); that we are to be fruit-ful and multiply (Gen. 1:28); that we are not made to be alone (Gen. 2:18);

26. Aquinas, "Supplement," *ST,* q. 41, a.1.
27. Aquinas, "Supplement," *ST,* q. 42, a.3.

and that a man is to leave his parents, cleave to his wife, and become one flesh with her (Gen. 2:24). But then, as we have seen, Luther insists that these are not commands; they are the result of a "divine ordinance *(werck)* which it is not our prerogative to hinder or ignore."[28] With special reference to the ordinance to "Be fruitful and multiply" (Gen. 1:28), Luther writes,

> From this passage we may be assured that man and woman should and must come together in order to multiply. . . . it is not within my power not to be a man, so it is not my prerogative to be without a woman. Again, as it is not in your power not to be a woman, so it is not your prerogative to be without a man. For it is not a matter of free choice or decision but a natural and necessary thing.[29]

I do not quote this passage to promote a theory of gender essentialism or the decisively un-Christian idea that all should marry. In fact, Luther himself qualifies these remarks with his discussion of eunuchs that are such for the sake of the kingdom of God.[30] My point, rather, is to show that Luther advances statements that have the logical status of being factual assertions about nature. But, in contrast to Aquinas, he based these statements not on a direct analysis of nature itself but on his interpretation of the creation narratives recorded in the book of Genesis. Listen to Luther when he says about our sexual and procreative urges that "wherever men try to resist this, it remains irresistible nonetheless and goes its way through fornication, adultery, and secret sins, for this is a matter of nature and not of choice."[31] This, however, is nature revealed more by Genesis than by rational experience.

A man, woman, and a child living in a covenant relation to each other and with God was for Luther the "estate of marriage," an ordinance of creation and willed by God in the way we are made. This, according to Luther, is what is intended by God as the goal and ideal organization of our natural tendencies. The revelation of the ideal, for Luther, is found in God's will for creation and this was shown in scripture.

28. Luther, "The Estate of Marriage," in *Luther's Works*, vol. 45, p. 18.

29. Luther, "The Estate of Marriage," in *Luther's Works*, vol. 45, p. 18.

30. Luther, "The Estate of Marriage," in *Luther's Works*, vol. 45, p. 17. Luther's discussion of the three kinds of eunuchs qualifies this position. Note Luther's strong words indicating that if you do not belong to one of these three kinds of eunuchs — eunuchs by birth, by man, eunuchs "for the sake of the kingdom of God" (Matt. 19:12) — then "Renew your natural companionships without delay and get married" (p. 27).

31. Luther, "The Estate of Marriage," in *Luther's Works*, vol. 45, p. 19.

What is missing in this view that we find in Aquinas? In Aquinas we find the doctrine of creation but more sketchily developed. But in Aquinas, the category of nature is far more differentiated. Hence, one finds actual naturalistic descriptions of what evolutionary psychologists today would call kin altruism. And we find in Thomas perceptive characterizations of what modern biologists call the asymmetrical reproductive patterns of males and females. In Aquinas, in short, the categories of creation and nature are more clearly differentiated; they are not conflated. Furthermore, the ideals revealed in the creation story function to bring the contradictory tensions of nature into a higher order, one that maximizes a higher good, especially the good of having and educating children. Luther tells us why, in the sight of God, children are a central good. Aquinas does the same, but also *explains* why the reality of children may be crucial for overcoming the male problematic and bonding couples together in the first place.

This book sides methodologically more with Aquinas than with Luther on this specific point, i.e., the proper way to conceptualize the relation between the categories of nature and creation. Those who start their reflection on families from a Christian perspective must take seriously what their faith, in its theology of creation, teaches about marriage and family. But with Aquinas as our model, we can also move into a conversation with the cultural disciplines of the modern world — psychology, biology, economics, history, anthropology — and have a critical dialogue about what both the biblical tradition *and* ordinary experience teach about the meaning of marriage and family and the reasons for their close connection.

The Archaeology of Marriage in Judaism and Islam

To speak about the naturalistic foundations of marriage is not to say that marriage is natural. It is, rather, to suggest that marriage organizes natural tendencies and places them into wider and more properly moral patterns of organization — ones that increase respect and equal regard for all parties and that also increase and coordinate a wider range of premoral goods. To speak of the natural foundations of marriage is not, as well, to argue that monogamy is natural or to imply that it is more natural than polygyny. There may be naturalistic considerations in discussing the relative advantages of monogamy and polygyny. But, following Aquinas, the more weighty and decisive arguments are moral ones; they pertain to how the two organizations of sexuality and procreation handle the questions of both the well-being of children and the dignity and respect of both women and men, husbands and wives.

In this chapter and the preceding one, we have been examining how observations about the regularities of nature have informed judgments about marriage and family in Greek thought as typified by Aristotle and in Christian thought as seen in Aquinas and Luther. As I have stated time and again, these natural inclinations do not dictate what is a moral organization of sexuality, but they may suggest the realities of natural inclinations that should be taken into account if a moral organization of it is to be found and sustained. It is beyond the scope of this book and the competence of its author to make an analysis of the naturalistic archaeology — the core assumptions about natural inclinations in human males and females — found in a wide range of the world religions.

But I do want to extend the analysis in a small way by drawing illustrations from both Judaism and Islam, the other two great religions of the "book" — religions that feed off the wisdom of the Hebrew scriptures and the Abrahamic tradition. I turn to the biblical commentary of Nachmanides, a rabbinic scholar from the era of the Rishonim — the early authorities of the Jewish law (halakha) who lived between the eleventh and the fourteenth centuries in North Africa and various parts of Europe. Let us consider his commentary on Genesis 2:24. His translation is capitalized in the text: "Therefore Shall A Man Leave His Father And His Mother And Shall Cleave To His Wife." In the following quote, many of the themes of today's evolutionary psychology are found even though they are bent and redirected toward his normative goals. Assumptions analogous to the concepts of inclusive fitness, kin altruism, sexual inheritance, and the unique bonding of human males and females in contrast to most other animals can be found in the following lengthy passage.

AND THEY SHALL BE ONE FLESH. The child is created by both parents, and there in the child, their flesh is united into one. Thus the words of Rashi. But there is no point to this since in beast and cattle too, their flesh is united into one in their offspring.

The correct interpretation appears to me to be that in cattle and beast the males have no attachment to their females. Rather, the male mates with any female he finds, and then they go their separate ways. It is for this reason that Scripture states that because the female of man was bone of his bones and flesh of his flesh, he therefore cleaves to her and she nestles in his bosom as his own flesh, and he desires to be with her always. And just as it was with Adam, so was his nature transmitted to his offspring, that the males among them should cleave to their women, leaving their fathers and their mothers, and considering their wives as if they are one flesh with them. A similar sense is found in the verses: 'For he is our brother, our flesh; to any that is near of his flesh.' Those who are close members of the family are called *sh'eir basar* (near of flesh). Thus man will leave "the flesh" of his father and his mother and their kin and will see that his wife is nearer to him than they.[32]

The ideas that in the birth of a child the flesh of the two parents are "united into one" suggests in nontechnical terms the idea of inclusive fitness. In the life of the child, the stuff or substance of the parents lives on. Ancients had little idea of what this stuff was. They certainly had no theory of genes or just how it was that natural parents seemed incarnated in some mysterious way in their children, but they made the observation nonetheless. Nachmanides is not the only rabbi saying such things; he refers to Rashi (Rabbi Shlomo ben Yitshaki), also of the Rishonim period, in support of his interpretation of the "one flesh" concept of Genesis 2:24. Rashi writes with stark but decisive simplicity as if he were settling centuries of rabbinic debate in his declaration, "Both parents are united in the child."[33] It should be noticed that in contrast to the Aristotelian understanding that the male somehow uniquely communicates the active seed that produces the infant, these two Jewish writers seem to credit male and female with equal contributions.

But Nachmanides has much more to say about this matter than Rashi. Nachmanides makes an observation similar to those found in evolutionary psychology and also made by Aquinas. "Beast and cattle" are united in this sense in their young, but their "males have no attachment to the females." The ancients knew that human males were in some way unique in comparison to most all other mammals (with the exception, perhaps, of elephants and gibbons) in their tendency under many conditions to bond with their consorts and offspring. This then leads to his second version of the "one flesh" doctrine — "that the female of man was bone of his bones and flesh of his flesh." Notice that this exegesis of Gen-

---

32. Nachmanides, *Commentary on the Torah: Genesis,* vol. 1 (New York: Shilo Publishing House, 1971-1976), p. 80.

33. Rashi, "Commentary on the Pentateuch," in *Eve and Adam: Jewish, Christian, and Muslim Readings on Genesis and Gender* (Bloomington: Indiana University Press, 1999), p. 208.

esis 2:23 does not emphasize the subordination of female to male so much as it does the affinity, solidarity, and continuity between the human male *(ish)* and female *(ishshah)*, both of whom are *Adam*. This solidarity emerges in the narrative structure of the verses; in the case of the male-female relation itself, considered independently of their offspring, it is less a biological reality than a calling or vocation willed by God. It is this that decisively makes the human male and female different from the other animals. Humans are distinct because the males remain with child and consort. I say more about this below.

The idea of sexual transmission by parents to children of inherited characteristics is also implicit in the passage that says, "And just as it was with Adam, so was his nature transmitted to his offspring." The reference may be to both male and female transmitting their "nature" to their children. But it also may have special reference to the male because of the following clause, "that the males among them should cleave to their women, leaving their fathers and their mothers." There seems to be a link — maybe a causal link — between Adam's transmission of his nature to his offspring and the subsequent move of the males to "cleave to their wives." Is this an implicit gesture toward the idea of paternal recognition and, perhaps, some acknowledgment of the role of infant dependency? Does the male remain with the wife partially *because* he knows that there is something of himself in this infant and partially *because* of the baby's dependency, vulnerability, and needs, all of which call for his additional support and protection of offspring and consort?

But then the passage takes one more step that clearly goes beyond the bounds of naturalism even though it also builds upon it. It says that males should cleave to their wives, "leaving their fathers and their mothers, and considering their wives as if they are one flesh with them." This remarkable move seems to assume the binding affinities of blood relations — father and mother with child and even adult males with their families of origin. *But it analogizes from this biological affinity and extends it to a relation with spouse which is not itself a biological kinship relation.* Biology becomes the ground for the symbolism and then, significantly, for the transformation of the aims of biological tendencies. I use here the word "transformation" instead of the word "transcend." The inclinations of kin altruism are not transcended in the sense of completely left behind; they are transformed in the sense of analogically extended to nonkin. Man and woman become one flesh and, in the process, become *as if* they were biological kin. In the process, they become husband and wife. The dialectic between the archaeology of desire that Ricoeur speaks about, and the teleology of the symbolism of these passages is exhibited in Nachmanides' interpretation. The energies of natural inclination are built on and extended, but in some ways transformed.

The passage concludes with an additional commentary on a social reality that evolutionary psychology would unambiguously call kin altruism. He writes, "A similar sense is found in the verses: 'For he is our brother, our flesh; to any that is near of his flesh.' Those who are close members of the family are called *sh'eir basar* (near of flesh). Thus man will leave 'the flesh' of his father and his mother and their kin and will see that his wife is nearer to him than they." These words seem to acknowledge the realities of kin altruism and kin preference as natural inclinations. But with husband and wife becoming of one flesh in their relation to each other and in their offspring, the passage's descriptive grammar also reveals a normative vision. This is a vision that portrays the new conjugal family, whatever its actual physical proximity to the extended family, as one in which the obligations and affinities of the paternal (and patriarchal) line of the husband are transcended by making "his wife nearer to him than they."

It should be acknowledged that although this remarkable passage points to many of the inclinations in human nature that we found in our analysis of Aquinas as well as many human characteristics discussed by contemporary evolutionary psychology, it has a unique way of resolving the tensions that these inclinations create. The one-flesh concept as applied in this text covers three sets of relations — (1) the parents' solidarity with the child and through the child with each other, (2) the direct solidarity of husband and wife independent of their union through the infant, (3) and the relation of a man with his wider kin. Noting this should not blind us, however, to the subtle ways in which each of these is redirected and guided by the very symbolism of one flesh itself.

Human males and females, we are first told, share with the other animals a joint contribution and investment in their offspring. But, second, humans handle this shared contribution to the infant in a different way from the other mammals such as "beast and cattle." The male and female create another, and analogous, direct one-flesh union with each other distinguishable from their union through the infant. The words "and they shall become one flesh" are later qualified; we are told of males "considering their wives as if they are one flesh." The "as if" is illuminating; it acknowledges that Nachmanides knew that the male and female are not actually one flesh in the biological sense in their direct interpersonal relation to each other as they are *de facto* in their shared procreation of their offspring. There is the combining of flesh in the act of sexual intercourse between husband and wife, but the relation is not in any other way one flesh. The statement is basically a *symbolic* statement; it points to both a permission and an imperative. It suggests that God offers this second kind of one-flesh union between male and female as a way to build on yet reorganize the more directly natural inclinations of both male and female. The new symbol of one flesh referring to the relation of husband and wife creates a bond that models biology but guides and transforms it.

Finally, the entire passage acknowledges the reality, and indeed the propriety, of the natural attachments of the consanguineous conjugal and extended family. But, in a way that may be unique for its era in world comparative family history, this passage *elevates the conjugal couple in status and obligation over the extended family, and this in a society that strongly emphasized the importance of paternal lineage. Lineage, even in this commentary on the ancient Genesis text, is both affirmed and transcended.*

A sampling from Islam might also be suggestive. Before doing this, more needs to be said about the androcentric character of all ancient religion. Judaism and Islam, as well as early Christianity, were typically stated and developed from a male point of view. Even when breakthroughs occurred that elevated the status of women — and they did occur — they nonetheless were still elaborated from the male perspective, at least as far as most extant literary sources are concerned. The voices of women do not appear in the authoritative sacred texts of either Judaism, Christianity, or Islam. Hence, we should not be surprised that even if naturalistic themes appear in some of these texts, they will generally be presented from the male angle of vision and most often to the male advantage.

It is difficult not to notice an interesting naturalistic archaeology in the pages of the Qur'an. This great sacred book contains many literary genres — poetry, narrative, legal pronouncements, legend, and more. But throughout all of these genres, the concern with male lineage plus the recognition of and subsequent care of fathers for their offspring are constant themes. Notice surah 2:228:

> Women who are divorced shall wait, keeping themselves apart, three (monthly) courses. And it is not lawful for them that they should conceal that which Allah hath created in their wombs if they are believers in Allah and the Last Day. And their husbands would do better to take them back in that case if they desire a reconciliation.[34]

34. Qur'an 2:228.

The text makes no elaboration of why there might be concern if a woman remarries while early in her pregnancy. But both Aquinas and evolutionary psychology might be able to provide the explanations. One reason appears directly within the text: from the male point of view, the first husband might decide that he preferred his lineage — his offspring — to grow up under his direction and care rather than that of some other man. He might even be inclined to take the woman back, especially since, in the Islamic system of divorce, he most likely would have initiated the divorce in the first place, and possibly because she was thought to be childless, even barren. Furthermore, once again from the male point of view, the unsuspecting new husband might prefer not to raise another man's child since he has none of himself in the child; as such, the child would not directly help perpetuate the second husband's line of descent. Hints of a concern with paternal certainty, paternal recognition, and even inclusive fitness and kin altruism reverberate throughout this short passage and provide a background to the ethical obligations of both male and female as it is expressed in the text.

The concern with lineage and the continuity of self through offspring are tremendously powerful themes in Islam, probably even more prominent than they are in Judaism. The introduction to al-Ghazali's *Book on the Etiquette of Marriage* lays out perennial themes of Islam.

> In the Name of God, THE MERCIFUL AND COMPASSIONATE, Praise be to God the marvels of Whose creation are not subject to the arrows of accident, for minds do not reflect on the beginnings of such wonders except in awe and bewilderment, and the favor of Whose graces continue to be bestowed upon them (creatures) whether or not they (creatures) wish to receive them (graces). One of His marvelous favors is creating human beings out of water (Kor. 21:30), causing them to be related by lineage and marriage, and subjecting creatures to desire through which He drove them to tillage *(hirāthah)* and thereby, forcibly preserved their descendants. Then He glorified the matter of lineage, ascribed to it great importance, forbade on its account illegitimacy and strongly denounced it through restrictions and reprimands, making the commission thereof an outlandish crime and a serious matter, and encouraging marriage through desire and command.[35]

The themes of inclusive fitness and kin altruism are strikingly present in this passage. They are also surrounded by a vision and narrative about

35. Al-Ghazali, *Book on the Etiquette of Marriage*, p. 45.

God's greatness and grace in providing a good creation in which these values are provided for and enhanced. "One of His marvelous favors is creating human beings out of water, causing them to be related by lineage. . . ." More than anything else, the relation and continuity of parents to children and grandparents to grandchildren testify to the goodness of God's hand in creation. But even within this sentence, a moral element appears. It is not just having children that is good; it is having them within "marriage." This institution of marriage — whatever it amounted to in the mind of Islam and al-Ghazali at that moment in history — was deemed as also a great good given by God and the proper context within which to responsibly pursue the good of lineage. Furthermore, this passage celebrates the goodness of sexual desire and "tillage," which seems to suggest the repeated and dutiful sowing of seed in the man's wife — a thought that doubtless sends shudders down the spines of many women today. Nonetheless, it is playing out a particular theory of naturalistic tendencies, one conceptually illuminated by Aquinas and contemporary evolutionary psychology. Notice, for instance, the horror of illegitimacy, i.e., the distaste of having children that fall outside the clear markers of paternal certainty and paternal recognition — a certainty and care that seem to demand some regularized and institutionalized method of exercising responsibility and care.

But in spite of the passage's high valuation of what today's scientific mind would call kin altruism and inclusive fitness sanctioned and conceptualized as a gift from the heavenly creator, according to this text these inclinations should be guided and organized by marriage. Of course, marriage could be polygynous in this context. And it is difficult always to know just how it was recognized and publicized. But it existed, and there were clear markers between marriage and nonmarriage. But as important as were progeny, lineage, and marriage in al-Ghazali's Islam, they were still subordinated to loyalty to God. Aquinas and al-Ghazali both agree: family and lineage must never gain priority over faithfulness to God. Al-Ghazali once wrote, "Whatever distracts [one's attention] from God — whether wife, wealth, or offspring — brings misfortune upon the possessor."[36] Aquinas, as we saw above, could say something quite similar.

In this chapter, I have tried to amplify further the natural foundations of matrimony. These natural inclinations provide some of the basic premoral goods of this institution. They also provide some of the constraints. If some form of publicly sanctioned marriage, preferably also sanctioned and blessed by a religious tradition, does not organize and

---

36. Al-Ghazali, *Book on the Etiquette of Marriage*, pp. 73-74.

guide these inclinations, they will find expression nonetheless in diffuse and destructive alternative ways. These tendencies contain preliminary directions and ordering, but they do not have their own full organization within themselves, and they certainly do not contain within their own nature a moral organization. They contain conflicting impulses — the conflict between the desire of one person and the possible resistance or reluctance of another, the conflict between pleasure and the consequences of pleasure such as the grinding burden and expense of caring for infants, and the asymmetrical if not agonistic reproductive patterns of males and females that may have been a premoral good from the standpoint of proliferation of the human race but which, nonetheless, render females so terribly vulnerable.

These religious traditions — Judaism, Christianity, and Islam — saw sex as good. They saw conception and children as good. Judaism and Islam saw desire and pleasure as good; Christianity, on this score, was more ambivalent and during part of its history saw pleasure as a special point of entry for inordinate self-seeking and sin. Social patterns, communities of tradition, cultural norms, and religious narratives with their sanctions and blessings are needed to secure and render accountable these powerful and productive inclinations. But it may be precisely the strains of modernization that are rendering it so difficult to achieve the responsible patterning of these powerful natural tendencies into a viable form of marriage.

Archaeology and Teleology of Marriage in Musonius Rufus

I conclude these illustrative remarks by returning to the Roman Stoic Musonius Rufus. Here we find additional insight into how ancients conceptualized the natural inclinations that go into marriage and how these inclinations are transformed and given a new and more stable structure by the institution itself. It is not always clear what constituted marriage in much of the ancient world. It is wrong always to think in terms of formal church weddings and due registration of the event before civil authorities, as was the accomplishment of the interaction between religion and the state in modern societies. It is clear, however, that some public advertisement before extended families and community — often accompanied by a contract, a ritual of some kind, and appropriate financial transactions — generally signaled that a marriage had occurred and a certain set of social obligations had been assumed by the respective parties.

Musonius Rufus is often thought to provide evidence that certain trends in sexuality and family were highly parallel in Stoicism and early Christianity. Paul himself, as we saw above, may have absorbed Stoic views on sexuality and marriage. In the comments that follow, I am less concerned with questions of historical causality than I am about the subtle interplay between Musonius's theory of nature and his understanding of the religiocultural complements and transformations of nature provided by marriage.

Musonius, like Aristotle, held a view of kin altruism and how it motivated parental affection. This is powerful enough to lead parents to feed their young and raise them to maturity even in hard times. Poverty is no excuse for not discharging the responsibilities of parenthood: "But pray, whence do the little birds which are much poorer than you, feed their young, the swallows and nightingales and larks and blackbirds?"[37] Are birds smarter, better, stronger? No, humans have the same inclinations but need additional moral commitments to stabilize and discharge them. Musonius also recognized how kin altruism can be extended to reciprocal altruism and how cooperation and mutuality, in turn, can lead to wealth and social strength. He disdained parents who killed their newborn infant so that their older children could have more material wealth. Don't these parents know that brothers and sisters are more important for personal security than wealth? "What good would one compare to the good will of a brother as a pledge of security? What better disposed sharer of common goods could one find than a good brother?"[38] On the other hand, although kin altruism was a great good, the love between a husband and a wife was even greater. "All men consider the love of man and wife to be the highest form of love."[39]

Musonius invoked the gods to bless this union. This was not the God of Abraham, Jacob, Moses, and Jesus. This was not the God that sacrificed himself through the cross of Christ. This was not the God that beckons Christian men to love their wives and children as Christ loved the church. Nonetheless, the gods Musonius had in mind also called men to love their wives with perfect mutuality, to do more for their wives at times than their wives did for them, and also to care for their children. He wrote,

> How great and worthy an estate is marriage is plain from this also, that gods watch over it, great gods too, in the estimation of men;

37. Cora Lutz, ed., *Musonius Rufus: The Roman Socrates,* p. 99.
38. Lutz, ed., *Musonius Rufus,* p. 101.
39. Lutz, ed., *Musonius Rufus,* p. 95.

first Hera (and for this reason we address her as the patroness of wedlock), then Eros, then Aphrodite, for we assume that all of these perform the function of bringing together man and woman for the procreation of children. Where, indeed, does Eros more properly belong than in the lawful union of man and wife? Where Hera? Where Aphrodite? Where would one more appropriately pray to these divinities than when entering into marriage?[40]

In addition to connecting the energies and attractions of *eros* to marriage, Musonius is also endowing this institution with divine sanction. He is aware that *eros* is full of contradictory yearnings and that many men "crave a variety of loves, not only lawful but unlawful ones as well."[41] There is no straight line between the vagaries of *eros* and marriage; it takes culture, institutional patterns, and divine sanction to bring the attractions of males and females to the settled outcome of marriage. But marriage as institution must build on *eros*. Marriage is consistent with the structure of nature in two ways; it expresses the energies of *eros* and fulfills the will of the creator.

For, to what other purpose did the creator of mankind first divide our human race into two sexes, male and female, then implant in each a strong desire for association and union with the other, instilling in both a powerful longing each for the other, the male for the female and the female for the male? Is it not then plain that he wished the two to be united and live together, and by their efforts to devise a way of life in common, and to produce and rear children together, so that the race might never die?[42]

Musonius tweaks the nose of the pagan male masters of his society. He agrees with the commonly held, and decidedly androcentric view, that having sex with another man's wife is wrong because it may "rob" the other man of "hope of children." He knows that some men used this reasoning to say sex with a courtesan or maidservant was permissible; presumably the prerogatives of other males were not involved. One senses behind this pattern of thought ancient naturalistic insights to the effect that males are naturally, although not inevitably, reluctant to care for the offspring of others and deeply resent the betrayals that might force them

40. Lutz, ed., *Musonius Rufus,* p. 95.
41. Lutz, ed., *Musonius Rufus,* p. 88.
42. Lutz, ed., *Musonius Rufus,* p. 93.

unknowingly to do this. But Musonius says sex with a courtesan or maid-servant is wrong even if it does not lead to the cuckolding of another man. To clinch his argument he invokes a variation of the golden rule or what Kant, Lawrence Kohlberg, and Jürgen Habermas in our day would call a species of reversible, if not universalistic, moral thinking. If a master thinks it is all right to have sex with his maidservant, especially if she has no husband, then "let him consider how he would like it if his wife had re-lations with a male slave."[43]

So, indeed, marriage is for procreation, but not just that alone. "Quite apart from marriage," conception and birth "could result from any other sexual union, just as in the case of animals."[44] Marriage is a distinctively human affair. Procreation, yes. But even more, "in marriage there must be above all perfect companionship and mutual love of husband and wife, both in health and in sickness and under all conditions, since it was with desire for this as well as for having children that both entered upon mar-riage."[45] In sickness and in health — here we find the patterns of the clas-sic wedding vows. It shows Christians were not the only ones who believed that marriage should endure and be permanent even through tough times. But it may have been that Christians had deeper and more power-ful symbols to make this point, symbols that sometimes were overstated and taken too far.

But the issue of permanence, and the Christian symbols of sacrament and covenant, are not the main points of this chapter. My message here has been that Christian symbols, and the symbols of other religions as well, make sense partially because they built upon and transformed profound naturalistic insights into regular features of male and female sexuality. The ancients got many things wrong, and the idea that female passivity is a nat-ural given was certainly one of them. But, on the other hand, they often had deft insights into the asymmetrical patterns between human males and females and how the symbolism of marriage must build on, compen-sate for, yet redirect the ambiguities of male and female sexuality.

43. Lutz, ed., *Musonius Rufus*, p. 88.
44. Lutz, ed., *Musonius Rufus*, p. 89.
45. Lutz, ed., *Musonius Rufus*, p. 89.

Chapter Six

A Practical Theology of Families

I move in this chapter from history and description to theology. I will begin outlining a practical theology of marriage and families. For those of you not familiar with the practical theology genre, and possibly not even sure you want to learn about it, allow me to say this. Practical theology is a kind or style of Christian theology. From my perspective, it has the following three characteristics: (1) it begins with an analysis of issues or problems facing church and society in their full historical, social, and cultural context, (2) it has a concern with application and practical strategy from the beginning of the reflective theological task, and, as I will argue, (3) it should be public, critical, and apologetic. This latter point means that in addition to being confessional and uplifting for the inner life of the church, it should attempt to give reasons for the practices that it recommends that can gain credibility with diverse publics both within and outside the ecclesial community.

I want to begin by recommending four criteria for an adequate practical theology of marriage and families. I will state these criteria briefly and elaborate them more fully in the remaining chapters.

First, an adequate practical theology of families must address the worldwide trends toward both modernization and globalization. As we have seen, these two phenomena are not identical processes and their implications for families differ as well. Modernization is the spread throughout the world of technical rationality and its efficiency-oriented and cost-benefit logics and patterns. Globalization in its contemporary form is a far more interactive process that is driven in part by the communications revolution. It is a process by which information, images, symbols, and styles of life zigzag back and forth across the world in unpredictable patterns. Whereas modernization tended to move from Western nations to the rest of the world, globalization is a process whereby the East and South can influence the West, poor societies can project images that shape the rich, and exotic (to our Western eyes) family practices of Africa and the Middle East can influence Europe and the United States. Modernization and globalization can occur simultaneously. All families can be touched by the spread of market-oriented modernization just as many families can be affected by images of family life from other parts of the world. An adequate practical theology of families must address both of these world trends.

Second, an adequate practical theology addressing these issues must have command over a double language. One of the languages should be confessional, i.e., the language of what the doctrines of both creation and redemption suggest about families. In addition, however, a good practical theology must have a language that can give a more public account of the regularities of human sexuality, procreation, and family formation and advance some philosophical plausibility for what Christian symbols contribute to marriage and family. It was because Thomas Aquinas had both languages that he serves as something of a model for my position. This double language will make it possible for the church to speak about the family both to itself and the wider public.

Third, an adequate practical theology must think analogically about families. Family patterns and family well-being are not equivalent to what Christians call salvation or redemption, although salvation and redemption can contribute to family well-being. Nonetheless, the Christian tradition has had implications for family well-being and family patterns. In the new interactive global society, Christianity will confront a variety of family patterns not associated with traditional Christian patterns. The task of a critical practical theology is to provide guidelines for seeing analogies between Christian patterns and other ways of family life. It must also provide guidelines for making evaluative judgments about which family trends it can support and which it must criticize, which are fulfilling and which are more destructive or less viable.

Fourth, an adequate practical theology of families should have confessional and critical resources to address the central consequences of present world trends, i.e., what I have called the male and female problematics. These have to do with the global drift toward men and women increasingly working out their reproductive strategies independently of enduring marital commitments to one another. In short, an authentic practical theology on family matters must have theological and strategic grounds to resist the *dehumanization* of the human family, i.e., the regression to a stage prior to egalitarian hunter-gatherer societies — to the time of prehuman mammalian existence when males were disconnected from their offspring and the females who bore them.

Liberal Practical Theologies of the Family

I hold that theology should base itself on historical-critical readings of the Bible and also critically interact with modern philosophical and social-science disciplines. This makes me a kind of theological liberal. But much of contemporary liberal theology has been unable to address the major problems in world family trends. Most North American mainline theology accepted the attitude of the liberal social sciences, at least until the early 1990s, and counseled that the church adapt to trends toward increased divorce, out-of-wedlock births, and other features characteristic of the emerging "culture of nonmarriage."[1] From the writings of sociologist Jessie Bernard in the 1970s until recent years, most of the social scientists in the U.S. acknowledged that major family changes were occurring but said that, on the whole, they were benign. Furthermore, many social scientists believed that these changes might even be positive, offering adults — and especially women — a vast new panoply of choices for expressing their sexual and reproductive interests.[2] In the late 1980s and the early 1990s, social science reports by Nicholas Zill, David Popenoe, Norval Glenn, demographer Sara McLanahan, and most recently Paul Amato and Alan Booth in their respected *A Generation at Risk: Growing Up in an Era of Family Upheaval* (1997), showed that significant numbers of children were suffering from these family shifts.[3] In addition, work by Lenore Weitzman and others demonstrated that large numbers of women were undergoing precipitous drops in income due to divorce and single parenthood.[4]

---

1. For a discussion of the phrase "culture of nonmarriage," see *Marriage in America: A Report to the Nation* (New York: Council on Families in America of the Institute for American Values, 1995). For a discussion of the interaction of liberal Protestant theology and liberal social science, see Don Browning, Bonnie Miller McLemore, Pamela Couture, Bernie Lyon, and Robert Franklin, *From Culture Wars to Common Ground: Religion and the American Family Debate* (Louisville: Westminster/John Knox, 1997), pp. 43-48.

2. Jessie Bernard, *The Future of Marriage* (New York: World Publishing, 1972).

3. Paul Amato and Alan Booth, *A Generation at Risk: Growing Up in an Era of Family Upheaval* (Cambridge, Mass.: Harvard University Press, 1997).

4. Lenore Weitzman, *The Divorce Revolution* (New York: Free Press, 1985). Although it

During the 1970s and 80s, the liberal churches reflected the optimistic attitudes of the social sciences during those decades. Their ecclesial studies and reports on family and sexuality reflected this cheerful mood toward family change. Furthermore, although the social sciences have become more somber in their assessment of these trends, much of liberal theology in the U.S. has continued its positive, if not celebratory, attitudes toward these new family directions.

Most liberal Protestant theology on family renounced the use of two classical Christian moral traditions — Roman Catholic natural law and the Protestant use of moral arguments based on the "orders of creation." Not only did liberal Protestants reject Aquinas and the nineteenth-century Catholic manualist tradition, they also rejected the powerful theologies of family by the twentieth-century Reformed theologians Karl Barth and Emil Brunner as well as the German Lutheran Helmut Thielicke. Catholic natural law seemed to liberal Protestants far too static to comprehend the dynamics of modern family changes, but so did the classic Reformation idea that social ethics should be grounded in the command of God revealed in creation.

Notes on Barth and Thielicke

I will discuss Barth and Thielicke first and then turn to Brunner. Karl Barth departed from Luther's understanding of God-ordained ordinances that revealed how daily life, including marriage and family, should be ordered. Barth did not speak directly of estates of creation, orders of creation, or ordinances. He acknowledged occasionally that there were differentiated "spheres" of life such as family, government, and business. He also believed that God's commands addressed these different spheres or orders. But Barth denied that these divine commands contained norms, laws, or orders that could be abstracted from God's command and gain a life of their own as independent principles of governance. In fact, Barth charged his contemporary Emil Brunner with virtually equating the classic Protestant orders of creation with Catholic natural law arguments; both wrongly bestow norms to marriage and family, Barth con-

---

was later discovered that the cost of divorce for women calculated by Weitzman was too high, other studies still show women's income goes down and men's goes up after divorce. See Richard Peterson, "A Re-evaluation of the Economic Consequences of Divorce," *American Sociological Review* 61 (June 1996): 528-36.

tended, independently of the direct will of God.[5] Marriage and family, Barth taught, receive their normative meaning through the direct command of God as revealed in the history of creation, reconciliation, and most definitively in the redemptive activity of Jesus Christ.[6]

Barth's ethic of marriage and the family is riddled with the language of command. We are "commanded" to be "male" or "female," but not necessarily to marry. As male and female, we are "commanded" to be in copartnership with one another. God's command means that we can only be man in relation to woman and only woman in relation to man.[7] This command of God extends to both the male-female differentiation and the basic male-female relationship. Barth writes, "We have to say both that man is necessarily and totally man or woman, and that as such and in consequence he is equally necessarily and totally man *and* woman."[8]

Of course, for Barth the language of command is more indicative than imperative; it announces our definition and status before God more than it imposes an external moral demand. It is, as Paul Ricoeur has insightfully pointed out, more *"gift" than arbitrary divine edict.*[9] Commands for Barth are intended to free human beings more than they are to restrict and control them. Nonetheless, a command for Barth makes Christian ethics (even in the sphere of marriage, family, and sexuality) a matter of direct encounter with the Word of God and quite independent of the regularities of reason and nature — independent, that is, of anything approaching a theory of natural law. God's command for creation, revealed in the creation stories in the first chapters of the book of Genesis, basically transcends nature and was in no way derived from nature. From the standpoint of the liberal theological mentality — steeped as it is in historicism, cultural relativism, deconstructionism, and comparative anthropology — Barth's ethics of command seemed both arbitrary and ethnocentric and was quickly set aside as a resource for dealing with social trends affecting marriage and family.

Helmut Thielicke's ethics of sexuality suffered a similar fate. Thielicke makes direct use of the classic Protestant orders of creation argument. But whereas Barth collapsed the orders of creation into the immediate command of God, Thielicke saw the orders more as completing and

5. Karl Barth, *Church Dogmatics* III/4, *The Doctrine of Creation,* ed. G. W. Bromiley and T. F. Torrance (Edinburgh: T. & T. Clark, 1961), pp. 19-23.

6. Barth, *Church Dogmatics* III/4, p. 18.

7. Barth, *Church Dogmatics* III/4, p. 117.

8. Barth, *Church Dogmatics* III/4, p. 118.

9. Paul Ricoeur, "The Logic of Jesus, the Logic of God," *Criterion* 18, no. 2 (Summer): 4-6.

perfecting certain natural regularities of human nature. The Genesis stories revealed to Thielicke, as they did to Barth, that male and female in cohumanity and copartnership with God is the divine will for humans at the origins of creation.[10]

But once Thielicke places human sexuality within this biblical anthropology (or what he calls a theological phenomenology), he goes further and identifies certain natural and pervasive tendencies of human sexuality that Barth ignores. For instance, he follows Freud in describing sexual human experience as phasic; it rises to a climax and then declines as tension is discharged. He also had affinities with contemporary evolutionary psychology in viewing males with polygynous tendencies and females as having more of an orientation to monogamy. It must be admitted, however, that because his descriptions preceded the more sophisticated explanations for, and exceptions to, these asymmetrical male-female orientations that evolutionary psychology provides today, his words on this subject sound stereotypical, if not chauvinistic. But they may not have been so much wrong as simply inadequately developed. Furthermore, humans, for Thielicke, have no estrus and therefore, in contrast to other animals, are in principle sexually ready at all times.[11] But these regularities of human sexuality are described by Thielicke, not explained. Nothing like the theories of kin altruism, inclusive fitness, or, as I indicated above, asymmetrical male-female reproductive patterns are invoked to account for what he describes. Without such explanations, Thielicke's descriptions sound quaint and unconvincing. But they were, in fact, consistent with observations about human sexuality that have appeared with consistent regularity throughout the history of Christian thought and that can also be found, as we saw in Chapter Five, in samples of Jewish and Islamic thinking as well.

Thielicke's phenomenology of sexuality is not a natural law theory. It does, however, have affinities to this ancient approach. Time and again, Thielicke uses these descriptions to show how natural functions of human sexuality in procreation and pleasure lead to and disclose the selfhood of the sexual partner, thereby carrying sexual exchange beyond its pleasurable and procreative functions to an initial, although fragmentary, sense of respect for the other.[12] For this reason, he argues that human sexual intercourse anticipates, and indeed calls for, the monogamous organi-

---

10. Helmut Thielicke, *The Ethics of Sex* (New York: Harper & Row, 1965), pp. 3-13.

11. Thielicke, *The Ethics of Sex*, pp. 35-58.

12. Thielicke, *The Ethics of Sex*, p. 89.

zation of sexuality willed by God in creation and completed in the self-sacrificial love of Jesus. For Thielicke, the orders of creation build on yet complete our natural human sexual tendencies. Thielicke's view of the orders of creation seems less arbitrary than Barth's commandments. For Thielicke, family and marriage, as orders of creation, capture and redirect certain inner tendencies of natural human sexuality. Thielicke understands the orders of creation as being closely related to the regularities of nature and functioning to build on them and direct them toward the human good.

Liberal Contractualism and Relationality

Liberal Protestantism, in the United States and around the world, rejected twentieth-century variations on Reformation theology represented by Barth and Thielicke, at least as they pertain to the areas of sex and marriage. As religious liberalism emerged from the 1960s battle over civil rights for African Americans, it analogically applied its new emphasis on universal justice and equal respect to relationships between men and women. I believe that there was much that is theologically sound in this liberal Protestant perspective. But liberalism tended to equate the civil rights struggle over the rights of minorities with the issue presented by changing family patterns; it believed that all family forms were equal in the same way as all races and all persons are equal. It was difficult for it to grasp the error in this analogy. Just as equal respect for all individuals does not mean that the actions of each person are of equal moral worth, so too the principle of respect for all families does not mean that they all are equally able to perform their various tasks.

Liberal Protestantism's ethic of justice love was stated without reference to Reformation theology's emphasis on the orders of creation or the command of God. This can best be seen in the 1991 Presbyterian report titled *Keeping Body and Soul Together.*[13] Families were not defined by form or function but by whether they exhibited the relational qualities of love and justice. This view promoted a family ideal marked by a fair and affectionate contractualism that blurred distinctions between nonsexual friendships, sexual friendships, cohabiting couples, legally contracted marital couples, and couples both legally contracted and covenantally or sacra-

---

13. *Keeping Body and Soul Together: Report to the 203rd General Assembly* (Presbyterian Church USA, 1991).

mentally blessed and sanctioned. A new democracy of fair and affectionate relationships replaced older boundary-creating understandings of
marriage as a publicly witnessed covenant, sacrament, and contract between man and woman in their copartnership with one another and God.

The Presbyterian report was actually the culmination of a trend that
began much earlier. Daphne and Terence Anderson have chronicled the
evolution of the United Church of Canada over the last three decades. Before 1978, the study documents of that denomination emphasized the importance of marriage, the centrality of parenthood, and the problems of
divorce. After that date, these documents generally discussed sexuality
rather than marriage, intimacy in contrast to parenthood, personal fulfillment rather than obligation, and family issues as private decisions
rather than matters of ecclesial and public accountability.[14] Historian
Joanna Bowen Gillespie shows a similar recent history among U.S. Episco-
palians. She writes, "Today, the former denominational focus on family
delimited by seed and marriage" has been subsumed under the more inclusive concept of "household." "The emerging theology of family sports
a new terminology: 'household' replaces an outmoded, stereotyped 'family.'"[15] What Gillespie was overlooking is that the modern reality of
household for the most part dismantles or sets aside the centrality of the
conjugal couple. The ancient model of household — inclusive of grandparents, slaves, and others — still made the conjugal couple central to its
meaning.

Even the World Council of Churches joined this trend when it wrote
the following words in one of its official study documents: "Families take
many forms. We tend to idealize the family form we know. Yet no single
structure captures the heart of the family."[16] Although there is truth in
this statement, without qualification this declaration and others like it
typical of liberal Protestantism functioned to blind the churches to what
has actually been happening to families, i.e., the impact of divorce and
out-of-wedlock births on children and mothers and the worldwide drift
of fathers away from their children. The liberal emphasis on the quality of
family relations, rather than the actual presence of fathers and mothers

14. Daphne and Terence Anderson, "Kingdom Symbol or Lifestyle Choice," in *Faith Traditions and the Family*, ed. Phyllis Airhart and Margaret Bendroth (Louisville: Westminster/
John Knox, 1996), pp. 126-42.

15. Joanna Gillespie, "Episcopal: Family as the Nursery of Church and Society," in *Faith
Traditions and the Family*, pp. 148-49.

16. As quoted in Gilbert Meilander, "What Families Are For," *Family Affairs* (October
1990): 35.

parenting their children, contains an insight. A harsh and rejecting biological parent may be worse than a loving and affirming stepmother or foster parent. But it also obscures both the testimony of tradition and the recent insights found in the social sciences that show all too clearly that both quality of relation and intensity of parental investment are reinforced by kin altruism. In the name of egalitarianism and fairness, liberal family theology has been, on the whole, blind to worldwide family disruption except when these were created by wars, famine, and such events as the explosion of airliners into the World Trade Center leaving hundreds of children without one or more of their parents. In the name of respect for all families, it has been blind to the reality of family disruption.

Roman Catholic Personalism

Although Aquinas, like Luther and Calvin, made reference to God's intentions as revealed by the Genesis stories, he reinforced this argument by making use of Aristotle's theory of kin altruism and its implications for parental investment. One can see this Aristotelian and Thomistic argument in the writings of Pope Leo XIII on the family at the end of the nineteenth century. With the marriage and family writings of Pope John Paul II, the values of Leotine neo-Thomism have been restated increasingly in more personalistic philosophical categories. This personalism has helped save Catholic thinking from a crude naturalism; it has also, however, left Catholic family theory deprived of the realism of its traditional naturalism.

The 1880 papal encyclical *Arcanum* is considered to have been the great statement of Leo XIII on marriage, but his 1891 *Rerum Novarum* on Catholic social teachings is the more revealing. Unfortunately, in grounding his theory of the importance and rights of natural parents, he perpetuated as well the Aristotelian-Thomistic emphasis on the natural and God-given authority of the father. In spite of this, we should not be blind to his insights into both the nature of families and their relation to the state. The seeds of the very important Catholic doctrine of subsidiarity were sown in *Rerum Novarum*. This is a theory of the relation of family and state that I believe is crucial for addressing the world situation of families today.

Leo XIII saw an analogy between parents' relation to their children and laborers' rights to the fruits of their bodily blood and sweat. He believed it to be a law of nature that humans should have certain *prima facie* rights and responsibilities to both the issue of their bodily labor *and* their procreation. With regard to natural parents, this was partially true because they by nature were the most invested in their children. Natural parents would care for their children more because they would see themselves in their children; they therefore should have both the primary responsibility to discharge this care and the rights needed to do this without undue interference from the outside forces of state and market. He paraphrased Thomas Aquinas, but unfortunately perpetuated Aquinas's theory of paternal authority. He wrote,

> A most sacred law of nature ordains that the head of a family should provide for the necessities and comforts of the children he has begotten. That same nature leads him to want to provide for his children — who recall and in some sense extend his personality.[17]

He recalled Aquinas's implicit theory of kin altruism when he wrote, "Children are naturally something of their father. . . . they are held under the care of their parents until they acquire the use of free will."[18] Of course, as we have seen, nature is not as single-minded about programming parental care as Aquinas thought; it is more that nature provides parenting tendencies that can be developed and built upon even though, at the same time, they can be easily disrupted and squeezed out by other natural tendencies. Furthermore, to rescue Leo's and Aquinas's point, we today would certainly acknowledge that mothers as well as fathers have these inclinations to care for their children. But since, in so many parts of the world, fathers more than mothers have become detached from the parental task, it is helpful to be reminded by Leo and Aquinas of the natural, although fragile, grounds of this male inclination and responsibility.

In these passages, however, Leo XIII established the framework for the Catholic theory of subsidiarity. Let us hear his early statement on this teaching.

> It follows that to want to see the state's power arbitrarily at work within the intimacy of household is to make a great and pernicious mistake. Of course, when a family happens to be in a state of great

17. *Rerum Novarum*, in *Proclaiming Justice and Peace: Papal Documents from Rerum Novarum through Centisimus Annus*, ed. Michael Walsh and Brian Davies (Mystic, Conn.: Twenty-Third Publications), para. 11 and 12.

18. *Rerum Novarum*, para. 12. (The quote from Aquinas comes from *ST*, II-II, q. 10, article 12.)

distress, helpless and utterly unable to escape from its predicament, it is right that its pressing need be met by public aid. After all, every family is a part of the state. Similarly when within a family there is grave dispute about mutual rights, it is for the public authority to insist upon each party giving to the other its due. In doing this the state does not rob citizens of their rights, but rather strengthens them and supports them as it should.[19]

But if the state goes too far and begins to replace the responsibilities and privileges of parents in the fashion of Plato's *Republic,* then Leo sounds quite Aristotelian in writing, "Thus, when socialists set aside parental care and put that of the state in its place, they offend against natural justice and dissolve the bonds of family life."[20] In these statements, Leo is criticizing the excesses of both state and market when they disrupt the initiatives and responsibilities of families and workers. In taking this stand, a position amplified later by Pius XI in *Casti Connubii* (1931) and *Quadragesimo Anno* (1931), he sets the stage for a critique of the two grand solutions to the world domestic crises — the family dominated by the state (the Nordic solution and the solution of Goode) and family dominated by the market (the American solution and the solution of rational-choice economists).[21]

The themes of Leo's concern with the family and subsidiarity are taken up one hundred years later in John Paul II's *Centisimus Annus* (1991) as well as his many writings on marriage. But the philosophical personalism of John Paul II suppresses the naturalistic dimensions of Leo XIII. In his early book titled *Love and Responsibility* (1960) as well as his many letters and communications such as "Faithful and Responsible Love" (1978), *Familiaris Consortio* (1981), and "Letter to Families" (1994), John Paul II approaches sexuality through the status of humans as persons.[22] The naturalistic emphasis on kin altruism as a foundation to parenthood, found in Leo XIII and Pius XI, is never completely forgotten in the writings of John Paul II. It is almost buried, however, within his great

19. *Rerum Novarum,* para. 12.

20. *Rerum Novarum,* para. 12.

21. Pius XI, *Casti Connubii* (New York: The Barry Vail Corporation, 1931), and Pius XI, *Quadragesimo Anno,* in *The Papal Encyclicals* (McGrath, 1981).

22. Karol Wojtyla, *Love and Responsibility* (New York: Farrar, Straus and Giroux, 1960, 1981); "Faithful and Responsible Love" (1978); "Letter to Families" (New York: Origins CNS Documentary Service, 1994); *Familiaris Consortio: Apostolic Exhortation on the Catholic Family* (Chicago: Archdiocese of Chicago, 1981).

emphasis on how humans are constituted through their intersubjective acts of self-giving and how the birth of a child should not be considered as a biological phenomenon alone but a creative culmination of the love of husband and wife for one another.[23] And even though he continues to celebrate the doctrine of subsidiarity, he nearly loses the central reason why the state should support, but not undermine, the rights and responsibilities of parents. The central point is this: kin altruism as a biological reality on average inclines natural parents, more than substitutes, to nourish and care for their children. Had not John Paul II nearly lost sight of this, his personalism — his view that we are historical creatures shaped by interpersonal interaction and love — would have balanced more evenly the threat of naturalistic reductionism that plagued his neo-Thomistic predecessors.

Nature and Creation in Brunner

Barth rendered the command of God in creation as disconnected from the regularities of nature. Thielicke, on the other hand, understood the orders of creation as completing natural regularities that he described phenomenologically but could not explain fully. Both Barth and Thielicke could be easily dismissed by the Protestant liberalism and Western intellectual elites as confessional, ethnocentric, and untutored by the postmodern currents of cultural relativism, historicism, and deconstructionism. In a similar spirit, Roman Catholic personalism of the kind represented by Pope John Paul II was so ambitious to correct the naturalism and scholasticism of nineteenth-century neo-Thomism that it too failed to state an adequate balance between nature and creation in its theologies of marriage and family. Nature almost disappears in its theory of the person, and increasingly in this body of literature the category of nature loses any dialectical tension with God's will for the person in creation. In different ways than was the case with Barth, creation and the person in late Catholicism swamp all and lose their dialectical relation to the known rhythms of nature.

Emil Brunner, a contemporary of Barth, is an important but poorly understood exception to these trends. Brunner honored the classic Protestant argument from the orders of creation. Marriage and family together constituted for him one of the many spheres of society that Christians should

23. Karol Wojtyla, *Love and Responsibility,* pp. 224-30.

order on the basis of God's command in creation. The male-female differentiation of Genesis 1:27, the command that it is not "good for the man to be alone" (Gen. 2:17), and the declaration that a man leaves "his father and mother and clings to his wife, and they become one flesh" (Gen. 2:24) were in his theology features of God's order of creation for marriage and family.

All this for Brunner was the marital ideal as seen by the eyes of faith. *But he did not stop with this. Brunner believed that the fundamental social spheres of life — marriage, government, and market — evolved out of basic human interests that could be known and analyzed by reason.*[24] These interests are based in the "psychophysical nature" of human beings. The sphere of marriage and family was built on the psychophysical interests of sex and procreation. The sphere of economics "arises out of the impulse to work for a living" and to advance one's economic power through social systems of exchange. And finally, the sphere of government arises from the natural interest to achieve security for the first two concerns of family and work.[25]

Brunner made a claim that was quite upsetting to Barth. He held that these three forms of communal life could be understood, in some senses, independently of "faith." Brunner said, "These forms of community . . . are all independent of faith, and of the love which flows from faith." But then he continues by saying, "This does not mean that their significance and their true nature can be rightly known outside the sphere of faith."[26] These natural impulses toward the different spheres of communal life "conceal within themselves the Divine orders of creation" — God's intention for the future fulfillment of all humans.[27] Furthermore, these natural forms of community constitute something like divine training schools for higher and more fulfilling forms of life that God wills in creation. From the perspective of human reason, these spheres function to articulate and meet human needs; from the perspective of faith, they are gifts of God in creation. This is true in spite of the fact that they are constantly changing, broken, and sinful.[28]

On the specific issue of marriage, Brunner occupies a conceptual space somewhere between Thomas Aquinas on the Catholic side and Helmut Thielicke on the Protestant side. The natural interests of sex and

24. Emil Brunner, *The Divine Imperative* (Philadelphia: Westminster Press, 1957), p. 335.
25. Brunner, *The Divine Imperative*, p. 333.
26. Brunner, *The Divine Imperative*, p. 333.
27. Brunner, *The Divine Imperative*, p. 336.
28. Brunner, *The Divine Imperative*, pp. 336-37.

procreation in humans anticipate and are fulfilled in the monogamous relation between husband and wife willed by God in creation. Yes, Brunner acknowledges that there are natural polygynous impulses in humans, especially men. Yes, there is the reality of infidelity and divorce. But there also are impulses in human nature that lead us toward the personhood of the other and to exclusive commitment. Hence, there is a teleology toward monogamy in the nature of human sexuality and procreation, as ambiguous and easily disrupted as it may be. Or to say it differently, there is a natural although unsteady tendency for humans to conform to the norm of monogamy as this was revealed in God's will for creation.

Brunner, like Aquinas and today's evolutionary psychologists, emphasizes the importance for the emergence of monogamy of "parental recognition," i.e., the human recognition that this child is mine, someone I brought into the world, and indeed someone who is literally part of my very being. *But it is for Brunner a three-way recognition entailing father, mother, and child.* Aquinas and the evolutionary biologists would agree, as we saw above, that the mother's recognition that the child is hers comes more easily and that a father's recognition of this fact is more a matter of probability and hence subject to a variety of additional contingencies. Brunner affirms the importance of these various recognitions, but emphasizes not only the recognition of mutual responsibility of husband and wife for the child's physical life, but the recognition as well of their responsibility for the child's existence — the child's *"Dasein,"* to use Heidegger's concept. Brunner adds the importance of the child's recognition that this woman and this man are responsible for the child's existence. The trinity of recognitions of this bio-existential reality throws mother, father, and child together in irrevocable ways. Brunner writes,

> Since I, the father, as well as the mother and the child, know irrevocably that this fact is irrevocable, then we three persons are bound together in a way in which no other three persons have ever been bound together, in an unparalleled and indissoluble relation. . . . This trinity of being we call the human structure of existence.[29]

Brunner further sounds like both Aquinas and evolutionary psychologists when, with reference to the child once again, he discusses the meaning of the long period of infant dependency. Human infants are dependent physically and existentially far longer than the offspring of other

---

29. Brunner, *The Divine Imperative*, p. 346.

creatures. This too points to the need to hold mother, father, and infant together. Hence, the need to educate the child is a crucial natural tendency pointing to God's intentions in creation.

In short, Brunner believes that nature itself both anticipates and is completed by God's intention as revealed in creation that husband and wife become "one flesh." Jesus himself, in his commentary on Genesis, seems to advance the idea that this one-flesh union should be lifelong. Remember the words recorded in the Gospel of Matthew: "So they are no longer two, but one flesh. Therefore what God has joined together, let no one separate" (Matt. 19:6). We do not need to harden this into a totalistic anti-divorce stance to realize this passage is the culmination of the Christian ideal of marriage as revealed in the story of creation.

Karl Barth thought that Brunner had sold out to an inadequate Roman Catholic theory of natural law. He called Brunner's idea of orders of creation a "horizontal" ethic that had lost contact with the transcendent. He once wrote,

> But we cannot help feeling that at the root of his conception of "order" there lies something akin to the familiar notion of *lex naturae* which is immanent in reality and inscribed upon the heart of man, so that it is directly known to him.[30]

But Barth is wrong in his interpretation of Brunner. Brunner says that reason can discern the human interests motivating the spheres of creation, including the order of family and marriage. But its full normativity is revealed in scripture and the ongoing testimony of the Spirit of God. Reason helps us understand the substructures of the spheres of life. It helps us discern the premoral goods that must be properly ordered in human life. It gives us hints about their fulfillment. But the ideals and goals of marriage, according to his point of view, are themselves revealed.

Barth has none of this kind of thinking in his theology and ethic of the command of God. For this reason, Barth cannot enter into dialogue with other perspectives and disciplines on aspects of human life such as marriage and the family. He can only confess what he presumes to be the command of God witnessed to in scripture and apprehended by faith in the moment. By claiming too much for the Word of God, Barth marginalized Christianity from modern discourse and, finally, even marginalized his point of view, as we saw, from ongoing deliberations of

---

30. Barth, *Church Dogmatics* III/4, p. 20.

the contemporary church. As a consequence, he made Reformation theology appear irrelevant to the contemporary ecclesial and social debate about the meaning of marriage and the family.

Family and Analogical Thinking

The preceding arguments lead us to this conclusion: *some ways of organizing family life are more consistent with Christian values than others even though family as such is not an ultimate value within a Christian view of things.* We are saved by God; not principally by our families, and certainly not the form of our families. Our families may witness to the source of life in God and may mediate this life, but they cannot in themselves take the place of the central affirmations of the Christian faith.

Family, for Christians, must be seen as a finite, in contrast to an ultimate, value. Christianity's emphasis on the sacrality of the person, its positive attitude toward both nature and creation, its twofold ethic of creation and salvation, and its high valuation of children and the task of raising them to enjoy God — all of these values may have led Christian cultures increasingly to celebrate what I have called the equal-regard family.

I can imagine a note of discomfort, however, with the idea of associating Christianity too closely with any particular family pattern. We know of the Christian polygynous families in sub-Saharan Africa. We know of matriarchal families of Indonesian cultures, some of which are Christian. We are aware of joint families in India, most of which are Hindu but some of which are Christian. We know of single-parent families, blended families, stepfamilies, families with adopted children, and even gay and lesbian families. We see among Asian Christians in China, Korea, and Japan the remnants of Confucianism with its high valuation of tradition mediated by patterns of male hierarchy and cherished generations of special father-son obligations which often marginalized other family relations.

We should not assume — as some sociologists of modernization do when they project the worldwide drift toward the companionate marriage and family — that the entire world will, and therefore should, emulate what we have called *the intact, equal-regard couple and their children interacting with extended family and civil society.* But, at the same time, I have argued that if we are to counter the near universal drift toward family disruption, there must be developed a powerful worldwide religiocultural vision that advocates a new critical familism.

Spreading this vision should come about through dialogue and analogy. With the words "dialogue" and "analogy," I am invoking the hermeneutical traditions of Hans-Georg Gadamer and Paul Ricoeur and the use of these resources in the correlational theology of David Tracy and others.[31] I will say more about these philosophical and theological methods in the next chapters. Let me say this, now: family issues must become a matter of worldwide dialogue. It is triumphalist to demand an immediate conversion of the world to the companionate and stable equal-regard family. But it is possible to look for analogies to it, aspirations toward it, and transformations reaching in that direction. We also must be sensitive to genuine patterns of mutuality and equal regard that exist in unfamiliar cultural and religious wrappings.

We should examine the deeper historical traditions that lie behind specific cultural and social practices. For instance, Islam as a tradition may contain analogies to the equal-regard family that Islamic fundamentalism and the Afghanistan Taliban have attempted to suppress. Since family issues are finite goods, analogies can be pursued and nurtured without making the family an ultimate test of religious orthodoxy. The analogical and dialogical perspective does not roam the world with abstract sets of rights labeling as deficient family patterns and forms that do not conform to its rigid requirements. It examines instead the internal histories of various traditions and tries to find the analogies that exist between them. This interpretive approach works to find overlaps and points of consensus that are not, as a matter of fact, identities as such. But they are points of contact around which to have dialogue and develop bridges of commonality for future understanding, cooperation, and loose consensus.

Analogy and the Example of Islam

For instance, the Islamic legal scholar Azizah al-Hibri argues for the cogency and legitimacy of finding principles of gender equality within Islam. We already have seen how Islam contains principles of paternal care and a high valuation of children. But does it contain the seeds of gender

31. For discussions of the hermeneutic tradition in contemporary philosophy, see Hans-Georg Gadamer, *Truth and Method* (New York: Crossroad, 1982), and Paul Ricoeur, *Hermeneutics and the Human Sciences* (Cambridge: Cambridge University Press, 1981). For a discussion of how this perspective is used in a revised correlational and analogical method of theology, see David Tracy, *Blessed Rage for Order* (New York: Seabury Press, 1975), and *The Analogical Imagination* (New York: Crossroad, 1981).

equality and an ethic of equal regard? Al-Hibri believes it does. Furthermore, she fiercely resists the idea of importing these values from strictly Western or liberal feminist perspectives. Her argument is intriguing. I present it at length not to argue for the validity of her detailed translations and interpretations. I do it to demonstrate that scholarly efforts do exist that are working to retrieve and reconstruct a non-Christian tradition that at least shows analogies, if not actual identities, between it and liberal interpretations of Christianity.

Her work demonstrates how the analogical process can proceed between liberal Christian reconstructions and those now occurring within a religion such as Islam. This is particularly important to notice in view of the arguable assumption that the conflicts that engulfed the world after September 11, 2001, although principally about conflicting models for relating religion and public life, had behind them additional deep antagonisms between highly patriarchal patterns of sexuality, marriage, and family to be found in Islam and emerging egalitarian models characteristic chiefly of the Christian and politically liberal West. The work of professor al-Hibri suggests that these two traditions, both of which are Abrahamic religions, have resources within them that point to important analogies — analogies that are sufficiently close to one another to provide for cooperation and the creation of overlapping, if not identical, cultural frameworks.

Al-Hibri believes that the law of Islamic nations must be based on the Qur'an and the *sunnah* (recorded deeds of the Prophet) and the *hadith* (or his recorded words). The *sunnah* and the *hadith* are secondary sources, and when there is apparent conflict between these sources or when the Qur'an and the *sunnah* do not address an issue, then Muslim scholars resort to *ijtihad* — "the science of interpretation and rule making."[32] According to Islamic law, if Qur'an and *sunnah* were completely silent on the issue at hand, then jurists could resort to local custom to make their final decision. This is where the patriarchal mischief gradually began to set in, according to al-Hibri. Most of the heavy patriarchal features of Islam are not to be found in the Qur'an, she insists, but rather have crept into Islamic family law from the long years of medieval legal interpretations — interpretations rendered by male jurists, done sometimes for the advantage of males, and reflecting the androcentric bias of their surrounding feudalistic societies of the time. Certainly, we saw parallels to this in the Christian

---

32. Azizah al-Hibri, "Islam, Law, and Custom: Redefining Muslim Women's Rights," *The American Journal of International Law and Policy* 5, no. 12 (1997): 6.

West. In fact, al-Hibri claims that "Muslim Arab patriarchy was greatly influenced in its development by the neighboring Byzantine and Persian empires. It took women centuries before they could even begin challenging it successfully."[33]

Al-Hibri believes, however, that the current distortions in Islam on gender issues can be challenged and changed. She turns directly to the Qur'an. The most basic evidence for a deep gender equality in the Qur'an can be found in the verses that say men and women are created of the same substance, the same soul, and with the same *nafs* (soul). She translates *ayah* 4:1 to read, "O people! reverence God (show piety towards God) who created you from one *nafs* and created from her (the *nafs*) her mate and spread from them many men and women; and reverence God, through whom you demand your mutual rights, and the wombs (that bore you), (for) God watches you." Or again, "It is He who produced you from a single cell, and appointed a place of sojourning (the womb of the mother), and a place of depositing (the grave)" (6:98).[34] And even more, "It is He who created you from a single cell, and from it created its mate, that you may live as companions" (7:189). These *ayah* establish what al-Hibri calls the Equality Principle in the Qur'an.[35]

But not all the Qur'an is thought to be consistent with the Equality Principle. There is one major exception, *ayah* 4:34, to which al-Hibri gives careful attention. She refers to this particular passage as a Complex Phrase. With the crucial Arabic words inserted, it goes like this: "Men are *qawwamun* over women *bima* God *faddala* of them over others, and *bima* they spend of their own money. . . ." The key words in this passage are *qawwamun*, which al-Hibri believes should be translated as "advisors," *faddala*, which should be rendered as "some," and *bima*, which conveys a causal connection in particular circumstances. One modern, but inadequate translation, goes like this: "Men are the *protectors and maintainers* of women, because God has *given the one more (strength) than the other,* and because they support them from their means."[36] With the more accurate translations that al-Hibri recommends, she thinks the passage should read: "Men are the (advisors/providers of guidance) to women (because/in circumstances where/in that which) God made some of them different

---

33. Al-Hibri, "Islam, Law, and Custom," p. 5.

34. These additional quotes from the Qur'an, when they do not come directly from al-Hibri, come from *Al-Qur'an: A Contemporary Translation,* trans. Ahem Ali (Princeton: Princeton University Press, 1993).

35. Al-Hibri, "Islam, Law, and Custom," p. 27.

36. Al-Hibri, "Islam, Law, and Custom," p. 27.

from some others and (because/in circumstances where/in that which) they spend of their own money. . . ."[37]

In light of the Islamic principle that when different passages seem to conflict they "must be carefully studied in search of a meaning that makes them consistent with each other,"[38] she thinks that the Equality Principle is the more general meaning to be respected and preserved, and the special circumstances under which men become advisors have to do with those more contingent social and economic conditions that require women to be economically dependent upon their husbands — a condition that does not always obtain. She concludes by saying,

> In other words, the Qur'an was describing (and not recommending) in this *ayah* a situation akin to the traditional one existing at the time, where some women were financially dependent. In those circumstances, the *ayah* informs us, God gave the man supporting her the responsibility (*taklif,* not privilege) of offering the woman guidance and advice in those areas in which he happens to be more qualified or experienced. The woman, however, is entitled to reject both (otherwise the advisory role is no longer advisory).[39]

With al-Hibri's interpretation of the Equality Principle in Islam, we can imagine how such a dialogue designed to discover and enhance analogies between two traditions might begin. It certainly requires a sense of the contextualization of one's own ideals and that of the other tradition. It requires a critical analysis of the meaning of the ideals or normative claims of both traditions. Are these traditions really saying what it often has been assumed they are saying? As in the case of both al-Hibri's interpretation of Islam and my own interpretation of Christianity, there is good reason to think that traditional interpretations that emphasize gender inequality are at fault. If this is the case, then reconstruction, i.e., a more adequate systematic interpretation, must take place. Such an enterprise then looks for analogies that can be identified, enhanced, and stabilized.

This retrieval and reconstructive task does not force identities where they do not exist. Gender equality in Islam is based on the idea that male and female come from the same stuff, the same substance, the same cell, the same *nafs* (soul). This is the meaning assigned to the Genesis 2:22 "bone of my bones, flesh of my flesh," fully ascribed to by Islam as well as

37. Al-Hibri, "Islam, Law, and Custom," p. 29.
38. Al-Hibri, "Islam, Law, and Custom," p. 29.
39. Al-Hibri, "Islam, Law, and Custom," p. 30.

Christianity and Judaism. This passage, often interpreted in Christianity (although not always) to say woman is subordinate to man because of her derivation from Adam's rib, is in fact given by Islam a more egalitarian interpretation. A distinctively Christian interpretation of the religious and social equality of women would more likely be based on the second half of the Great Commandment that says "You shall love your neighbor as yourself" (Mark 12:31). Or it might be based on the Galatians affirmation that for those baptized in Christ "There is no longer Jew or Greek, there is no longer slave or free, there is no longer male and female; for all of you are one in Christ Jesus" (Gal. 3:28). Or it might turn to the Ephesians passage that says husbands and wives should "Be subject to one another out of reverence for Christ" (Eph. 5:21). The love ethic of equal regard in these passages is variously grounded on the love command, mutual baptism, and mutual reverence *(phobos)* for Christ. These passages are not saying quite the same things as the various *ayah* dealing with the one-cell substance of male and female quoted by al-Hibri. But they are highly analogous and good grounds for further dialogue.

Another retrieval and reconstruction agenda can be found in the Islamic legal scholar Abdullahi Ahmed An-Na'im. In his *Toward an Islamic Reformation* (1990), he makes a claim that at first sounds very strange to Western ears. He contends that the values of human rights and gender equality must for Islam be derived from the Qur'an. In other words, the law of Islamic countries must be informed by the Qur'an, the *sunnah,* and the *hadith.* But the Islamic state must no longer be viewed as theocratic — as derived directly and solely from God's revelation to the Prophet. An-Na'im is interested in reform — in bringing human rights, gender equality, and pluralism (respect and protection for non-Islamic persons) into Islamic societies. He insists that maintaining "Islamic validity is . . . essential for the political viability of the proposed reforms."[40] But the state in primarily Islamic societies can no longer be grounded solely on the Qur'an, the *sunnah,* and the developed bodies of law called Shari'a. The state in Islamic countries must be grounded on constitutional theories of human rights. *The Qur'an and the Shari'a can contribute to a theory of human rights, he claims, but they can no longer be the only determining voice.* Shari'a, as it has been conceived and practiced in the past, must itself now be reformed. The Qur'an, the *sunnah,* and Shari'a must be shown to be unique and independent sources for the values of gender equality and human

40. Abdullahi Ahmed An-Na'im, *Toward an Islamic Reformation: Civil Liberties, Human Rights, and International Law* (Syracuse, N.Y.: Syracuse University Press, 1990), p. xv.

rights. An-Na'im thinks that this can be done. They should be guides to a deeper and more humane set of values that do indeed exist in Islam and the Qur'an. But other voices, and other insights into the human, will and should also inform Islamic societies and Islamic law.

His strategy, although similar to al-Hibri's in its ultimate goal, uses different means to get there. An-Na'im believes that a distinction can be made within the Qur'an between the Prophet's revelations received at Mecca and those thought to have been received at Medina — the city to which the Prophet and his company fled because of persecution in Mecca. He claims that the message of Mecca emphasized "the inherent dignity of all human beings, regardless of gender, religious belief, race, and so forth."[41] The Qur'an of Medina addresses the faithful and those inside Islam; the passages recorded during the Mecca period, we are told, always address the whole of humanity, using such phrases as "O, children of Adam," and "O, humankind." More specifically there is *ayah* 17:70 where God has "honored the children of Adam; provided them with transport on land and sea; given them good and pure things for sustenance; and preferred them over many parts of Our (His) Creation."[42] With regard to male and female relations, the Mecca period scriptures say, "O, humankind, We have created you into male and female, and made you into peoples and tribes so that you may be acquainted (and cooperate) with each other."[43]

When An-Na'im turns to 4:34, the one commented upon extensively above by al-Hibri, he does not translate it to be consistent with al-Hibri's Equality Principle; he says, instead, it came from the Medina period, not the early and more authentic stage of Mecca. At Medina, the Prophet began to accommodate to the social and tribal circumstances around him; his more uncompromising message given at Mecca had backfired. Its more ideal dimension conveyed in Mecca, the Prophet determined, had to be delayed in its implementation. Hence, the loss of the earlier equal dignity of women and men. The crucial verse 4:34 gets recorded; it was a passage that constituted the bedrock of conservative Shari'a judgments unfavorable to women. An-Na'im interprets it to read, "men have *qawwama* (guardianship and authority) over women because of the advantage they (men) enjoy over them (women) and because they (men) spend their property in supporting them (women)."[44] An-Na'im does not so much try to

---

41. An-Na'im, *Toward an Islamic Reformation*, p. 52.
42. An-Na'im, *Toward an Islamic Reformation*, p. 54.
43. An-Na'im, *Toward an Islamic Reformation*, p. 54.
44. An-Na'im, *Toward an Islamic Reformation*, p. 55.

reinterpret the passage to be more egalitarian, as did al-Hibri; he locates it, instead, in a less authoritative and less authentic strand of the Qur'an.

Christian interpreters do much the same thing as An-Na'im when they argue that the teachings of Jesus and Paul are more authoritative than the reactionary hierarchical and gendered messages of the later pastoral epistles. They make the same maneuver as al-Hibri when they argue that fresh translations of old and familiar passages offer new insights. I will not here try to determine whether al-Hibri or An-Na'im have the better method. I only intend to show that interpretive moves similar to those found in Christian theology today can be identified among interpreters of Islam. *This invites the analogical process that I think is necessary for the development of the emerging global and critical marriage culture — a new worldwide critical familism.*

An Ontology of Gift

I conclude this chapter by identifying a theme that I believe runs through Christianity but that is shared analogously with Judaism, Islam, and as we will see in the concluding chapter, possibly other world religions as well. It may help identify what is unique in these traditions in its language about sex, family, and marriage, especially when compared with some dominant discourses of modernity. Although overstated and disconnected from the rhythms of nature, Barth's theology of creation does contain an insight into the fundamental character of Christianity and it may throw light on Judaism and Islam as well. I will identify this insight now and qualify it later.

It has to do with what I call, following Barth, and even more the thought of Paul Ricoeur, the narrative of creation in the Hebrew scriptures that discloses the goods of life as a gift from God. I call this an "ontology of gift." The narrative dimension of a tradition is important to understand even if we cannot always fully account for how it interacts with practices and even if we cannot understand the full historical situation of the original narrative. Ricoeur, who learns from Barth's theology of creation, takes another step beyond Barth. He is interested in knowing what public philosophical sense can be made out of the core narratives and symbols of a great confessional tradition. Barth thought that such philosophical ambitions were inconsistent with a religion first grounded in revelation and the confession or avowal of its truth. Ricoeur has advanced the argument that public philosophical points of view always first of all start with people's confession of the illuminating nature of the metaphors and narratives that form the classics of a great tradition. He summarizes this view with his celebrated formula "the symbol gives rise to thought."[45] This is his way of saying that myth, narrative, and symbol give rise to philosophy, hence give birth to all discursive thought — including moral and legal thought. I think this is true.

Judaism, Christianity, and Islam have a common narrative tradition in the creation stories. They interpret them somewhat differently, but not categorically so. One key element that these traditions have in common because of these shared creation stories is a similar moral ontology — what Ricoeur would call an "economy of gift" but I choose to call an ontology of gift.[46] This ontology of gift makes praise and thanksgiving the fundamental predicate of moral action and legal thought for those who faithfully appropriate these traditions. God creates a good world (a well-resourced world in the premoral sense) prior to the revelation of specific commandments to people. The Hebrew scriptures attest to the goodness of the world when the book of Genesis sets down after each major act of creation such words as, "And God saw that it was good" (1:12) or even, "God saw everything that he had made, and indeed, it was very good" (1:31). The Christian scriptures regularly repeat such affirmations. The Qur'an is almost obsessive in asserting this ontology of gift. Notice, for example, "All praise be to Allah, Lord of all the worlds, most beneficent" (1:1); "All praise be to God who created the heavens and the earth" (6:1); "All that is in the heavens and the earth sings the praises of God" (62:1); and "Oh children of Israel, remember the favors he bestowed upon you" (2:40).

In interpreting metaphors and narratives, Ricoeur agrees that it is important to put them into historical context. The historical context of a narrative and its symbols is important, but the meaning of a metaphor, symbol, or story cannot be located only behind the text, i.e., in the motivations of the author or in the conflicts of history within which the text is situated. The meaning of the metaphor and narrative, according to Ricoeur, is found in the "mode of being-in-the-world" projected in "front

---

45. Paul Ricoeur, *The Conflict of Interpretations* (Evanston, Ill.: Northwestern University Press, 1974).

46. For an excellent summary of Ricoeur's thought on what I have called the ontology of gift and which could more accurately be called an "economy of gift" at least from the perspective of Ricoeur's thought, see John Wall, "The Economy of the Gift: Paul Ricoeur's Significance for Theological Ethics," *Journal of Religious Ethics* 29, no. 2 (Summer 2001): 235-60.

of the text."[47] In the case of these three traditions, the basic mode of being-in-the-world is most appropriately one of "gratitude." Furthermore, our respect and active helpfulness for the other, including the marital partner, is based on the "anterior gift" that all humanity and all others, be they male or female, are parts of God's good creation.[48]

Ricoeur summarizes this biblical ontology with the following words: "Because (existence) has been given to you (by God), give in turn."[49] This suggests that the moral obligation to love the other, to show equal regard for the other, is rooted in a prior sense of being given the gifts of life and love. This gives us insight into how our fundamental visions of life (our ontologies) are linked to our sense of moral obligation — a point I will elaborate more fully in the next chapter. *This affirmation of the gift of life conveyed by these religious traditions may sound trivial, but in light of the competing ontologies of scarcity and competition found in many of the dominant discourses of modernity such as neoclassical economics, classical psychoanalysis, Marxism, and most interpretations of evolutionary psychology, this ontology of gift is significant indeed.*

This shared ontology of gift animates other common elements quite visible in Christianity and observable in Judaism and Islam as well. Sex and procreation are gifts of creation (products of this ontology of gift) that are both intrinsically good and instrumentally useful. In and through the processes of birth, humans share in the divine creativity. The fatherhood of earthly men, as John Miller has pointed out, should model itself after the fatherhood of the infinite, caring, and righteous God — Creator and Preserver of the gifts and goods of life. This identification with the model of the caring parenthood of God helps overcome male ambiguity about bonding with their offspring. It does this by guiding the conflicting inclinations of men and reinforcing those that can be directed toward the care and support of the children they help create rather than toward their own satisfactions and short-term interests. This ontology of gift, when rightly understood, can also provide the grounds of an ontology of equality between all human beings and certainly between husband and wife in the marital relation. The dignity and honor of being created by God in the image of God is a gift bestowed equally to both male and fe-

47. Paul Ricoeur, "Philosophical Hermeneutics and Biblical Hermeneutics," in *From Text to Action* (Evanston, Ill.: Northwestern University Press, 1991), pp. 89-101.

48. Wall, "The Economy of the Gift," p. 247.

49. Paul Ricoeur, "Love and Justice," in *Radical Pluralism and Truth: David Tracy and the Hermeneutics of Religion*, ed. Werner G. Jeanrond and Jennifer Rilke (New York: Crossroad, 1991), pp. 187-202.

male (Gen. 1:27). Much the same thing is said in the Qur'an: "It is He who created you from a single cell, and from it created its mate, that you may live as companions" (7:189).

In the chapter to follow, I will try to illustrate the dialogical and analogical process developed in this chapter by discussing the worldwide drive of feminism to enhance the situation of women in families throughout the world. This story of the new voice of women raises all the relevant issues about the emerging world conversation about families.

Chapter Seven

Feminism, Family, and Global Trends

I have argued that Christianity has an investment in marriage and the form that families take, even though it holds that neither marriage nor family form are conditions for salvation. True as this is, Christianity has views of nature and the person that suggest some marriage and family patterns are more fulfilling and ethically responsible than others. I hinted in the last chapter that this stance implies that a Christian practical theology should take an analogical attitude between its view of families and those of other traditions. More specifically, practical theology should find analogies and promote commonalities with other religions and other perspectives through dialogue. This requires a framework of interpretation and a model for doing ethics. In this chapter, I will both clarify and illustrate the interpretive and ethical perspectives that have been implicit in this book from its beginning.

An Interlude on Method

I have waited until late in the book to bring forth my point of view on methodology in practical theology. Discussions about method in theology and ethics are trying and difficult. If readers have gotten this far, I hope they are sufficiently interested in the substance of the issues I am addressing to wonder about the rules that might govern interpretation and ethical engagement between different perspectives. I think the perspective I outline here will enhance the dialogue needed to create the new world marriage culture that I have been proposing.

I propose a philosophy of hermeneutic realism as the most adequate

155

epistemological framework for the practical theology needed to accomplish this interpretive and ethical task. Don't let the specialized phrases "hermeneutic realism" and "practical theology" put you off. Take the phrase "practical theology." Some of you may say, "Oh, I am not interested in practical-theological method. I simply do theology, and of course it is practical. I ignore issues of method." Or some may say, "I just want to compare, contrast, and critique various religious and nonreligious views of marriage and family. I wouldn't call it theology at all." I claim, however, that any comparative or critical task will inevitably become involved in religious issues. Since the institution of marriage is such an imminently concrete and practical social reality, comparison will soon get one into a practical and religious enterprise as well. It will entail coming to terms with one's own history and the ethical and religious ideas that shaped that history. Sooner or later, it will involve a critical assessment of this tradition. But this also is true when confronting another tradition in dialogue; eventually, you and your interlocutors must be open to a critical assessment of the customs, practices, and teachings of that tradition as well. For shorthand, I will call this a practical-theological task since in both cases the interpreter has to make decisions about the religious horizons of these customs and practices, both in one's own tradition and in others'.

"Hermeneutic realism" is the other obscure term that I mentioned above. This refers to an epistemological and philosophical stance that makes it possible to illustrate the thickness and multidimensionality of both the process of understanding and the task of ethics entailed in good practical theology. Part of this multidimensionality includes references to the natural regularities of human life. These are regularities that we first of all see and experience through the language and symbols of the cultures we inherit, but the regularities are there nonetheless, even if rendered in somewhat distorted ways by the linguistic traditions we use to represent them. These language traditions house assumptions, more or less adequate, about these regularities that provide the background for all of our practical judgments.

Definitions

Even though I have said much already about practical theology, I now need to get far more specific. Practical theology increasingly is being defined as critical and correlational reflection on the church's transformative praxis in the world. The focus of practical theology's reflection on the needs and orders of the world beyond the church is not designed to suppress reflection on the internal life of the church.[1] Nor should it obscure the truth that the promises of God include but transcend the scope of finite life. It is, rather, to locate the scope of practical theology in its most comprehensive context — ministry to the world. It is, in effect, to claim that a fully critical and correlational practical theology must necessarily be a public practical theology. A public practical theology aspires to demonstrate how theology can analyze and critique the practices of both religious and nonreligious groups as they impact the public or common good.

Furthermore, this definition of practical theology as public is not designed to dissociate it from the traditional domains of that discipline such as pastoral care, religious education, homiletics, worship, missions, and service (diaconia). It is simply to suggest that these traditional subdisciplines should have both an inner-ecclesial and a public expression. To take just one example: practical theology must not only be concerned about the pastoral care of families within the church, it also must be critically attentive to the health of families in the wider society and, indeed, the wider world.

Hermeneutics, Ethics, and Practical Theology

For several years I have argued that the descriptive and normative interests of both practical theology and theological ethics should be pursued within a framework of "hermeneutics," a word that begs for further clarification. By using the troublesome word "hermeneutics," I follow such scholars as Hans-Georg Gadamer, Paul Ricoeur, and Richard Bernstein in seeing all attempts at human understanding as unfolding within a context of dialogue or conversation.[2] Of course, dialogue or conversation, within this philosophical tradition, has a rather precise meaning. It holds that understanding begins with questions shaped by the traditions that have constituted one's experience. Understanding, therefore, is a kind of synthesis or fusion between the historically shaped questions of the inter-

---

1. Recent discussions have distinguished beween practical theology done within the clerical, ecclesial, and public paradigms. It is my position that the public paradigm is the most inclusive and can and should contain the clerical and ecclesial. For a discussion of these distinctions, see Edward Farley, *Theologia* (Philadelphia: Fortress Press, 1983).

2. For an excellent summary of Gadamer, see Richard Bernstein, *Beyond Objectivism and Relativism* (Philadelphia: University of Pennsylvania Press, 1983).

preter and the meaning of classic texts or monuments of an identifiable tradition.[3] It is my claim that both practical theology and theological ethics should be conceived as proceeding within such a historically contingent dialogue. That is true even if the primary object of study is family and marriage, i.e., what these institutions have been in the past and should become in the future.

But I move toward Ricoeur and my colleague William Schweiker in calling for a kind of critical hermeneutic or "hermeneutic realism."[4] This move, as I will show below, is especially important for studies in sexuality, marriage, and family. Hermeneutic realism, to use that phrase for the moment, acknowledges that all understanding — including scientific understanding — is historically and linguistically shaped. But it also holds that it is possible, through various methodological maneuvers, to gain degrees of what Ricoeur calls "distanciation."[5] The concept of distanciation is Ricoeur's happy substitute for the positivist concept of objectivity. The idea of objectivity holds that understanding must begin with a cognitive self-emptying of one's assumptions or prejudgments and, through controlled experiment, conclude with objective propositions about states of affairs.[6] Hermeneutic realism argues against the idea that understanding can be achieved when guided by positivistic assumptions about objectivity.[7] But it does believe that we can gain some distance from our historically conditioned starting points and achieve glimpses of the stable structures of reality (kinds of regularities within the human and natural world), even though one can never grasp them completely untouched by culturally and historically shaped prejudgments. This is important for family studies; even though family patterns vary around the world and certainly are historically and culturally conditioned, there are relatively

3. Hans-Georg Gadamer, *Truth and Method* (New York: Crossroad, 1982), p. 273.

4. The phrase "hermeneutic realism" is more associated with the work of William Schweiker. See his *Responsibility and Christian Ethics* (Cambridge: Cambridge University Press, 1995), p. 4. In one place Schweiker defines hermeneutic realism as follows: "It grants descriptive relativism with respect to how moral values are understood and interpreted; it insists on historical and pluralist consciousness in ethics. Yet I want to show that this does not entail normative relativism with respect to the diversity of goods rooted in created life. The way forward is through a multidimensional theory of value rooted in natural needs and relations" (p. 24).

5. Paul Ricoeur, *Hermeneutics and the Human Sciences* (Cambridge: Cambridge University Press, 1981), pp. 155-58.

6. Ricoeur, *Hermeneutics and the Human Sciences,* pp. 64-65.

7. For an excellent discussion of the nature and limitations of positivism, see Bernstein, *Beyond Objectivism and Relativism,* pp. 115-18.

stable natural structures that good family patterns accommodate, actualize, and channel, even though in somewhat different ways.

In short, hermeneutic realism is a form of critical realism, as this term is used by philosophers of science. It is not naïve realism, with its correspondence theory of the relation between understanding and reality.[8] Nor does it hold that all knowledge is nothing but human construction with no relation to the regularities of reality. Critical realism admits that even the best scientific knowledge is constructed in some sense. Nevertheless, it contends that in spite of this constructed element in all understanding, good knowledge has degrees of approximation to reality. For these reasons, hermeneutic realism believes that understanding as dialogue, when done well, can increase a shared public sense of workable approximations to the descriptively true and normatively good, even though absolute objectivity on these matters is impossible.

Hermeneutic realism lessens the distinction between descriptive and normative inquiries. Both types of understanding begin with historically shaped preunderstandings and language traditions, function in the context of dialogue, and achieve varying degrees of distanciation. Even though descriptive statements of the kind pursued by the social sciences specialize in the question of "What is the case?" and normative statements specialize in the question "What should be the case?," hermeneutic realism denies the possibility of conceiving of these distinctions as absolute. This is true even when studying marriage and family, a point that positivistic social scientists studying these subjects should take more seriously.

Hermeneutic realism's consistent concern with questions of "What is the case?" as a dimension of understanding has implications for how rough public consensus is achieved between different cultures and traditions, even on highly charged issues pertaining to sex, marriage, and family. I will clarify this point by comparing hermeneutic realism with three commanding contemporary views on the nature of public discourse. Hermeneutic realism should be distinguished from Foucault's idea that apparent public agreements are really arbitrary enforcements of dominant centers of social power. He claims that this is especially true on matters dealing with sexuality.[9] Although this is often true, hermeneutic realism believes that cognitive and moral truth exists, however fragmentarily per-

8. For an excellent discussion of critical realism, see Ian Barbour, *Myths, Models, and Paradigms* (New York: Harper & Row, 1974).

9. Michel Foucault, *The History of Sexuality*, vol. 1 (New York: Vintage Books, 1990), pp. 99-100.

ceived, and that such truth is likely eventually to expose and undermine arbitrary power.

Hermeneutic realism also is different from Richard Rorty's view that public agreement is mere consensus achieved by communal conversation with no relation to stable structures of the true and good.[10] Although hermeneutic realism acknowledges a huge place for conversation and the conventions it produces (just as it admits a significant place for tradition), it also believes that the obdurate regularities of reality often force their intrusive noses into human affairs and provide boundaries to the arbitrariness of what communities just happen to agree on.

And, finally, hermeneutic realism's belief that conversations can achieve approximations to the good and true is different from the idea of consensus found in Habermas, with its skepticism that statements about the regularities of human desires and needs can be rationally redeemed in uncoerced discourse. It is true that propositions about the regularities of human wants and needs are difficult to redeem rationally, but agreements about similarities in natural needs between different cultural contexts are in fact often achieved.[11] Hence, consensus about what is crucial and central about human needs, regularities, and corresponding goods is achieved partially on the basis of rational and scientific evidence and not just on the basis of what seems generalizable because of its consistency with the interests of the relevant parties.[12]

Hermeneutic Realism and the Thickness of Moral Thinking

If hermeneutic realism is the most adequate framework for the interpretive and normative tasks of practical theology, then a strong separation between practical theology and theological ethics is untenable. Customarily, practical theology has been conceived as specializing in the description of contexts into which norms defined by theological ethics are to be mediated. Theological ethics, on the other hand, often was thought to specialize in clarifying and grounding the norms that practical theology applied.

10. Richard Rorty, *Philosophy and the Mirror of Nature* (Princeton: Princeton University Press, 1979).

11. Jürgen Habermas, *Knowledge and Human Interests* (Boston: Beacon Press, 1971), pp. 214-45. For a critique of the tendency to linguistify human needs and wants, see Russell Keat, *Politics of Social Theory* (Chicago: University of Chicago Press, 1981), pp. 84-91.

12. Robin Lovin and Frank Reynolds, *Cosmogony and Ethical Order: New Studies in Comparative Ethics* (Chicago: University of Chicago Press, 1985), pp. 20, 26-32.

If, as hermeneutic philosophy suggests, the normative and descriptive aspects of understanding cannot be so easily distinguished, then the customary separation of practical theology and theological ethics should be discouraged. A distinction between them should be maintained, at best, for certain intellectual and institutional conveniences. Each discipline, however, should take full responsibility for articulating both the norms of practice and the description of practice in its various contexts. Both disciplines should have interest in transformation. When this happens, their absolute separation will become tenuous.

With this in mind, I have simplified my task throughout this book by bringing practical theology and theological ethics together into a single inquiry. If this task is to be named, and indeed, names help us keep track of what we are doing, I would call it "practical-theological ethics." Such an inquiry combines into a single discipline the tasks of description, normative critique, and a concern with transformation. Such an inquiry does not consume or preempt the other practical-theological disciplines of pastoral care, religious education, homiletics, etc. But it contributes a significant and often neglected dimension to these subdisciplines, i.e., a contextualized and critical ethic, or at least a methodology to arrive at one.

What I am arguing here may seem to apply only to the inner working of Christian theology, and such methodological concerns may be of little interest to many of my readers. But the argument I am advancing applies just as well to the relation of the social sciences to the normative disciplines of moral and political philosophy. Gadamer and Ricoeur's view of understanding makes the task of understanding inseparable from practical reason in whatever context it is used — ethics, politics, or theology. Practical interests, as Gadamer reminds us, guide understanding from the beginning, thereby making a strong distinction between descriptive and normative disciplines in the human sciences impossible to hold.[13] Several contemporary social scientists have adopted this point of view, not the least of which is Robert Bellah and his colleagues in the widely read *Habits of the Heart* (1985) and *The Good Society* (1991).[14] *I apply the insights of Gadamer, Ricoeur, and Bellah to weaken customary boundaries between the theological disciplines of practical theology and theological ethics. I also use these same insights to*

13. Paul Tillich articulates a rather sharp distinction between theology, theological ethics, and practical theology in *Systematic Theology* I (Chicago: University of Chicago Press, 1951), p. 33.

14. Robert Bellah et al., *Habits of the Heart* (Berkeley: University of California Press, 1985); Bellah et al., *The Good Society* (New York: Knopf, 1991).

*weaken the categorical distinction between the social sciences and normative disci-
plines such as moral philosophy and, indeed, even theological ethics.*

The task of practical-theological ethics is complicated by what I call the "thickness" of practical-moral reflection. By using the metaphor of thickness, I am arguing that all practical-moral thinking, whether alleg-edly secular or religious, has many distinguishable, overlapping, and in-teractive dimensions. In a series of essays and books stretching from the early 1980s, I have identified five levels or dimensions of moral thinking or practical reason, (1) a visional level generally conveyed by narratives and metaphors about the character of the ultimate context of experience, (2) an obligational dimension guided by some implicit or explicit moral principle of a rather general kind, (3) a level of assumptions about basic regularities of human tendencies and needs that give rise to many of the premoral goods we search for in life, (4) a dimension of assumptions about pervasive social and ecological patterns, more or less set, that chan-nel and constrain our search for these premoral goods, and finally, (5) a level of concrete practices, virtues, and rules that are informed by all the foregoing dimensions. These concrete practices, virtues, and rules are thick and can be analyzed in terms of all four of the other dimensions. A practice is not just a practice, and the rules that guide it are not just rules. Virtues, which are not quite the same as practices or rules, are similar in their concreteness. They too can be analyzed in terms of the other four as-sumptions. They are thick and assume much that is often inarticulate. Practices, virtues, and rules are weighty. This is because they are imbued with a multitude of meanings of a metaphysical, moral, social, and natu-ral kind. The reader will have noticed me using these levels somewhat stealthily, I must admit, in the preceding chapters. I have at times ana-lyzed the vision of a marital practice, its ethical obligations, the tenden-cies and needs the practice organizes, its implicit views of context, and its actual behaviors. These levels were especially prominent in my analysis of the marriage theory of Thomas Aquinas but were visible in my analysis of Nachmanides and al-Ghazali as well.

In a loose sense, these dimensions are organized hierarchically. The visional or narrative level, which projects general meanings of life, influ-ences all the other dimensions. The visional level is the most comprehen-sive. From another perspective, judgments about any one of the five di-mensions can become highly influential for the other dimensions because of the particular life challenge confronting a person or group at the mo-ment. For instance, the American debates over the ordination of homo-sexuals or the legalization of gay marriage generally center on the third level of practical-theological thinking, the tendency-need level. This dispute is regrettably preoccupied with the relevant, but not determinative or sufficient, question as to whether there is a pervasive tendency in some people toward homosexuality that is either biologically determined, psychologically determined, or perhaps only a difficult-to-break habit comparable to smoking cigarettes. The preoccupation of this debate with level three of practical-moral thinking neglects relevant judgments at the other four levels.

A hermeneutically conceived practical-theological ethics should proceed as a dialogue involving all five of these dimensions. According to this view, practical-theological ethics begins with a problem, crisis, or question that challenges the practical thinker's (or community of practical thinkers') preunderstanding at each of the five levels. When I teach practical-theological ethics to students in introductory courses, I ask them to discover and describe, at each of the five dimensions, the preunderstanding behind the practical question they chose to study. This is often a difficult assignment; they are not accustomed to examining their own questions and preunderstandings. Nor are they accustomed to describing their preunderstandings in terms of these five dimensions. I then ask them to give a thick description, at each of the five dimensions, of the witness of the classic Christian texts that they believe have a normative relevance to their primary question. I invite them finally to enter a third critical dialogue between the witness of the classic Christian text and an alternative cultural answer to their primary question, once again at each of the five levels. This exercise invariably produces an intensely pursued high-quality paper that enables students to focus the central issues of practical-theological ethics around a concrete question of importance to them and the wider public.

Practical-Theological Ethics
and the Dialogue over the Family

I will illustrate this hermeneutically conceived practical-theological ethics by referring, once again, to the Religion, Culture, and Family Project that I described in Chapters One and Two. The project was stimulated by the question, Is there a family crisis in the modern world, and, if so, what are the interests and resources of the Christian faith for addressing it? To begin thinking about this question is to activate ideas and assumptions at all of the five dimensions I have mentioned. It entails wondering about what vision of life underlies our assumptions about families; what principle of obligation orders relations between husband and wife and parent and child; what tendencies and needs families guide, fulfill, redirect, or fail to address; how social patterns such as modernization and new employment possibilities affect families; and, finally, what concrete practices are guiding families in the present and should guide them in the future.

To bring each of these dimensions of practical thinking into dialogue with the normative claims of the Christian faith entails a wide range of inquiries and judgments. For instance, how does the biblical vision (or narrative) of a good creation, a fall into sin, and the possibility of redemption shape normative judgments about families? With regard to the obligational level, does the principle of neighbor love apply to families, or should families be ordered by some idea of proportional justice as claimed by theories of male headship in Aristotelian philosophy? At the third level, do families primarily satisfy our needs for interpersonal intimacy, as many liberal theological views claim, or do they also regulate stouter tendencies such as asymmetrical male-female reproductive patterns and the energies of kin altruism, as Christian views informed by Aristotle and Aquinas have argued? Or do families satisfy both intimacy needs and reproductive strategies, while subsuming the latter to the former, as the revisionist marriage writings of John Paul II argue? At the fourth level, practical ethics might inquire into how Greco-Roman honor-shame social patterns influenced families in the Jesus movement, as I did in Chapter Three, and how, in turn, these early Christian families resisted, and, to some extent, transformed these male-dominated and female-constraining family social patterns of the antique pagan world.

Finally, what actual early Christian practices existed, and what do they suggest for viable practices today? Here the practical interpreter must not fail to take account of the stunning innovations of the common meal in the early Christian house church, located as it was in the boundary-breaking space (the peristyle) between male and female quarters and presided over by both men and women.[15] These concrete practices and rituals suggest how profoundly, yet subtly, early Christianity was a family revolution when compared to the surrounding culture. They also reveal the density and thickness of these practices and how the acts of the common meal reveal the narratives of both the good gift of Creation as well as Christ's sacrificial love, the obligations of brother and sister Chris-

---

15. For a discussion of the likely location and function of the common meal in the early church, see Carolyn Osiek and David Balch, *Families in the New Testament World* (Louisville: Westminster/John Knox, 1997), pp. 6, 20, 193-214.

tians to one another, and the needs of life that are both fulfilled and transformed. All of these questions, following the five dimensions of practical-theological thinking listed above, have been illustrated implicitly, at various times, throughout the preceding chapters.

Challenges confront the practical-theological ethicist at several of these levels. I will illustrate some that pertain to the fourth of the five dimensions — the social and environmental context of both interpreter and gospel. Practical-theological ethicists with liberal preunderstandings are likely to react negatively to the lingering Greco-Roman honor-shame patriarchal patterns that surrounded early Christianity and are still visible in its sacred texts. For that reason, they are also likely to ignore how families in the Jesus movement subtly resisted these social forms by resorting to alternative family practices.[16] On the other hand, practical-theological ethicists with conservative preunderstandings are likely to absolutize the male honor codes of antiquity and their vestiges in Christian scripture, assume they are intrinsic to early Christianity, and miss more egalitarian social patterns in the Gospels, the pre-Pauline Jesus movement, and in Paul himself.[17] Understanding the social patterns of the Greco-Roman world is crucial to understanding what is being said about families in the New Testament. These patterns constituted social constraints on families in these ancient societies. As is often the case, these patterns looked inevitable, totally natural, and perhaps even built into the very fabric of reality. They were indeed constraints of such magnitude that early Christianity never completely liberated itself from them even though it did indeed disrupt them and point the way to liberation.

But these honor-shame patterns were not eternal and unchangeable; the tensions between them and the impulses of early Christianity were such that Christianity, even within its own time, was viewed as subversive of these codes — a subversion that has gradually realized itself over time. If space permitted, I could illustrate copiously the dialogical tensions on the family issue between interpreter and classic texts at each of the five levels of practical-moral thinking. A reading of the appendix to the sec-

---

16. Stephen Barton, "Paul's Sense of Place: An Anthropological Approach to Community Formation in Corinth," *New Testament Studies* 32 (1986): 74.

17. For evidence of trends toward gender equality in early Christian communities, see Elizabeth Schüssler Fiorenza, *In Memory of Her: A Feminist Theological Reconstruction of Christian Origins* (New York: Crossroad, 1983); Don Browning, Bonnie Miller McLemore, Pamela Couture, Bernie Lyon, and Robert Franklin, *From Culture Wars to Common Ground: Religion and the American Family Debate* (Louisville: Westminster/John Knox, 1997), pp. 129-56; and Osiek and Balch, *Families in the New Testament World,* pp. 103-55.

ond edition of *From Culture Wars to Common Ground* reveals how my co-authors and I worked at all of these levels in our critical dialogue with the classic texts of the Christian faith in their relevance to family questions.[18]

Rights Feminism and Practical-Theological Ethics

I will illustrate the thickness of practical-theological ethics by discussing a group of renowned women scholars who are addressing the rights of women in cross-cultural contexts. I have in mind the moral philosophers Martha Nussbaum of the University of Chicago, Susan Moller Okin of Stanford University, Catholic moral theologian Lisa Cahill of Boston College, and the Harvard legal historian Mary Ann Glendon. Each of these scholars is, in some sense, a feminist. Each is a theorist of human rights, especially as they relate to women. Each is nonrelativistic in her ethics, even though they all attempt to account for the relativizing influences of culture, tradition, and language. Each rejects thoroughgoing constructivism, historicism, and deconstructionism — whether proclaimed by Foucault, Derrida, or feminist literary critics such as Judith Butler — as both philosophically false and inimical to the interests of women throughout the world.[19] These thinkers believe some kind of rights-oriented realist ethics is necessary to protect women from such abuses as genital mutilation, discrimination in employment and education, and, in some cases, the starvation of mothers and their children. They claim that cultural practices that lead to these consequences must be critiqued and changed, however so gently, respectfully, and slowly. All of these writers are concerned with the reconstruction of marriage — a key concern of this book — even though they differ dramatically in how central this topic is to their respective agendas.

Nussbaum and Capability Theory

The thought of Martha Nussbaum is having considerable impact on international feminist discussions under the auspices of the United Na-

18. Browning et al., *From Culture Wars to Common Ground,* pp. 335-41.

19. This unnuanced reading of early Christianity is the error of the men's movement in the United States called the Promise Keepers, the highly influential Focus on the Family led by James Dobson, and the convention of the Southern Baptist Church which, during June of 1998, made the submission of women to their husbands a matter of church doctrine.

tions. Nussbaum is a feminist Aristotelian. She uses Aristotle, in combination with selected modern human sciences, to go simultaneously in two directions that are often thought to be contradictory. On the one hand, she shows powerful evidence of how our needs and emotions are constructed by the cultural and linguistic interpretations placed upon them.[20] On the other hand, she argues for a significant inventory of natural human capabilities which, no matter how diversely they are shaped by different cultural contexts, are still universal and should therefore be cultivated and actualized.[21] These two directions give her considerable ammunition for developing a social philosophy of sex, marriage, and family and a powerful understanding of the respective roles of religion and state in giving normative shape to these human realities. Her writings are relevant to the polity of the U.S., but she also addresses societies around the world, particularly India.

Nussbaum grounds her theory of rights in this theory of capabilities. She argues that basic, yes, innate human capabilities should be recognized and actualized by socially protected human rights. Societies should be assessed by how fully they safeguard and realize these capabilities. Nussbaum's list of human capabilities is gender neutral and includes such items as bodily capabilities (hunger, thirst, sexual desire, and needs for shelter and mobility); the capacity for pleasure and pain; and the cognitive capabilities to perceive, imagine, and think. She also lists practical reason, the need for affiliation, the need to relate to nature, humor and play, and the need for separateness or individuality as fundamental human capabilities.[22] She is aware that all of these capabilities are marked by human finitude, the reality of death, and the impossibility of realizing them all at any one point in time or at any time in the future.[23] Although this list of capabilities is not directly, or exclusively, derived from Aristotle, he is her inspi-

20. Martha Nussbaum, *Sex and Social Justice* (New York: Oxford University Press, 1999), p. 38.

21. Martha Nussbaum, "Constructing Love, Desire, and Care," in *Sex, Preference, and Family*, ed. David M. Estund and Martha Nussbaum (Oxford: Oxford University Press, 1997), pp. 19-29.

22. For this list of human capabilities, see Martha Nussbaum, "Nonrelative Virtues: An Aristotelian Approach," in *The Quality of Life*, ed. Martha Nussbaum and Amartya Sen (Oxford: Clarendon Press, 1993), pp. 263-65; Nussbaum, "Human Capabilities, Female Human Beings," in *Women, Culture, and Development: A Study of Human Capabilities*, ed. Martha Nussbaum and Jonathan Glover (Oxford: Clarendon Press, 1995), pp. 76-80. For a more updated list, see her *Women and Human Development* (Cambridge: Cambridge University Press, 2000), pp. 78-80.

23. Nussbaum, "Human Capabilities, Female Human Beings," pp. 76-80.

ration for the concept of capabilities and for the general idea that their actualization is the goal of life and the measure of a good society.

Nussbaum claims that her Aristotelianism teaches her to be sensitive to contexts. For instance, the capability for practical reason and the cognitive capacities for perception, imagination, and thought are universal but will be expressed differently in various social and cultural contexts. Some people will express these capabilities through philosophy or art. Others will express perception, imagination, and thought through religion. The same is true of the capability of affiliation. For some this may be expressed almost exclusively through family, friendships, or clubs. For others, it may become manifest through their religious commitments.[24] Nussbaum does not advance a clear definition of religion. She does view it, however, as a valid arena in some social contexts for the exercise (although sometimes the suppression) of human capabilities. To further make her point about the culturally variable patterns for the expression of universal human capabilities, she shows that efforts by international organizations to distribute educational material to poor rural women in Bangladesh failed when first tried because the resources seemed detached from their everyday pursuits and the culturally specific ways they expressed their capabilities. When, however, literacy was introduced as part of efforts to form a cooperative that addressed these women's economic needs, their cognitive and reasoning capabilities were awakened, and the literacy program succeeded.[25] Hence, Nussbaum's ethic of universal capabilities acknowledges that they are expressed differently in various contexts, but this concession to relativism does not dismantle her basic essentialism. These capabilities are universal, and their development is fundamental to what it means to be human.

From the standpoint of the five dimensions of practical-ethical thinking that I discussed above, *Nussbaum's list of capabilities is her way of fleshing out what I have called the tendency-need level of practical thinking.* Her list is powerful and has been adopted by a variety of thinkers in the field of international development. The capabilities approach to international human and economic development has led to a particularly fruitful collaboration

24. Nussbaum, "Human Capabilities, Female Human Beings," p. 76.

25. Nussbaum, *Women and Human Development,* pp. 295-96. Nussbaum, "Nonrelative Virtues," in *The Quality of Life,* p. 258; see also Martha Chen, "A Matter of Survival: Women's Right to Employment in India and Bangladesh," in *Women, Culture, and Development,* pp. 37-57.

between Nussbaum and the Nobel Prize winning Cambridge economist Amartya Sen.[26]

But both her list and her general ethical position are not beyond criticism. From my standpoint, Nussbaum's practical ethics is extremely thin on the other levels of practical thinking. She gives little or no attention to the visional and narrative level of either her own perspective or that of the cultures she examines. Contrary to her position, I would argue that to respect a person is to, in principle, respect his or her religion. But religion for her seems principally to be a matter of "beliefs," a set of moral teachings offered to the young, or a framework for defining the meaning and purpose of life.[27] The powerful narratives — especially in the Abrahamic religions about the goodness of God and creation, the reality of sin and the fall, and the divine resources for overcoming sin — are of little interest to her. This neglect is not without consequences. Because Nussbaum has no ultimate story to frame her ethics, and because she tends to neglect the narratives of others, her own system lacks an ontology that provides the deep positive valuation to the goodness of human capabilities that her position assumes. Why are capabilities good in some premoral sense of the term? Nussbaum's answer seems only to be that they are good because humans universally feel them or perceive them as good. But religions, especially theistic Abrahamic religions, support and stabilize the experienced goodness of such premoral values by also claiming they are good in the sight of the ultimate power of the universe, i.e., good in the sight of God. In fact, they are gifts of God. Nussbaum is primarily interested in the point at which religions frame codes of behavior, codes that can conflict with the constitutional systems of modern secular societies and be seen either to suppress or support the realization of human capabilities, especially those of women. Her theory of human capabilities is commendable; something like this theory is fundamental to the tendency-need dimension of practical ethics (my third dimension) and is often sadly lacking in some of the most powerful religious and secular ethical theories of our time. But her list can be criticized, both with regard to its content and how it was derived. And it lacks an explicit narrative view of life surrounding it that conveys why we should honor these capabilities so highly.

We learn more from Nussbaum about a principle of obligation, my second dimension of practical reason. She speaks in her more recent writ-

---

26. Amartya Sen, *Inequality Reexamined* (Cambridge, Mass.: Harvard University Press, 1992), p. 49.

27. Nussbaum, *Women and Human Development*, pp. 179-80.

ings about the idea of "capability equality." This points to the fact that she is a kind of Kantian, but one who tries to get human needs and purposes together with the Kantian principle of universal respect for persons, a combination that Kant himself never explicitly tried to develop. Nussbaum calls this reformulated Kantian principle "the principle of each person's capability." Nussbaum explains that this entails treating "each person as an end," but this means not only respecting their capacity for freedom and rationality but also their more concrete endeavors to realize the full range of their capabilities.[28] Nussbaum interprets these principles in highly individualistic ways. They apply specifically to each individual. She writes, "As with politics and the family, so here: an organic good for the group as group is unacceptable if it does not do good for then one by one."[29] Yet, from another perspective, the principle is highly communal; each group, family, political community, or religious body must finally have that solidarity needed to enhance the capability realization of each of its members. In short, the good society helps all of its members equally to develop their capabilities. Although, as we see, Nussbaum develops a principle of obligation, she does not relate it to a coherent story or narrative of life, especially one that accounts for both the ontological goodness of our capabilities as well as the inevitability of human loss.

Finally, we hear little about dimension four — the social and natural conditions that pattern and constrain our human practices. To be fair, we do learn that Hindu and Muslim social systems restrict most women from participation in the educational and wage opportunities of their societies. We also learn that Nussbaum is no friend of market capitalism, especially if it functions to restrict our list of fundamental human goods to a slender list of economic values.[30] She is not sympathetic to the rational-choice economics of Gary Becker and Richard Posner and what it implies for either an analysis of modern societies or a course that they should follow. Other than that, there is no fundamental analysis of the impact of modernization on women in traditional societies or, for that matter, is there an analysis of the effects of modernization on the well-being of women and families in more advanced industrial societies. Nor is there in Nussbaum an analysis of modernization and globalization on the institu-

---

28. Nussbaum, *Women and Human Development*, pp. 12-13, 188.

29. Nussbaum, *Women and Human Development*, p. 188.

30. Nussbaum, "Human Capabilities, Female Human Beings," in *Women, Culture, and Development*, p. 90.

tion of marriage. In fact, there is little attention to the issue of marriage at all in Nussbaum's philosophical writings. On the whole, Nussbaum's agenda centers around equipping women to participate in the fast-paced, efficiency-oriented rationalities of modern societies by developing their capabilities. For this, they need freedom, education, and respect as individuals. This, according to my view, is part of what is required, but is it sufficient?

To sum up, Nussbaum's moral and political philosophy is weighted on my third dimension of practical-moral reason and underdeveloped at the other levels. And, as we will see below, there is an individualistic tone even to her list of capabilities. Nonetheless, she gives us a powerful perspective from which to judge the adequacies of societies and religious traditions on both the subject of human rights and issues of gender, family, sexuality, and marriage, although this last topic receives scant attention. Nussbaum writes from the perspective of her political philosophy. She takes seriously the belief that liberal political philosophy must support and defend both religious rights and human rights, both the freedom to exercise one's own religious conscience and the right to actualize one's human capabilities. The dilemma of political liberalism is that these two sets of rights often conflict. More specifically, religious traditions, at least some of their specific codes, appear to conflict at particular moments in history with human rights as generally defined by the international community.[31] For instance, women in Islam have less freedom to divorce than do Islamic men. Marriages are still arranged among many Hindus, thereby infringing on the practical reason and control of one's own body for both young men and women. Inheritance laws have often been discriminatory against women in almost all religions. So, how would Nussbaum use her moral and political philosophy to resolve the dilemma between religious and human rights that confronts political liberalism?

Nussbaum would begin by measuring religious traditions against her principle of treating each individual as an end, interpreted, of course, as respect for an individual's pursuit of his or her inalienable capabilities. But Nussbaum supplements this principle with another that she calls the "principle of moral constraint."[32] She nowhere gives a precise definition of this principle, but it seems to mean "that any cult or so-called religion that diverges too far from the shared moral understanding that is embod-

31. Nussbaum, *Women and Human Development*, p. 168.
32. Nussbaum, *Women and Human Development*, p. 190.

ied in the core of the political conception does not deserve the honorific name of religion."[33] Where is the core of the political conception? It seems to rest, in Nussbaum's view, in the modern constitutions of such countries as the United States, South Africa, and India. For Nussbaum, these constitutions, and their specifications of human rights, appear to give more detailed embodiment to her first principle pertaining to respect for persons as ends and as agents pursuing the good of their capabilities. If religions conform to this principle of constraint, Nussbaum is willing to take a generous attitude toward them. After all, they teach some brand of morality, mold the young, and pursue some ideal of justice (although frequently an inadequate one). But they often contain conflicting moral subtraditions, some of which are more worthy than others of state encouragement for what they can contribute to the common good. But if a religion obstructs the free exercise of the capabilities of individuals, especially women, then the right to the unburdened pursuit of its religious ideals must be constrained.

Nussbaum adds to these two principles some additional guidelines. The law of modern societies must realize, as I hinted above, that religions are complex and possess conflicting themes and practices. Some of these get more to the classic core of a tradition than others. She does not believe female genital mutilation gets to the core of the African religious traditions that practice it. She does not think that patriarchy or polygyny gets to the core of either Hinduism or any of the Abrahamic religions. If, for instance, the state required in the U.S., South Africa, or India that patriarchal inheritance laws favoring males, female genital mutilation, or polygyny all be outlawed, these governments probably would be simply emphasizing one highly plausible interpretation of their religious traditions rather than another.[34] Many people in these traditions would agree with and applaud these state decisions. Nussbaum does not invoke Gadamer and Ricoeur's view of the classical within a tradition, i.e., that which is central and commanding and that sooner or later reasserts itself. She speaks of something similar to this with her idea of the "core" of a tradition. But even this concept, as useful as it is, is not developed nor does she understand the narrative form that the classical center of a tradition generally takes. There is little evidence in Nussbaum's view of religion that she thinks it has value beyond what can be grasped by her principle of respect and her principle of constraint. Religion may help

33. Nussbaum, *Women and Human Development*, p. 190.
34. Nussbaum, *Women and Human Development*, pp. 194-97.

motivate people to be better, it may be good for the moral formation of children, it may be a preferred arena for the exercise of one's capabilities, and it may give us a sense of life's meaning.[35] But, for Nussbaum, all of these functions can be performed by other social and institutional functions.[36] I will say more about Nussbaum in a few paragraphs.

Okin and Justice in the Home

The political theorist Susan Moller Okin, in my terms, concentrates on the second dimension of practical-moral reason — a principle of obligation. She agrees with the Kantian principle of respect advanced by Nussbaum, but has a more restricted interpretation of its meaning. By the same token, she neglects nearly all the other four dimensions of moral thinking. She presents a powerful moral principle by adapting for feminist purposes John Rawls's neo-Kantian theory of moral obligation, namely, his theory of justice as fairness. This principle, as is widely known, is derived from the thought experiment that models fairness on the idea of making decisions that would be considered just even if one were blind to the results of the decision when viewed from the perspective of one's gender, race, or social position.[37] Okin uses this principle to guide her feminist analysis of international development and its impact on women. She has more to say on the issue of justice than Nussbaum. And, from the perspective of practical-theological ethics, we should acknowledge the analogies, although not identities, between the Christian principle of neighbor love (with its reversible relation between self and neighbor) and Rawls's principle of justice.[38] There is as well at least an affinity or analogy between Okin's neo-Kantian theory of justice and Christian principles of moral obligation defined, as I have suggested it should be, around love as equal regard.

But Okin is weak where Nussbaum is strong. Okin has a thin theory of human needs and capabilities and hence a weak theory of the premoral goods of life (dimension three) that moral obligation must guide and actualize for both others and self. She does not support fully Nussbaum's view that human capabilities ground a theory of human rights. She is interested only in the basic right to exercise the capability for practical rea-

---

35. Nussbaum, *Women and Human Development*, p. 190.

36. Nussbaum, *Women and Human Development*, pp. 206-7.

37. John Rawls, *A Theory of Justice* (Cambridge, Mass.: Harvard University Press, 1971).

38. Susan Moller Okin, *Justice, Gender, and the Family* (New York: Basic Books, 1989), pp. 17-24.

son as Rawls defines it. She argues that this right is precisely what is denied to women throughout the world. This happens to women first in the home — with their fathers and husbands — and second in the public world of wage employment, politics, and education. There can be no fully reversible fairness in these public realms, Okin argues, unless there is first gender justice in the home. Okin is so driven to protect women's right to exercise practical reason that she leaves unthematized any list of additional capabilities and rights of the kind advanced by Nussbaum. The right to exercise practical reason as a formal pursuit of justice is so central for Okin that she fails to specify the needs, capacities, and goods that practical reason should promote and adjudicate. Hence, she neglects the third dimension of practical reason — the tendency-need level — and becomes preoccupied with the second, the obligational level.

Okin also seriously neglects the first dimension — the visional and narrative level. First of all, she does little to clarify the vision of life motivating her own thought. And, for the most part, she either neglects or is critical of the visions and narratives of others, especially if that vision is recognizably religious. Like Kant in *Religion within the Limits of Reason Alone*,[39] Okin measures various historical manifestations of both the Abrahamic and other religions from the perspective of how they conform to the principle of justice as fairness. Judged by this perspective, she finds Judaism, Christianity, and especially Islam as deficient — all of them being principally responsible from her viewpoint for the patriarchy in the families of their followers. She is equally unapologetic in condemning Hinduism, Confucianism, and various folk religions.[40] To put it bluntly, Okin sees multiculturalism, and the religions that feed various non-Western cultures, as "bad for women." Western religious traditions have been harmful to women, but at least they have been influenced by the emerging Western philosophical traditions of human rights. Most non-Western traditions, she contends, have not benefited from this influence and should therefore be all the more mistrusted by women.[41]

---

39. Immanuel Kant, *Religion within the Limits of Reason Alone* (New York: Harper & Brothers, 1960).

40. Okin, "Religion, Law, and Female Identity," p. 31, a lecture given at the Seminar on Religion, Law, and the Construction of Identities, Divinity School, University of Chicago, 1997.

41. Okin, "Is Multiculturalism Bad for Women?," *Boston Review* (October-November 1997): 25-28. This essay was organized into a book with a large number of responses from various social critics. See Susan Moller Okin, *Is Multiculturalism Bad for Women?*, ed. Joshua Cohen, Matthew Howard, and Martha Nussbaum (Princeton: Princeton University Press, 1999).

When she considers, however, actual strategies of transformation, Okin's antagonism toward religion is more subdued. She acknowledges the possibility that the world religions might be reformed. This would require what she calls "inside-outsider" individuals and groups who have critical distance from these religions but also the empathic sensibility of an insider. With reference to Islam, a variation of this strategy might be found in Abdullahi Ahmed An-Na'im's argument, reviewed in Chapter Six, that the Qur'an's strong patriarchy stems from the Medina period of early Islam, rather than the earlier and less compromised Mecca period. For that reason, this later patriarchy should be rejected in favor of the earlier and deeper gender equality of Islam's founding vision elaborated by the Prophet at Mecca.[42] We saw a similar "insider's" strategy in the reinterpretation of *ayah* 4:34 by Azizah al-Hibri. Both Okin and Nussbaum acknowledge that the core of a religious tradition might be distinguished from various forms of its debased practice. Both, however, appear to agree that one only knows whether the inner core, i.e., the classical center, of a tradition is trustworthy on the basis of its consistency with the external principles of moral obligation that Okin and Nussbaum respectively uphold.

Okin is clearly skeptical that such a deeper stratum honestly can be found in Islam, just as she is wary of finding a ground for women's rights in Judaism or Christianity. She prefers the strategies of the organizations called Women Living Under Islamic Law or Sisterhood Is Global. Both groups try to raise the consciousness of Islamic women by confronting them with the diversity of women's rights as they are empirically known and practiced in today's various Islamic societies and by juxtaposing United Nations theories of women's rights with Qur'anic views of their rights. Such groups, then, encourage Islamic women themselves to search for the analogues, identities, and differences between the two views of rights.[43] None of these three strategies — that of Nussbaum, Okin, or An-Na'im and al-Hibri — is designed to dismantle Islam, but only the approach of An-Na'im or al-Hibri hopes to reform it from within its classical tradition. Nussbaum and Okin at best hope to effect social improvement

42. See also Abdullahi Ahmed An-Na'im, *Toward an Islamic Reformation: Civil Liberties, Human Rights, and International Law* (Syracuse, N.Y.: Syracuse University Press, 1990).

43. An-Na'im, *Toward an Islamic Reformation*, p. 335; see also Farida Shaheed, "Controlled or Autonomous: Identity and the Experience of the Network, Women Living under Muslim Laws," *Signs: Journal of Women in Culture and Society* 19, no. 4 (1994): 997-1019; Mahnaz Afghami and Haleh Vaziri, *Claiming Our Rights: A Manual for Women's Human Rights Education in Muslim Society* (Bethesda, Md.: Sisterhood Is Global Institute, 1996).

for women without instigating reactions from Islamic fundamentalists. Their strategies are not based on serious interpretations and reconstructions of the tradition itself.

Parental Capabilities in Glendon and Cahill

Three criticisms are relevant to the practical-moral thinking of Nussbaum and Okin. In developing these criticisms, I will make use of the rights theories of Lisa Sowle Cahill and Mary Ann Glendon. First, both Nussbaum and Okin have thin theories of the human goods relevant to women viewed in the global context. Okin, as we have seen, is particularly weak here, primarily limiting her moral theory to my second dimension of practical ethics — a principle of obligation developed along Kantian and Rawlsian lines. Nussbaum is richer in her theory of goods with her extensive list of human capabilities and their corresponding rights. But, as Cahill points out, one set of capabilities is downplayed by Nussbaum — that set associated with parenthood. In her *Sex, Gender, and Christian Ethics* (1996), Cahill makes use of evolutionary psychology's theory of kin altruism, as I did in Chapters Five and Six. This is the idea that parents love their children in part because their offspring are literally (in the genetic sense) part of them. She goes on quickly, as I do, to assure us that Christian parents should love their children for other reasons as well, not the least of which is that they are gifts of God and human beings worthy of care and protection. She argues, however, that parenting too is a universal biologically grounded capability and that this ground for parental care should be taken seriously along with these other reasons. It should be ranked among the fundamental capabilities that humans should be free to safely exercise. It is because kin altruism is a fundamental element of our psychobiological nature that parenting is perceived to be a highly desirable capability by most people throughout the world.[44] Kin altruism, as we already have seen time and again in this book, shows up at various points in most of the great religious traditions of the world. It constitutes background assumptions in Aristotle, Nachmanides, al-Ghazali, and Aquinas about the naturalistic archaeology that humans both project into their religious traditions and, in turn, have transformed by the central symbols of those traditions. Hermeneutic realism tells us that we need not be content with restricting our investigation of this natural archaeology by reading the texts

44. An-Na'im, *Toward an Islamic Reformation*, p. 59.

of contemporary evolutionary psychologists, as helpful and suggestive as they may be. It may be even more rewarding to uncover these natural inclinations and capabilities as they are contextualized and redefined by the ethical and metaphysical intuitions of the great religions.

It is only when under the spell of the more confined epistemologies of Western secular individualism that this parental capability — and its corresponding rights, responsibilities, and implications for the institutions of family and marriage — could be neglected in Nussbaum's list. It is due to her disregard of this capability that Nussbaum speaks eloquently about the protection and development of women's rights but has hardly a word to say about the protection and reconstruction of parenting within the context of marriage in modern and postmodern societies.

Mary Ann Glendon shows that familial and parental rights are not excluded from several versions of human rights, especially continental European theories with their higher indebtedness to Rousseau rather than Locke.[45] Cahill echoes Glendon's point by showing how it would seem bizarre to women from India, China, and especially Africa to exclude parenthood from the list of capabilities and rights to be respected. Glendon makes a similar criticism, not about Nussbaum specifically, but about the human rights documents (strongly influenced by feminists such as Nussbaum) issued from the 1995 Fourth Conference on Women held in Beijing, China. They dedicate much space, Glendon points out, to women's rights to reproductive health but give little mention to parenting as such, especially parenting within the context of marriage and family.[46] The practical-theological ethicist need not absolutize parenthood, nor the institution of marriage designed to organize it, but the narrative and tradition of the Christian faith clearly values both as highly central finite values even though it makes neither of them essential for full Christian personhood and salvation. Nonetheless, these capabilities and tendencies should not be excluded from the list of vital premoral goods and capabilities designed to undergird a theory of human rights.

Second, neither Nussbaum nor Okin is sufficiently dialogical in her respective ethical methodology. Because of this, they are too quick to impose liberal Western feminist views on non-Western women. Hermeneutic realism holds that traditions have a right to influence and even convert

45. Mary Ann Glendon, *Rights Talk: The Impoverishment of Political Discourse* (New York: Free Press, 1991), pp. 32-39.

46. Mary Ann Glendon, "Feminism and the Family: An Indissoluble Marriage," *Commonweal*, February 14, 1997, p. 12; see also Glendon, "The Bitter Fruit of the Beijing Conference," *Wall Street Journal*, September 21, 1995, p. A22.

one another in the name of attaining higher degrees of the good and true; to understand, as Gadamer contends, is to influence others just as it necessarily entails practice and change. But practical-theological ethicists should first try to uncover the respective points of analogy common to diverse traditions before they move on to critique and transformation. For instance, there are clearly analogies between Nussbaum's theory of capabilities and assumptions about human nature found within other traditions. This is the presupposition, as we have seen, of An-Na'im in his *Toward an Islamic Reformation* (1990); he argues that analogues to Western human rights traditions can be found in Islam but ensconced there in religious symbols, metaphors, and narratives. Nussbaum's list of capabilities is not a product of abstract and unconditioned reason; it reflects a dialogue with Aristotle, the Stoics, modern psychology, and the recent experiences of American academic feminists — all Western traditions. Her list should not be used to rush to judgment about the adequacy or inadequacy of non-Western traditions but used instead to search for points of analogy between her own perspective and views of women's rights within other cultural strands. Indeed, as Cahill and Glendon suggest, the perspective of other traditions, especially on the importance of parenthood, should be used to enrich Nussbaum's list. Hermeneutic realism does not mean that criticism between two traditions is improper, but rather that it should occur on the basis of a deeper search for analogues between the best of our own and other traditions — deeper than Nussbaum and Okin envision.

Third, both Nussbaum and Okin, as I already have suggested, are neglectful of the visional aspects of practical ethics and therefore either dismissive of religion, as is Okin, or neglectful of the full contributions of religion, as is Nussbaum. Nussbaum measures narratives of religious traditions according to how they contribute to the equal actualization of human capabilities. Okin measures religious traditions from the perspective of their conformity to the principle of justice as fairness. Both Nussbaum's and Okin's frameworks for critiquing religion, I might add, have some philosophical legitimacy. There is much that can be said on the basis of generally accepted philosophical reasoning for the cogency of Okin's use of Kant to assess religion or Nussbaum's synthesis of Kant and Aristotle for the same purpose.

But on the whole, both positions are too narrow in their view of religion. The deeper intentionality of a tradition's religious vision must be taken into account. And the deeper religious foundations of their own respective philosophical positions must also be considered. Philosophy, as

Paul Ricoeur has argued, does not stand on its own two feet; it is a differentiated and distanced moment of reflection born out of deeper religious intuitions, symbols, and revelations. This is true for the philosophy of Nussbaum and Okin. Ricoeur's celebrated phrase "the symbol gives rise to thought" is highly pertinent to our deliberations; it suggests that supposedly rational philosophical arguments for such things as human rights are little more than the tip of a deep mountain of religious vision, symbol, metaphor, and narrative. This observation is important for a proper understanding of the grounds of the contemporary human rights revolution. It is also important for the adequate understanding of the foundations for the reconstruction of contemporary and future theories of marriage and family.

Legal historian John Witte probably has done more than any other contemporary scholar to properly locate the archaic religious grounds of contemporary human rights discourse. He reminds us of the powerful dialectic between the secular human rights movement and religion. Religious traditions, in their most authentic expressions, provide transcendental foundations for human rights, even as these are exercised in the arenas of marriage and family. On the other hand, religious traditions can be co-opted by repressive political regimes and cultural hegemonies and used to suppress the free exercise of nonreligious human capacities and rights. When this happens, the contemporary human rights movement's respect for religion can sometimes give license to corrupt, and even violent, religious movements that harm basic human rights. This is a danger that Okin and Nussbaum are aware of, and it explains their concern to closely monitor religion from the perspective of the state. They overlook, however, the many occasions when the state not only fails to restrain religion but actually encourages it to violate human rights, which was allegedly happening in Saudi Arabia when ruling families supported the repressive educational programs of the Wahabi wing of Islam. In some cases, however, the quest to achieve human rights took the form of securing religious rights. Witte shows how this happened when medieval Roman Catholicism fought to protect its own religious freedom from the control of the emperors and empires of that day. Okin and Nussbaum seem far more inclined to see the need for the state to control religion than they do the need to restrain the state in defense of human and religious rights.

Witte provides several reasons for why religion should, and can, be seen as a positive source for human rights and for religious claims beneficial for the human good. His points apply as well to the task of preserving and reforming marriage and family. First, the right to the free exercise of religion is the foundation of many other rights. He tells us, "the right to believe leads ineluctably to the rights to assemble, speak, worship, prose- lytize, educate, parent, travel, or to abstain from the same on the basis of one's beliefs."[47] Religious traditions are more likely than contemporary liberal philosophical perspectives to balance human rights with human responsibilities. "The classic faith of the Book," he contends, "adopts and advocates human rights to protect religious duties. A religious individual or association has rights to exist and act, not in the abstract, but in order to discharge discrete religious duties."[48] Furthermore, without religion, human rights become too captive to Western liberal philosophical ideals and the secularity generally attached to them. Witte believes that "Many religious traditions, whether Buddhist, Confucian, Hindu, Islamic, Taoist, Orthodox, Reformed, or traditional stock, cannot conceive of, nor accept, a system of rights that excludes religion."[49] If by religion, Witte means to refer to a sense of sacrality in contrast to a theism as such, he is doubtless correct in this assertion. Even more, without religion, the "state is given an exaggerated role to play as the guarantor of human rights. The simple state versus individual dialectic of modern human rights theories leaves it to the state to protect and provide rights of all sorts. In reality, the state is not (and cannot) be so omnicompetent."[50]

In the end, both Okin and Nussbaum, in their different ways, under- sell the importance of religion in providing a deeper ground for human rights, both inside and outside the family. There is little doubt that Kant was ingenious in his transcendental deduction of the categorical impera- tive that established a philosophical basis for respecting persons, as both Okin and Nussbaum would hold. But it is not clear that even Kant was completely free of religious motivations and visions in establishing the cat- egorical imperative; its similarities to neighbor love and the golden rule are all too obvious and have been observed by numerous commentators.[51] But even if it has an independent basis, many have argued still that grounding human rights on the concept of the *imago dei* (the idea that all humans are made in the image of God and therefore should be respected as sacred ends) renders them all the more serious, convincing, and powerful. Witte reminds us, "The ancient teachings and practices of Judaism, Christianity,

47. John Witte, "A Dickensian Era of Religious Rights: An Update on Religious Human Rights in Global Perspective," *William and Mary Law Review* 42, no. 3 (March 2001): 709.

48. Witte, "A Dickensian Era of Religious Rights," pp. 726-27.

49. Witte, "A Dickensian Era of Religious Rights," p. 717.

50. Witte, "A Dickensian Era of Religious Rights," p. 718.

51. Witte, "A Dickensian Era of Religious Rights," p. 718.

and Islam have much to commend themselves to the human rights regime. Each of these traditions is a religion of revelation, founded on the eternal command to love one God, oneself, and all neighbors."[52] Witte's main point is this: the human rights philosophy of the kind espoused by Okin, Nussbaum, and the entire human rights movement does not stand completely on its own two feet. It requires a "human rights culture" to be effective.[53] Religion and philosophy need not be pitted against one another in competition over which is the ultimate source of the insights that feed human rights in the areas of politics, religion, and family. The more likely truth is that they feed and correct each other. *Whatever the ultimate origin of human rights, it is the case that religious traditions and philosophies of human rights have become differentiated from one another. To develop the culture of human rights that Witte champions, these two discourses need to be in intimate dialogue, especially for the task of reconstructing twenty-first-century models of marriage and family.*

Marriage and AIDS in Africa: A Case Study

I will illustrate the multidimensionality of practical-ethical thinking and the relative thinness of the views of Nussbaum and Okin with reference to the indigenous religions of East Africa and what some anthropologists call "Africanity." Africanity is a term used by anthropologists Philip and Janet Kilbride in their *Changing Family Life in East Africa* (1990). This concept names and helps account for the high valuation that both men and women from Kenya and Uganda have for procreation, children, and parenthood. For people from these parts of Africa, having children is a way of realizing the divine in human life; children are gifts of God, indeed, expressions of God.[54] Of course, this religious vision was expressed traditionally within a family system that sanctioned polygyny, a freer sexual standard for men, and an elevated social status for men over women. The Kilbrides argue that the early phases of modernization "with its emphasis on mobility, urbanization, male pursuit of the wage market, and weakening ties with the extended family" have brought the East African family system to the verge of chaos. AIDS, child abandonment, fatherlessness, the emer-

52. Witte, "A Dickensian Era of Religious Rights," p. 718.

53. Witte, "A Dickensian Era of Religious Rights," p. 712. These themes are also expanded in Witte's *Religion and the American Constitutional Experiment: Essential Rights and Liberties* (Boulder, Colo.: Westview Press, 2000).

54. Philip Kilbride and Janet Kilbride, *Changing Family Life in East Africa: Women and Children at Risk* (University Park: Pennsylvania State University Press, 1990), p. 246.

gence of street children, the overuse of grandparents as surrogate parents, and the still too restricted access of many women to the wage economy have developed a family crisis in this part of Africa.[55] Poor women are becoming more desperate and less healthy and have little access to the jobs and education needed to help them and their dependent children survive.

How should either the church or public policy address the family situation in East Africa? This question illustrates the transformative purposes of practical-theological ethics. Nussbaum and Okin would doubtless emphasize changing the social system so that women can have access to education and the wage economy to support themselves and their children. This strategy is important, but is it sufficient? East African governments and some NGOs also emphasize education in condom use so that AIDS will not be transmitted and uncared-for children will not be born. Doubtless, as an emergency measure, this too is a valid strategy.

But both of these strategies may be limited and both neglect the vision of Africanity. The Kilbrides advocate a strategy that builds on Africanity. They believe that any effort to change patriarchy, to alter the double sexual standard, to enhance the situation of women, and to limit the disease-spreading potentials of formal and informal polygyny must respect the deep African vision of the relation of children to the divine. Shorter and Onyancha in their *The Church and AIDS in Africa* (1998) agree in part with the Kilbrides when they write, "For Africans, life is essentially reproductive life, and the transmission of life is both a social and religious obligation."[56] Both teams of practical thinkers contend that efforts to change behaviors must be anchored in the African belief in the sacrality of children, their reflection of the divine, and children's right to flourish.

Even though both the Kilbrides and Shorter and Onyancha agree that retaining the Africanity vision is essential if more concrete sexual practices are to be altered, they vary profoundly as to which practices should be changed. *This is truly interesting to observe because this agreement at the level of the visional and narrative — their shared emphasis on the importance of Africanity — does not prevent them from profoundly disagreeing at the level of strategies of intervention.* This points to something that all comparative practical ethics must keep in mind: encompassing visions influence but do not always determine in all respects subsequent levels of practice and behavior. There are many intervening judgments that have to be factored

55. Kilbrides, *Changing Family Life in East Africa*, pp. 13-19.

56. Aylward Shorter and Edwin Onyancha, *The Church and AIDS in Africa* (Nairobi: Pauline Publications Africa, 1998).

in, such as judgments about needs, relative goods, social and natural constraints, and principles of obligation.

But the plot thickens. Shorter and Onyancha see real analogies between the Roman Catholic sacramental view of marriage with its high valuation of infant life and the Africanity view of the sacredness of procreation. As we saw in Chapter Four, they could have invoked the authority of Luther as well as Roman Catholicism; he too saw procreation and parental care as participating in the action and life of God. But for Shorter and Onyancha, the analogy between the Catholic and East African visions leads them to believe that the Catholic view of sexuality can tap into the high African valuation of children and procreation to ground appeals for monogamy, paternal responsibility, the rejection of the double sexual standard, and the subsequent elevation and protection of wives and mothers. The message that Shorter and Onyancha would send to East Africans goes like this: "In order to protect your sacred children and your divine vocations in procreation, you should alter the destructive parts of your sexual and marital patterns." Shorter and Onyancha are not alone in this strategy. Sarah Ruden, a journalist from Cape Town, says much the same thing. With shocking frankness, and without special reference to the rhetorical usefulness of Africanity, she asserts, "The churches' strict view on sexual morality turns out to be the most realistic response to the AIDS crisis."[57]

The Kilbrides, on the other hand, are willing to settle for a rebirth of responsible polygyny, yet one that somehow might be consistent with the feminist values of women's education and participation in the job market.[58] Before the advent of industrialization, modernity, and colonialization, polygyny, as we saw in Chapter One, worked with its own set of rules and restraints. There is a difference, they argue, between the older normative polygyny and its contemporary debased and disorganized forms. The contemporary patterns are a result of the onslaughts of modernization — mobility in the job market for men and increasingly for women, less communal control of sexual arrangements, and the temptations of converting normed polygyny into informal liaisons by men with numerous women.

The Kilbrides want to build on Africanity to return to normative plural marriage in Africa. In fact, this would not only be for them a solution to the problems of sub-Saharan Africa. It would be a solution to the family crisis of modernity throughout the world. There would be more and

---

57. Sarah Ruden, "AIDS in South Africa: Why the Churches Matter," *The Christian Century,* May 17, 2000, p. 567.

58. Kilbrides, *Changing Family Life in East Africa,* pp. 225-50.

better polygynous marriages in Africa, but there would be, in their view of things, more plural marriages of all kinds throughout the world. This would be the way to handle the strains on matrimony everywhere.

It is beyond the scope of this chapter to solve the conflict between the Kilbrides and Shorter and Onyancha. My goal in discussing them was to demonstrate their attention to the visional level of moral thinking and how this might be important for practical-theological ethics in the fields of international development, women's rights, family, and sexuality. The case of Africa demonstrates the importance of taking the visional level into account — in this case the vision called Africanity — in ways that Nussbaum and Okin neglect. On the other hand, it demonstrates the various ways in which taking account of vision, although important, is never sufficient to gain definitive agreement on policy issues. Both the Kilbrides and Shorter and Onyancha agree that the vision of Africanity is crucial for understanding African behavior, but they also illustrate how a shared general vision is not enough to ensure accord on a common practical strategy. Somewhere amidst the four lower levels of practical-moral thinking, these two teams interpret things differently. Agreement at the visional level is important and influential on lower levels, but progress between these alternative approaches to African family disruption will require a careful review of their respective judgments at the lower levels of moral thinking. Here, the preoccupations of Nussbaum and Okin would doubtless and rightly enter the picture again, but, I would hope, with a higher degree of hermeneutic, dialogical, and religious sensitivity than either has employed up to the present.

It is likely that the strategy of the nation of Uganda and the message of Nelson Mandela have captured a direction that more subtly spans the distance between Africanity and concrete behavioral change. Both of these perspectives combine the high valuation and protection of children, the advocacy of abstinence outside of marriage, the backup use of condoms, HIV drugs, and education.[59] Glamorous and shocking Madison Avenue ad campaigns seem not to work.[60] Approaches that make contact with the fundamental values and religious sensibilities of people seem necessary.

Regardless of the final resolution of this international discussion, this conversation with these feminist thinkers illustrates the thickness of

---

59. Lawrence K. Altman, "Africa's AIDS Crisis: Finding Common Ground," *The New York Times,* July 16, 2000.

60. Daniel Halperin and Brian Williams, "South Africa's Misguided AIDS Campaign," *Washington Post* National Weekly Edition, September 3-9, 2001, p. 21.

practical-moral thinking and the potential contribution of a close relation between practical theology and theological ethics in what I have called practical-theological ethics. It illustrates the complicated nature of practical thinking and how agreements at one dimension do not necessarily preclude serious disagreements at another. Using a richer understanding of practical thinking should help us specify more accurately where the real conflicts can be found and help us discover more precisely how to address them.

Chapter Eight

Cultural, Social, and Educational Strategies

What is a viable world strategy for coping with the ambiguous impact of modernization and globalization on families? Some of you may think that this question is entirely too ambitious. My defense for asking it is based on the low expectations I place on myself for providing a satisfactory answer. In short, the question is designed to initiate a new world conversation and not immediately find the final answer.

From the beginning I have argued that the reformation and revival of marriage is crucial to a world strategy for families. I have recognized the importance of government supports for families along the line of those suggested by William Goode. I fully acknowledge the importance of viable family-friendly economies. Nothing I say to emphasize the importance of marriage itself is designed to detract from the significance of these points of leverage. Government programs and healthy markets are the bread and butter of public policy affecting family and marriage around the world. World peace, as recent events have shown, is also crucial.

These initiatives alone, however, will not do the job. The cultural work of reconstructing marriage is also crucial. This entails, most centrally, the mobilization of the institutions of civil society around the world. Since religious institutions are central forces in civil society, they must be the center of activity for marital reconstruction and revival. This book cannot speak directly for all of the world's major religions. Its goal, instead, is to articulate a Christian contribution to the world discussion and action.

In earlier chapters I characterized this reconstructive task as a complex cultural work. Indeed, I imagined creating an organization pretentiously called the Coalition of Marriage Reformation and Revival. Its tasks, according to my unruly fantasies, would be to do research and reflection on the Western marriage traditions, develop proposals for its reformation and revival, initiate conversations with other world religions, relate religious perspectives to government and market, maintain and deepen marriage as both a public and religious institution, address work and family issues, and promote the emerging world marriage education movement. This is a huge, and many will think unrealistic, agenda, and this book has not developed all of the various dimensions required to advance these tasks. I have concentrated primarily on the theological side of this cultural work, i.e., why and how Christianity is interested in equal-regard families, marriage, the involvement of both fathers and mothers in child care, the centrality of children to families, and a just relation between families and the world of paid employment.

In this chapter, I want to address one small aspect of the agenda of this Coalition of Marriage Reformation and Revival. This is the emerging world marriage education movement. In concentrating on this dimension for a few pages, I do not want to detract from the theological task of this reconstruction nor the importance of deepening and promoting the initiatives of religion, state, and market.

Chatting about Marriage Around the Globe

Almost every morning after eating breakfast and skimming the *Chicago Tribune* and the *New York Times,* like millions of people around the world I start the day by checking my e-mail. Downloading one's electronic communications is one of the new burdens of modernization and is increasingly an experience of globalization as well. Messages come to me from around the world — England, Scotland, Germany, Holland, Japan, South Africa, Australia. One set of messages I get regularly is from a new organization called the Coalition for Marriage, Family, and Couples Education. No more than a few years old, this association is a clearing house and promotion center for the burgeoning new marriage education and communication movement.

This movement is essentially a spin-off of the family-therapy movement associated with such towering figures as Virginia Satir, Salvador Minuchin, Nathan Ackerman, and Murray Bowen. The marriage education movement, however, is preparatory and preventative rather than curative and remedial. Rather than waiting until marriages are in deep difficulty as tends to be the strategy of family therapy, it believes good marriages depend on communication skills that can be learned prior to marriage, or at least before serious trouble begins.

This movement is one sign among many of an emerging world marriage movement. I receive two to four long e-mail communications each day from the enterprising president and founder of this organization. She also relays news and communications from around the world — Australia, New Zealand, England, Norway. These communications not only have to do with the spread throughout the world of the marriage education movement but also with efforts over the globe to reconstruct marriage as an institution and lived reality. I get news about the covenant marriage bill that became law in the state of Louisiana during the summer of 1997 and later in Arizona and Arkansas. I learn about the marriage preparation law that offers premarital inventories and marriage education to couples getting married in Florida and about that state's mandatory marriage education course for high school students. I am likely to read about the community marriage policy developing in Adrian and Grand Rapids, Michigan, and attempts in some English communities to do the same. I hear about the marriage education movement in Australia and how the government there is increasing funds to private organizations for more and better premarital education. I receive news that Howard Markman and Scott Stanley, the developers of PREP (Prevention and Relationship Enhancement Program) — one of the main marriage education programs in the United States — have spent three weeks in Norway teaching their communication techniques to marriage educators there. I learn about Char Kamper, who has developed a remarkable high school curriculum on marriage and relationship education that is widely used in California, Oklahoma, and several other states and also is beginning to be used in other countries. I am told that these marriage education programs are based on research out of the University of Washington, the University of Minnesota, and Denver University — research that is often handsomely funded by grants from the U.S. government. I learn, in short, that marriage is becoming a public health issue and that governments around the world are investing in it as such. I learn about the pros and cons of President George W. Bush's 2002 proposal to spend 300 million dollars on pilot projects on marriage education for welfare and low-income Americans.

Each year since 1997, hundreds of people from twenty countries or more gather at the annual conference called Smart Marriages that is sponsored by this Coalition. Most people who attend this increasingly international and intercultural conference are also hooked to the Internet website of this organization and receive the same daily messages that I receive. Indeed, the website is interactive: people write back, and some of these messages are shared with thousands of individuals who are on the Coalition's list serve.

What does this organization and its global clientele mean for strategies to address the world family crisis? This question can be answered by reflecting on the topic of the concluding plenary session at its 1998 and 1999 conferences. The topic was the question, Is there a marriage movement? It was assumed that the question was geographically limited in scope and meant, Is there a marriage movement in the U.S.? But as I observed the international diversity in the audience, I wondered whether the question should really be, Is there a world or global marriage movement? The group's answer for the U.S. scene was a qualified "yes," and I think that a qualified "yes" would be appropriate if the entire world were the referent to the question. Put more generally, this group is a symbol of a growing tendency to search for cultural — possibly even religiocultural — answers to world family disruptions in addition to, but not necessarily in contradiction to, governmental and economic answers. The Coalition for Marriage, Family, and Couples Education is an example of a cultural strategy. Behind its belief in the possibility of worldwide marriage education is its cultural conviction about the importance of marriage as both an institution and as part of the answer to global family disruption. Obviously, when I speak of a new Coalition for Marriage Reformation and Revival, I am imagining a more broadly conceived version of this American organization than one narrowly dedicated to marriage education alone.

The Coalition for Marriage, Family, and Couples Education is not the only such organization of its kind. In fact, it is something of a latecomer. Before it came along, there was the Institute for American Values, a neoliberal pro-family and pro-marriage organization whose 1995 study titled *Marriage in America: A Report to the Nation* is credited with placing marriage on the agenda of Washington politicians, both liberal and conservative.[1] It is also this organization, in cooperation with other groups, that released the June 2000 report titled *The Marriage Movement: A Statement of Principles* that summarized the need for, and the evidence for, the emergence of a loose coalition of social and cultural movements calling for a renewal of the institution of marriage.[2] And then there is the liberal Washington-based Resource Center on

---

1. The website for the Institute for American Values is www.americanvalues.org.

2. *The Marriage Movement: A Statement of Principles* (New York: Institute for American Values, 2000).

Couples and Marriage Policy that dedicates its energies to examining marriage as a public policy issue.[3] There are a variety of conservative organizations such as Focus on the Family and the Family Research Council. England has at least two research and policy organizations that examine marriage as a public policy issue — One Plus One and CARE and its offshoot, CARE for the Family.

Marriage Education as Supplement to State and Market Initiatives

In the first chapter, we examined two major world alternatives for addressing modernization's disruption of families — the state and the market alternatives. The state (or bureaucratic) answer — symbolized by the Nordic welfare societies and actively proposed by scholars as diverse as William Goode, Dizard and Gadlin, and Richard Posner — acknowledges that the dynamics of modernization are disruptive to families but can be mitigated through the supports of an extensive welfare network, one that would eventually be worldwide. The other answer is equally technical and economic: it imagines a worldwide spread of market-generated wealth to such a degree that families everywhere would have the financial resources to compensate for modernity's family and marriage disruptions. In short, it is easier to weather the stress of divorce, out-of-wedlock birth, and fatherlessness if you are rich than it is if you are poor. Although both solutions contain partial truth, they are limited as general solutions throughout the world and are unworkable without the support of a moral, cultural, and religious vision of the kind symbolized by, although not confined to, the Coalition for Marriage, Family, and Couples Education and the new organization that I am playfully imagining.

The Marriage Movement and Sphere Cooperation

The emerging world marriage movement is not just about marriage education, although that subject is central to it. Nor is it confined to the Coalition for Marriage, Family, and Couples Education, although many of its currents are visible through its range of interests. This growing

3. The director is Theodora Ooms. Address is Resource Center for Couples and Marriage Policy, Center for Law and Social Policy, 1015 15th Street, NW, Suite 46, Washington, DC 20005.

movement for the most part exhibits a cooperative mood among the sectors of government, market, and civil society not unlike what one can find, as we will soon see, in the alliance between the various sectors of society in the state of Oklahoma. Polarizing attitudes that say either government or market is the true source of family salvation are rejected. The contributions of both are affirmed, but they are set within the context of cultural revolutions carried principally by the institutions of civil society such as voluntary organizations, local churches, community organizations, and what these institutions can do to mediate between government and market forces. I see the nascent global marriage movement primarily from the perspective of the United States, but programs both similar and different are happening in other places around the world.

Insofar as religious organizations are involved in this movement, two theological models — the covenantal and the subsidiarity models — are sometimes turned to (although frankly, not often enough) to justify religion's cooperation with government, market, and other secular institutions of civil society. I discussed both of them in Chapter Six and tried to bring them together in a single coherent model. Some Protestants, as I noted, are likely to invoke the idea of covenant, and some religious groups actually use Calvin's idea of multiple covenants intersecting marriage and family. As John Witte points out in his *From Sacrament to Contract*, Calvin believed marriage was a matter of multiple covenants — between the bride and groom; between them and their parents, the state, the church, and witnesses; and between all of these parties and God.[4] From Calvin to the Dutch Reformed theologian and statesman Abraham Kuyper, and on to the twentieth-century Reformed theologian Emil Brunner, the Calvinist mentality has envisioned a society differentiated into relatively autonomous spheres with each having a covenant responsibility before God. Both mainline and conservative neo-Calvinists in the U.S. and elsewhere are developing this model even today and use it to conceptualize various ways in which government, family, market, church, and other sectors of civil society can cooperate without total control of one another. Even in a secular society such as the U.S., where government and market are increasingly seen by many people as having no religious foundations, Christians are entitled to ask from their point of view, what does God will for this sphere of life? Christians have a right to make this inquiry even though to advance their views in the public square, they must often interweave their

---

4. John Witte, *From Sacrament to Contract: Marriage, Religion, and Law in the Western Tradition* (1997), pp. 95, 96-112.

more encompassing theological rationales with various subordinate secular forms of reasoning.

The second classic Christian theological ground for a cooperative world marriage movement is the Catholic subsidiarity model. The Catholic model, as I explained in earlier chapters, respects the fundamental energies of God's created world, especially the cohesion-producing forces of kin altruism in families and the radiation of these energies outward into family networks in local communities. Subsidiarity theory sees government as a God-ordained support and complement to these local energies. In this view, families, civil society, and government should cooperate as interacting parts of God's good creation.

Each of these models can provide Christian theological grounds for a world marriage movement interweaving families, civil society, market, and government. Combining these two models, as I attempted to do in Chapter Seven, is even more powerful. In the combined model, subsidiarity theory's respect for the energies of kin altruism and its stimulus to local families and communities becomes a subordinate part of our wider covenant responsibility to God, spouse, neighbor, state, and market. One gains the power of both the special emotions of kin affections and more universal obligations founded on God's covenant love for all humankind. Such a model avoids envisioning a role only for the state, or only the market, or only for culture and belief carried by religion, or only for the natural affections of families for their own members. None of these reductionisms to either state, market, culture, religion, or kin will sustain a world marriage movement.

It is difficult to detect a functioning theological grounding to the public message of this new world marriage movement. The grand Christian theological resources in the ideas of covenant and subsidiarity are only vaguely visible at the ground level of the movement, even among its Christian supporters. This new movement is, for the most part, a lay phenomenon. Even though many of its leaders are driven by religious commitments, they have difficulty giving articulate public expression to them. Nonetheless, for churches to become a stable and enduring part of this emerging movement, the theological grounds of their participation will need considerable clarification. At the moment, mainline Protestant leaders have little relation at all to this movement. On the other hand, many of the ideas driving it have been borrowed from Roman Catholicism, and for this reason it should be considered a tacit partner.

Signs of the Movement

One of the most intriguing signs of the new marriage movement is the Community Marriage Policy strategy. This is an idea developed over the last decade by journalist and Presbyterian layman Michael McManus. The details of the concept can be found in his widely read 1993 book *Marriage Savers*.[5] From one perspective, his proposals sound trite; from another perspective, and in the hands of some interpreters, they are profound. In brief, McManus hit on the idea of adapting and extending the American Roman Catholic Common Marriage Policy to all churches willing to participate in an ecumenical venture. Most churches in the U.S., McManus concluded, had forsaken their role in serious marital preparation even though nearly 75 percent of all weddings were still conducted by ministers, rabbis, priests, and other religious officials.[6]

The exception to this neglect is the American Roman Catholic Church and its Common Marriage Policy. Of the 142 dioceses in the U.S, 124 implement this policy, at least as recently as 1993 when McManus wrote his book. In other words, young Catholic couples face a common front from their church on the meanings, ideals, and challenges of marriage and the proper preparation for it. Getting married in Chicago in a Catholic church is very similar to marrying in New York City, San Francisco, or Dallas. Getting married in one Catholic church in Atlanta is very much like getting married at another Catholic church on the other side of town. The priests in these places have the same standards, very much the same expectations, the same models of preparation, and impose the same waiting period.

The Roman Catholic common policy has five components: (1) a six-month minimum preparation period, (2) the administration of a premarital questionnaire (either PREPARE or FOCCUS), (3) the use of lay leadership and "mentoring couples" with the engaged and newly married, (4) the use of marriage instruction classes (Pre-Cana workshops or weekends, evenings for the engaged in the homes of mentors, and the use of Engaged Encounter and Marriage Encounter — all premarital and marital programs that Catholics have pioneered), and (5) engagement ceremonies held before the entire congregation.[7] McManus proposes bringing together Catholic, evangelical, and mainline churches to create a "Commu-

---

5. Michael McManus, *Marriage Savers* (Grand Rapids: Zondervan, 1993).

6. McManus, *Marriage Savers*, p. 24.

7. McManus, *Marriage Savers*, pp. 296-98.

nity Marriage Policy," i.e., an ecumenical common marriage policy that would help churches across denominations to develop a united front on standards of marriage preparation.

Ministers from over 147 cities have adopted McManus's idea of a Community Marriage Policy. They have had varying degrees of success. While some communities claim significant drops in the divorce rate, to date there has been little systematic study to distinguish the effects of the Community Marriage Policy from other social factors, although new efforts to study these distinctions are now emerging.[8] Mainline Protestant churches are often the last to participate in this movement. Nonetheless, the movement is growing and is widely considered to be a potentially powerful grassroots effort.

The most interesting aspect of this movement is its extension in some communities to include government, market, and secular aspects of civil society. Judge James Sheridan of Adrian, Michigan, initiated the first all-community marriage policy that included justices of the peace, family therapists, ministers, and the county marriage license bureau.[9] Church, government, and secular counselors join together to encourage many of the same features found in McManus's more church-based Community Marriage Policy.

An even bolder program has been started in Grand Rapids, Michigan. This program is guided by a 49-member steering committee chaired by mayor Bill Hardiman. Four task forces representing different spheres and professions of the community — religion, business, mental health, and law — have been formed and report to the central committee.[10] A public relations campaign achieved a wide community consensus based on arguments that used both the language of traditional religion and the language of community health. Leaders employed recent social-science research by Professor Linda Waite of the University of Chicago and others that shows that marriage is good for mental and physical health, sexual fulfillment, and wealth accumulation of both men and women and that

---

8. A workshop on how to study the success of community marriage policies was held at the year 2000 conference of the Coalition of Marriage, Family, and Couples Education. A report on the methodological problems connected with a study of the Greater Grand Rapids Marriage Policy was given by Mark Eastburg and Fred DeJong of Calvin College, Grand Rapids.

9. Judge Sheridan reported on this program at the June 1998 meeting of the Coalition for Marriage, Family, and Couples Education in Washington, D.C.

10. "Grand Rapids Erects a Civic Tent for Marriage," *Policy Review* (July-August 1998): 7-8.

children of two-parent families do, on average, much better in a whole range of life tasks.[11] In short, the leaders of the Grand Rapids Community Marriage Policy argue that marriage is good for individual adults and children and therefore good for the whole community. Stable marriages, the campaign contended, lower delinquency and health problems, and improve the quality of life of the entire community. Early reports indicate that seventeen other communities in the U.S. are considering starting programs similar to the Grand Rapids model. And there are reports that a small number of communities are beginning such programs in the United Kingdom.[12]

Although the theological underpinnings of the Grand Rapids initiative are broad, flexible, and vague, they are not entirely absent. From one perspective, one detects assumptions associated with the Calvinist understanding of the multiple spheres of society (law, business, medicine, education, etc.), all of which have their special functions and responsibilities — maybe even covenant responsibilities. It should come as no surprise to learn that Grand Rapids, Michigan, is in the heart of the Dutch Reformed Church, the home of Calvin College, and only a few miles from Holland, Michigan, the home of Hope College, another Calvinist institution. From another perspective, one detects elements of Catholic subsidiarity theory, with its emphasis on the integrity of the family and its need for support from government, business, and the institutions of civil society. It is my conviction that Brunner's synthesis of Catholic natural law and subsidiarity theory with a more inclusive covenant theology that applies to both marriage and other social spheres could do quite well in giving a theological account of what is happening in Grand Rapids. Some people involved in the program there actually explicitly champion that theological vision, but many do not.

The Greater Grand Rapids Community Marriage Policy is a bold experiment in intersector cooperation. Marriage there is no longer seen as a private affair. Nor is it viewed as simply a matter between church or synagogue and the individual couple. It is looked at as a personal commitment between husband and wife that also entails a public commitment relating them to the church, government, and several other spheres of society. The experiment holds that married couples should think of their commitment as including several spheres, but it also suggests that these

11. Linda Waite and Maggie Gallagher, *The Case for Marriage* (New York: Doubleday, 2000).

12. This information comes by way of verbal communication from Michael McManus.

spheres in turn should deepen their sense of obligation to each and every marriage.

The Community Marriage Policy movement also has influenced, as we will see more fully below, the state of Oklahoma. Cooperation between the various spheres of society at the city and county levels in Grand Rapids is now beginning to develop at the state level in Oklahoma. A hazy covenant theology may hover in the cultural horizon of Grand Rapids, but is it present in Oklahoma as well? Should it be? Would it be helpful for the faithful of various religions to have a covenant theology available to them?

The Community Marriage Policy movement generally brings together only Christian groups with other parts of the community. Occasionally Jewish synagogues join in. But would it be possible to have a local, and perhaps a statewide, community marriage policy with Muslims, Buddhists, Hindus, and other religious groups included as well? The state of Oklahoma, as we soon will see, is trying to do just that.

Marriage and the State

The rise of the Community Marriage Policy movement is one of the most striking, but certainly not the only, evidence of a new marriage movement. Governments themselves are not only legitimating marriage but some are now beginning to help prepare for it. State family policies designed to encourage natality, support families with children, or shore up single mothers and their children are widespread among the wealthier Western democracies. The 1996 welfare reforms in the United States were directly designed to encourage marriage and the two-parent family, to discourage welfare dependency, and to end decades of welfare mothers depending on the "Man" — a phrase these women themselves often use to refer to the government and the welfare check that comes from its good graces.

But only recently have governments at the level of the fifty U.S. states begun to use the law to encourage, rather than simply to regulate, marital commitment and marriage education. The most striking recent effort was the 1996 Covenant Marriage act first passed in the state of Louisiana, but with variations of the bill now adopted in Arizona and Arkansas. The Louisiana legislation created two kinds of marriages — no-fault marriage which has become standard throughout the United States since the late 1960s and a new covenant marriage. Some say that the new covenant marriage is simply the old marriage arrangement that existed prior to the time no-fault became standard. The standard no-fault marriage entitles the husband or wife to unilaterally initiate divorce with only a short waiting period required before the divorce can be finalized. But couples, if they wish, can freely elect in Louisiana this more demanding covenant marriage. It is, however, not forced upon them. Whereas no-fault divorces in the U.S. generally can be secured if either party declares the marriage to be "irrevocably broken," those electing covenant marriages in Louisiana must take a marriage education course before marriage and wait two years after separation before a no-fault divorce can be granted. In addition, couples can achieve a fault-based divorce if there is evidence of adultery, abandonment, physical or sexual abuse, or felony imprisonment.[13] Other states are considering laws similar to the covenant marriage provision passed in Louisiana, Arizona, and Arkansas. Covenant marriage legislation has passed one house, but not both, in Oregon, Georgia, Texas, and Oklahoma.

The most audacious alternative example of the state getting into the marriage education business is the law passed in the spring of 1998 in the state of Florida. All ninth- or tenth-grade public school youth are now required to take instruction in marriage and relationship education.[14] In addition, the state cuts in half the cost of a marriage license if couples show evidence of having taken a four-hour marriage education course. Couples also are provided a handbook discussing the rights and responsibilities of marriage. Divorcing couples with children must take a four-hour divorce-education course, and charges to file for divorce have been increased.[15] This is the first state to take an active, educational stance toward the support and improvement of all marriages. It is a sign of the growing belief that marriage is a public as well as a private good and that government should do more than simply allow and sanction it; the state should also prepare its citizens for marriage just as it does for the responsibilities of voting, driving a car, and other life tasks. As Elaine Bloom, sponsor of the Florida bill, said, "We prepare children for the world of work. We need to prepare them for the world of parenting and family relationships."[16] Since Florida passed its marriage education law, bills have been introduced in Maryland, Arizona, Connecticut, Kansas, and Michi-

13. Pia Nordlinger, "The Anti-Divorce Revolution," *Weekly Standard,* March 2, 1998.

14. Karen Peterson, "Wedlock 101: Florida Schools May Require It," *USA Today,* May 21, 1998, p. 7.

15. "Florida lawmakers pass marriage prep bill," *Associated Press,* June 4, 1998.

16. Peterson, "Wedlock 101," p. 7.

gan. A bill passed the legislature in Minnesota, but was not signed by Governor Jesse Ventura.

In the U.S., marriage and family laws are established and administered by the fifty states. For this reason, it is extremely difficult in this country to evolve a coherent national approach to marriage as a public good. Countries such as Australia are presently actively entering into the marriage enhancement field. In a recent comprehensive report titled *To Have and to Hold* (1998), the Australian House of Representatives Committee on Legal and Constitutional Affairs is forthright in saying that new marriage legislation should concentrate on strengthening marriage and not just setting the terms of divorce. The report aspires to establish a new national tone about marriage — a new culture of marriage — by urging "politicians, health professionals, marriage educators and clergy to focus on two key goals: to extol strong and happy marriages as a high value and encourage couples to take advantage of effective tools to make their marriages not just more stable, but truly better."[17] This report is urging a significant extension of the already existing national governmental support of marriage and parenting education by various agencies of civil society. The rationale is based on the community-health concept, i.e., strong marriages increase mental and physical health and lower crime, delinquency, and child neglect. Hence, the committee recommended, although did not mandate, national standards of six hours of premarital education based on scientifically credible couple-compatibility inventories and communication training. It recommended that the state should offer couples vouchers to pay for this marital training, and it advocated that government should establish training standards for both ministers and civil authorities who perform marriages.[18]

We should not be too surprised to hear of such initiatives in a Western-oriented country such as Australia. But to learn that the People's Republic of China is considering mandating marriage education is more arresting. With the new market freedoms now enjoyed in China, there also have come new family disruptions. Somehow, marriage education has caught the attention of communist party leaders in that country, further documenting that there is a world marriage movement. An Eastern Orthodox church of the Maronite patriarchate in Lebanon has recently instituted a policy that requires all engaged couples to take marriage education in a

---

17. *To Have and to Hold: Strategies to Strengthen Marriage and Relations* (Australian House of Representatives Standing Committee on Legal and Constitutional Affairs, 1998), p. xx.

18. *To Have and to Hold*, pp. xvii-xxiv.

class setting.[19] Cross-cultural use of marriage education in the U.S. has penetrated recent Vietnamese immigrants. In the spirit of respecting Eastern patterns of indirectness, groups taught in one Roman Catholic church used the Speaker-Listener technique, but did so by dividing husbands and wives into separate groups to talk through some of the issues difficult to handle in more face-to-face communication in that cultural setting.[20]

The Australian initiatives are like the Community Marriage Policies of Grand Rapids and the marriage legislation of Louisiana and Florida; they are all riddled with sanctioned cooperation between government, civil society in general, and religious institutions in particular. Rhetorical appeals calling for different community sectors to support marriage are advanced on several different grounds, but economic considerations constitute the dominant mode of reasoning. Good marriages — so goes the logic — lower social problems which in turn lower taxes, a step that is good for everyone, including business. Hence, the economic realm is implicitly part of the dialogue, and cooperation occurs across the various spheres of society. In all of these models, there are multiple centers of authority and initiative, even if in some cases government provides part of the money. A distinct Christian theological voice is frequently — and needlessly — absent in justifying and explaining this cooperation between the different spheres of life. Christian sentiments are often relied on, but Christian theological frameworks are generally invisible, even among the Christians who participate. Christians need not dominate the discussion in these local movements in order to contribute a powerful and distinctive language consistent with their own heritage.

Oklahoma: Calvin Without Covenant?

The most ambitious state-sponsored program in marriage education comes from Oklahoma. Governor Frank Keating believes research indicates that the high rate of divorce, nonmarital births, father absence, and related issues of alcoholism and drug abuse have contributed significantly to poverty in his state.[21] He is very explicit about the economic as-

19. Zayan Khalil, "Church Marriage Preparation Policies in Lebanon; Church Makes Marriage 101 Prerequisite for Tying the Knot," *Daily Star,* October 19, 1998.

20. Lynn Heitritter made this report to the newsletter of the Coalition for Marriage, Family, and Couples Education, May 22, 1998.

21. Katherine Anderson, Don Browning, Brian Boyer, eds., *Marriage — Just a Piece of Paper?* (Grand Rapids: Eerdmans, 2002), p. 335.

pects of the marital problems in his state. In an interview for the PBS documentary "Marriage — Just a Piece of Paper?" he says, "The first thing and the most important thing is sensitizing the public to the fact that our high divorce rate is not healthy. Our high divorce rate results in a lot of impoverished children and a lot of impoverished families. There is a challenge to health care and there's a challenge to education. . . . So we need a public awareness and public sensitivity."[22] Notice the economic aspects of the argument. Notice too that talk about the sectors of society — education, business, and medicine — begins to emerge in the very midst of his diagnosis. Observe as well that he says something that is strikingly true but widely unrecognized, i.e., that marital and family disruption create poverty and economic decline, both for individuals and for the wider community. Social science research for over a decade has shown that this is patently clear, yet the general public, and especially young people, still seem not to know this.[23]

Part of the solution in Oklahoma was for the state to invite religious institutions into a new cooperative effort with other sectors of society. Keating tells us,

> We also brought in the church community. This is a state where 70 percent or more of the people go to church twice a month or more. Virtually every denomination, the Catholic Church and the principal Protestant churches plus the Jewish and Muslim communities, signed a statement saying that the marriages they perform would require premarital counseling or training on conflict resolution, paying bills, fighting and arguing fairly, and those kinds of things. Again, with no force from the state, but a lot of voluntary persuasion from government and the private sector working together to say that marriage is a good thing, marriage is a lifetime contract, marriage is a way out of a poverty trap. Stay married, work through your problems, and before you get married make sure you have a course in marriage.[24]

But the Oklahoma strategy involves more than government encouragement for churches to do a better job of marriage preparation and marriage support. It is a multi-sector or multi-sphere approach. Education, business, medicine, and social work are also encouraged to support mar-

22. Anderson, Browning, and Boyer, eds., *Marriage — Just a Piece of Paper?*, p. 336.
23. Lenore Weitzman, *The Divorce Revolution* (New York: Free Press, 1985).
24. Anderson, Browning, and Boyer, eds., *Marriage — Just a Piece of Paper?*, p. 336.

riage. There is a great deal of emphasis coming from the governor's office on the idea that marriage education is something that all sectors of society should encourage, support, and use. This would entail high schools, colleges, and universities becoming involved in relationship education, the development of communication skills, and training in conflict resolution. Social workers should have these skills and be able to provide them for others. Doctors too should at least know how to refer patients to agencies that can provide education and training in these skills. The business sector should be concerned about work-related stress on families and do what they can to relieve them.

The Oklahoma initiative is more interesting theologically than it might first appear. John Calvin's Geneva developed a close relationship between civil society and government in the regulation and encouragement of marriage. But it functioned almost completely at the level of church law and the powerful influence that it had over civil law. John Witte shows how the church consistory established by Calvin developed elaborate moral and legal theories to govern the marriage and family life of the Genevan faithful.[25] At the same time, Calvin and his colleagues had enormous influence on the civil law of Geneva governing sex, marriage, and family that was embodied in the 1545 Marriage Ordinance and enforced by the so-called Small Council of the city government. The central church consistory worked "hand-in-hand with the Small Council in the governance of marital matters."[26] The church consistory, which the lawyer-theologian John Calvin both led and shaped, had no legal power; it could not imprison, fine, or exert other legal penalties. The town council could and often did levy legal penalties over a variety of indiscretions and injustices pertaining to sex and marriage. Troublesome church consistory cases were often sent to the Small Council of the city government for possible legal action. But the consistories themselves had the power of stigma, exclusion from communion, penance, and even excommunication. Often informal civil costs such as job loss and exclusion from neighbor associations fell on errant church members guilty of breaking the sex, marriage, and family rules of the church. Geneva's close association between religious institutions and the city state was built on a covenant theology — one that preceded such theories as Emil Brunner's reviewed in Chapter Six. Each sphere of society enjoyed a relative autonomy from one another, but every sphere also

---

25. Witte, *From Sacrament to Contract,* p. 80.
26. Witte, *From Sacrament to Contract,* p. 81.

had its covenantal obligations before God and toward the other sectors of society.[27]

Oklahoma's experiment exhibits remnants of the multi-sphere and multi-sector cooperation of Calvin's Geneva and its various permutations around the world.[28] In fact, the initial similarities between the two justify more careful comparison. First, Oklahoma today is far more pluralistic than Geneva in the sixteenth century. The Protestant denominations in Keating's state, some of which are offshoots of Calvinism, are indeed powerful and visible. But they are not the only religious players in Oklahoma. As the governor said, Roman Catholicism, Islam, Judaism, and other groups also joined into the pact. Second, there is in Oklahoma an emphasis on marital education and skills rather than ecclesial or legal regulations, pressures, and penalties, as was the case with Calvin's Geneva. *The Oklahoma initiative is an intersector and interreligious program that is totally voluntary.* The emphasis is on a high religious and cultural valuation of marriage along with the commitment and communicative competence needed to reach these aspirations. No laws are passed to enforce the program as such. Of course, the state of Oklahoma has its customary family-law codes, but this cooperative program between the sectors is not enforced as such by the state. The churches may use pressure and some stigma, but not so much with regard to marital failure itself but with regard to incomplete marital preparation and the continuing neglect of the conjugal relationship by the relevant spheres themselves. The tone of the various sectors, including the church, is positive and invitational rather than negative, judgmental, or penalizing. Such is the way churches, and many other parts of our society, enforce norms today — by the carrot and not by the stick, by education and appeals to a better life, not by civil or communal sanctions and penalties.

Governor Keating did not invoke the language of covenant to justify the Oklahoma program. Indeed, he used the language of economics. In the terms of Brunner's "psychophysical" analysis of the interests motivat-

---

27. Witte, *From Sacrament to Contract,* pp. 94-99.

28. The most audacious national experiment in sphere sovereignty occurred in Holland during the early decades of the twentieth century. It was initiated by journalist, politician, and Prime Minister Abraham Kuyper who organized the society around spheres or pillars that reflected both religious and political worldviews. These spheres were both to nurture their own traditions as well as cooperate together at the level of government for the common good. See John Witte, "The Biography and Biology of Liberty: Abraham Kuyper and the American Experiment," in *Religion, Pluralism, and Public Life: Abraham Kuyper's Legacy for the Twenty-First Century,* ed. Luis Lugo (Grand Rapids: Eerdmans, 2000), pp. 243-62.

ing the various spheres of life, he used the languages of the marketplace and government to justify intersector cooperation on marriage and family. Strong families are good for the government, the market, and the individual person — in short, good for the pocketbook. One might even say that Keating imposed the language of economics, and to some extent medicine's language of health, on the intimate spheres of marriage and family. He seemed aware that each of the great religions involved in the Oklahoma agreement had their own language, their own tradition, and their own justification for marriage and family. But he bracketed the specific language of the different religious traditions and used a broad, but rather thin, public language of economics and health.

It is entirely possible, however, for the eyes of faith to bring another language and perspective to bear on Oklahoma's intersector experiment. This is the language of our various covenant obligations before God to nurture the ideal values that should govern each of the spheres of life in which we live, including the sphere of sexuality, marriage, and family. Although the language of covenant is a more Protestant language, it has analogies to the perspectives of Judaism and Islam and has been recently retrieved by Roman Catholicism. It is a richer language than the language of economics and health; it introduces the elements of promise, commitment, duty, and response to the love of God and neighbor — concepts and meanings that reorganize and redirect the human interests of health and material well-being. The language of covenant does not displace the language of health and economics, but neither does it permit discourse motivating intersector cooperation to be reduced to that of health and wealth. Through the eyes of the religious traditions that have fed off the image of covenant, the Oklahoma experiment could be seen as a continuation and revision of the pluralistic covenant theology of Calvin's Geneva.

Marriage Education and the Federal Government

Even as I write these paragraphs, the president of the U.S. — George W. Bush — has proposed spending 300 million dollars funding experiments at the state level on marriage education, especially for the poor and those on welfare. Although there have been major initiatives in this direction in Australia, rumors that it might be tried in China, and some gestures toward such programs in England, only a short time ago the proposal of such a program in the U.S. would have been inconceivable. And even today, there are strong resistances to the idea of government, especially the federal government, encouraging marriage. This is strange from the perspective of modern European and American history. The transformations of the Protestant Reformation developed a cooperative relation between church and state that made the state a positive influence in the encouragement of marriage. Nancy Cott in her history of marriage in the U.S. shows how time and again the federal government encouraged marriage — in its policies toward freed slaves, toward Indians, and toward the polygynous state of Utah.[29]

The goal of this proposed legislation is to "finance experimental programs in the states — like education campaigns on the importance of marriage and premarital counseling for people who decline to wed — to find out what works."[30] This possible legislation is being discussed in close association with congressional debates about the renewal of TANF (Temporary Assistance to Needy Families) — the federal government's 1996 bill that replaced the old welfare program called AFDC (Aid to Families with Dependent Children). TANF, in addition to helping welfare poor to break the dependency cycle and enter the workforce, also wanted to "reduce the incidence of out-of-wedlock pregnancies" and to "encourage the formation and maintenance of two-parent families."[31] Jobs may help these latter goals, but many experts believe that more is needed.

This is why the federal government is now taking steps to experiment with marriage education. It wants to find the best models at the state level and spread them across the country. In many cases, this probably will entail experimenting with government-financed marriage education programs run by select voluntary organizations of civil society. In some cases, that is likely to be some form of faith-based institution. It is not the purpose of this proposed legislation, we are told, for the federal government to "run a dating service," to push poor women into "abusive marriages with their boyfriends," or to coerce people to marry against their will. But it is designed to face realistically the impact of modernization, joblessness, and discrimination on large portions of the population and to provide the educational resources and positive cultural supports needed to better prepare people for marriage — especially those who are economically disadvantaged. It is too early to determine just what actual shape this legislation will take or whether it will be successful. It is also too early

29. Nancy Cott, *Public Vows: A History of Marriage and the Nation* (Cambridge, Mass.: Harvard University Press, 2000), chs. 2-5.

30. Robin Toner, "Welfare Chief Is Hoping to Promote Marriage," *The New York Times*, February 19, 2002, p. A1.

31. Toner, "Welfare Chief Is Hoping to Promote Marriage."

to know what kind of partnerships the government will form with the various sectors of society in case the idea is passed into law. But the proposal does bring up many of the same issues and theological challenges that the experiments in Grand Rapids and Oklahoma illustrate.

Marriage Education: Movement or Mush?

I have referred several times to marriage education. There is a marriage education movement that is part of the world marriage movement I have been describing. But what really is marriage education all about? Is it something to take seriously, or just another liberal and upper middle-class luxury that can't really help the masses and possibly not even its privileged practitioners?

Marriage education has been in existence in some form for decades. The Roman Catholic Church has been a leader in marriage education. Its Marriage Encounter weekends that the Spanish priest Father Calvo designed in the late 1960s have now become ecumenical and global and are called Worldwide Marriage Encounter.[32] Since its inception in the 1960s, it has been built around weekend retreats for married couples during which spiritual lectures and personal sharing in group settings alternate with couples writing love letters and dialoguing about them in their individual rooms. In its early days, as many as 100,000 couples a year in the U.S. alone would experience Marriage Encounter weekends. Scientifically conducted surveys of couples taking these weekends show that they are highly valued and widely thought to have helped their marriages. It should be noted, however, that these surveys do not as such demonstrate that these couples do better in their marriages than those who have not been exposed to these programs. The surveys do show, however, that couples think such programs help.

But Marriage Encounter is thought not to emphasize training in communication skills in ways typical of programs based on more university-based research into what makes marriages succeed. Over the last two decades there have been several impressive investigations, of an intentionally scientific kind, into what makes for satisfying and enduring marriages. Three of these programs have been located in major universities and have received large grants from the U.S. Institute of Health and other sources. For years, these investigations have been buried in social-

---

32. McManus, *Marriage Savers,* pp. 171-94.

science journals. More recently, the results of these various programs have been published in more accessible books and promoted by professional organizations and other bodies. These educational programs are being implemented in countries throughout the world, both East and West, North and South.

I will touch on three of these research programs — the laboratory research of John Gottman of the University of Washington, the communication theories of Professors Howard Markman and Scott Stanley from Denver University, and the marital inventories of Professor David Olson from the University of Minnesota. Gottman is a leading grant winner of governmental funding, and since 1979 he has held a National Institute of Mental Health Research Scientist Award. Markman, a former student of Gottman's, has joined with Scott Stanley and worked on the details of marital communication in a premarital and marital communication program called PREP (Prevention and Relationship Enhancement Program).[33]

Stanley, a conservative evangelical Christian, is the lead author of a recent book called *A Lasting Promise* (1998) that brings Christian teachings together with the PREP communication program.[34] As is often the case with many theologically conservative syntheses of science and religion, Stanley's science is better grounded than his theology. Nonetheless, seen from a larger perspective, his synthesis of Christian marriage theology and PREP's Speaker-Listener communication concepts has analogies with political theology agendas that have correlated Christian theology with the communicative ethics (sometimes called "discourse ethics") of Jürgen Habermas — an observation that I will soon elaborate.

David Olson is internationally known primarily for the development of a marital inventory and education program called PREPARE/ENRICH, the first a premarital program and the second a marriage enrichment approach. Olson's premarital inventory is based on national norms developed from giving the test to 350,000 couples. The inventory claims to predict with approximately 85 percent accuracy those couples who will stay together and those who will divorce.[35] It is on the basis of these scientific and predictive claims, whether justifiable or not, that Florida has passed

33. Howard Markman, Scott Stanley, and Susan L. Blumberg, *Fighting for Your Marriage* (San Francisco: Jossey-Bass, 1994).

34. Scott Stanley, Daniel Trathen, Savanna McCain, and Milt Bryan, *A Lasting Promise: A Christian Guide to Fighting for Your Marriage* (San Francisco: Jossey-Bass, 1998).

35. Overview of PREPARE/ENRICH Program: Version 2000 (PREPARE/ENRICH, P.O. Box 190, Minneapolis, MN 55440-0190).

marriage preparation legislation and other U.S. states are considering it. It is also on the basis of these claims that countries such as Australia and England have considered doing the same and that leaders such as Gottman, Markman, and Olson roam the globe selling their wares. Foreign countries have their own adaptations of these programs, for example, Australian PREPARE/ENRICH and FOCCUS Australia, the latter being a Roman Catholic inventory devised in the U.S. but adapted for Australia.[36]

I expect it to become clear someday that, as important as are the skills they teach and their capacity to predict the likely compatibility of the couple, these communication programs help in part because they convey a high valuation of marriage. They help create a "culture of marriage" — a sensibility and ethos conveying that the institution of marriage is important and that good marriages are possible. In short, they take marriage seriously, communicate this to the public and to clients, and then convey hope. For decades it has been shown that new therapies are more effective when they are first invented, partially because their creators have such faith in their inventions and convey this faith and hope to their clients. Something similar may be true with the new marriage education. There is a high degree of belief abroad that they are effective, even though evidence for long-term results is only preliminary.

Although the marriage education programs vary from one another in small details, they are more alike than different. The first point is this: marriages stay together because couples learn how to handle conflict.[37] This does not mean that they necessarily solve the problems producing the conflict. But, and this is the second point, they learn to communicate in such way as to produce more positive over negative effects.[38] In fact, according to Gottman's electronic surveillance of the physiological patterns of communicating couples, good marriage communication has five times more positive than negative responses.[39] The third common feature is ownership of one's messages, thoughts, and feelings. In good marriage communication, each member of a couple is encouraged to express his or her own individual opinions and emotions rather than second-guessing the mind of the partner or ascribing negative motives to the other while defending oneself.[40] Holding or supporting the other when he or she is

---

36. *To Have and to Hold,* p. xxii.

37. Markman et al., *Fighting for Your Marriage,* p. 13.

38. John Gottman, *Why Marriages Succeed or Fail* (New York: Simon & Schuster, 1994), p. 28.

39. Gottman, *Why Marriages Succeed or Fail,* p. 57.

40. Markman et al., *Fighting for Your Marriage,* p. 64.

speaking and showing some validation of the partner's communications is the fourth common element. One need not always agree with the other, but one must validate the spouse's feelings and support or hold one's partner's sense of self-cohesion, even in the midst of serious disagreement. This, in many ways, is what good listening and a good summary of the other's communication is all about; it is what Markman and Stanley's Speaker-Listener technique tries to accomplish.[41]

There are differences between the various schools. Some marriage communicators, such as Markman and Harville Hendrix, believe active listening communicated through empathic rephrasing of the partner's communications is central to a stable marriage.[42] Gottman believes that it is not active listening but, as we have seen, the percentage of positive over negative responses in marital communication that truly makes the crucial difference.[43] Furthermore, Gottman and Markman agree in believing that men become more physically aroused by negative communications than women, and for that reason boyfriends and husbands more easily withdraw or become aggressive in the midst of verbal conflict. In view of this asymmetry between men and women, good marriages, according to Gottman's research, are those in which wives learn to state their negative responses gently and husbands learn to be influenced by their wives' point of view.[44]

But how do secular marriage educators ground their commitment in marriage? Why are they concerned to keep married couples together? In short, why all the fuss about the importance of good communication unless there are additional reasons for the importance of marriage in the first place? Secular marriage educators justify their commitment to marriage on a variety of grounds. Some take a market approach: since 95 percent of Americans want a happy marriage, marriage educators try to give people the skills for, as the title of Harville Hendrix's popular book goes, *Getting the Love You Want* (1988).[45] Others present justifications that are, in

---

41. Markman et al., *Fighting for Your Marriage*, p. 64.

42. Harville Hendrix, *Getting the Love You Want* (New York: Henry Holt, 1988), p. 216.

43. For an exchange between Stanley and Gottman on this issue, see Scott Stanley, Thomas Bradbury, and Howard Markman, "Structural Flaws in the Bridge from Basic Research on Marriage to Interventions for Couples," *Journal of Marriage and the Family* 62, no. 1 (February 2000): 256-64; John Gottman, Sybil Carrier, Catherine Swanson, and James Coan, "Reply to 'From Basic Research to Interventions," *Journal of Marriage and the Family* 62, no. 1 (February 2000): 265-73.

44. Gottman, *Why Marriages Succeed or Fail*, pp. 137-54.

45. Hendrix, *Getting the Love You Want*.

the terms of moral philosophy, more broadly teleological in logic. In short, they argue that marriage is a means to other ends, i.e., that marriage on average is good for one's health and wealth, that it is good for society, or that it is good for both the individual and society. Marriage educators often quote University of Chicago Professor Linda Waite's famous article titled "Does Marriage Matter?" and her more recent book, *The Case for Marriage* (2000); both give demographic evidence that married people live longer, are psychologically and physiologically healthier, have more sex, are more satisfied with their sex lives, and accumulate much more wealth than single people.[46]

These narrowly utilitarian or ethical-egoist reasons have enormous appeal to people in a secular age and to professions that have lost their religious and moral grounding. We should be reminded, however, that these prudential and social-utility justifications always have had some place in the Western religious tradition, although they were never the whole story. Roman Catholic marriage theory has always spoken of the goods of marriage, but they anchored these goods in God's will for creation and saw individual and social good as dimensions of the higher quest to enjoy the good of God. Even Luther and Calvin saw marriage as a social good, but one that first of all reflected the ordinances and gifts of the Divine. Marriage justified as a community health issue can easily be absorbed and reconceptualized within the traditions of both Catholicism and Protestantism.[47] But when this happens, the goods of health and wealth get subordinated to the moral and spiritual demands of covenant, sacrament, and the kingdom of God. According to this theology, God wills marriage for most of us because it is a human good. But it isn't the only human good, and sometimes the goods of marriage must find second place to the more inclusive goods and justice of God's kingdom. And to be faithful, sometimes our commitment to our marriages must endure even though the good things of marriage seem in short supply. *Such a wider theological framework is required if marriage as a community health measure is to resist degenerating into the calculation of costs and benefits on the same level as our reasoning when purchasing automobiles, insurance, and footwear.* Notice that in these

---

46. Linda Waite, "Does Marriage Matter?" *Demography* 32, no. 4 (November 1995): 483-504; Linda Waite and Maggie Gallagher, *The Case for Marriage* (New York: Doubleday, 2000).

47. For an excellent summary of the teleological goods that Roman Catholicism and Protestantism have thought to be a subdimension of marriage, see John Witte, "The Goods and Goals of Marriage: The Health Paradigm in Historical Perspective," *Marriage, Health, and the Professions*, ed. John Wall, Don Browning, William Doherty, and Stephen Post (Grand Rapids: Eerdmans, 2002), pp. 49-89.

mundane decisions, if we don't get what our calculations had hoped for, we are then likely not to buy that product again, or try to buy something better, or allow the product to fall into misuse. If the languages and logics of health and wealth are our dominant, and perhaps sole, justifications for marriage, the same fate will be in store for the marital institution as well.

This is the challenge facing the marriage education movement. It must learn to see itself within a larger context. It needs to think of itself as one important element within a larger cultural work consisting of many different elements. Marriage educators should learn more about the history of marriage. They must come to understand the contributions of Judaism, Roman Catholicism, Roman law, the Protestant Reformation, and the Enlightenment to the development of the modern institution of marriage. They need to comprehend how religion — Judaism, Christianity, Islam, and other faiths — can offer an intrinsic language of commitment that makes marital promises reflective of the fundamental features of the Divine rather than simply an instrumental language about the relative costs and benefits of certain finite satisfactions. These educators should acquaint themselves with how the language of religion can appreciate but also transcend language about the various utilities of marriage. The marriage education movement will not alone save marriage within the context of modernization and globalization. It is at best only one aspect of an emerging world marriage movement with many different features. It is one small but crucial part of a complex cultural work needed to revive and reconstruct marriage in the new global context.

Chapter Nine

World Family Strategies

Throughout this book, I have argued for a world dialogue on strategies for helping families cope with modernity. I am not the only person who has hopes for such an ambitious venture. There are others. And some of these are not just idealistic individuals given to speculation and day-dreams. Many of them are parts of powerful and respected institutions — institutions that have delved into the business of thinking about the worldwide needs of families.

In this final chapter, I plan to review some of these world programs and strategies. I will first sketch the informal and formal stances of such organizations as the World Council of Churches, the Roman Catholic Church, the United Nations, and the small but influential Howard Center. But I will spend most of my time analyzing and critiquing the research, ideas, and hopes of a scholarly project called the Religious Consultation on Population, Reproductive Health, and Ethics.

The Howard Center

Let's first start with the Howard Center. Its full name is The Howard Center for Family, Religion, and Society. Although located in the small Mid-western city of Rockford, Illinois, and under the savvy leadership of its president, Allan Carlson, this little-known organization is at the center of an emerging conservative religious and political world strategy on fami-lies. In its publications, books, and international conferences that it helps organize, the Howard Center has developed a distinctive position on fam-ily issues. It is leery of the processes of modernization, especially in the form of mass society, industrialization, urbanization, the globalization of market forces, and the growing influence of bureaucratic states into private life, families, and small communities. All of these forces are seen to undercut the cohesion of families, homogenize gender roles, undercut mutual dependence between family members, induce divorce and non-marital births, and damage both children and the well-being of adults.

The Howard Center's central strategy is radical. It does not so much propose to halt the march of modernization as it proposes to sidestep it or create pockets of local resistance. Allan Carlson is an emerging prophet for a rebirth of agrarian localism.[1] Big cities, big industry, mobility, rapid social change — these are the enemies of the family from Carlson's perspective. Industrialization by definition undermines the family as a mutually dependent economic entity. Economic dependency is the key factor, from his perspective, that produces family cohesion. Industrialization disrupts this mutual dependency by taking economic activity outside of the home and sending family members in a thousand directions in the pursuit of a livelihood. The answer? Return to the farm. Develop rural communes. Find ways to make the home and family a center once again of economic activity. We need more subsistence farming, more communal living, more home schooling of our children, and more people willing to jump off the speeding train of modernization and market globalization.

Carlson and his followers are not anti-intellectuals and do not oppose all aspects of modernity. Modern medicine is a plus. Excellent education for children, youth, and adults is deeply valued. But, finally, to restore strong families, to retain and enhance marriage, and to raise children in stable environments, the great expanse of our rural communities throughout the world must be revived. Governments through patterns of taxation, rewards, subsidies, and other encouragements should play a major role in the restoration of local communities, family farms, and agrarian communes.

The Howard Center is also pronatalist. The so-called threat of over-

---

1. Allan Carlson, "Third Ways, Middle Ways and the Family Way: The Quest for the Virtuous Economy," an address given to the North American College, The Vatican, March 11, 1996. See also his "Why Things Went Wrong: The Decline of the Family," an address given before Bishops of North and Central America and the Caribbean, January 31, 1994; Carlson's critique of socialist economies and their negative effects on families can be found in "Lessons from the Swedish Experiment," address to the Civic Institute's Conference on Family Policy, Prague, January 21, 1995. Finally, see Carlson's numerous essays in his journal *The Family in America*, especially his recent "The Changing Face of the American Family," 15, no. 1 (January 2001): 1-7.

population, it believes, has been greatly exaggerated and is rapidly curing itself as birthrates plummet around the world.[2] It holds that quite rapidly the elderly everywhere will outnumber the young, and modern economies will be crushed with the burden of sustaining the aging. The collapse of marriage and population-sustaining birthrates is, for the Howard Center, a far greater threat than overpopulation. The Howard Center's analysis of the world population problem is completely different, as we will see, from that of the Religious Consultation on Population, Reproductive Health, and Ethics.

Although the Howard Center sometimes seems extreme in its analysis of industrialization's contribution to the decline of the family, it overlaps with the Vatican's analysis. There are also analogies, as we will later see, between Carlson's solution of returning to agrarian life and the Vatican's principal antidote to industrialization — the idea of the family wage. Pay the family's main wage earner (thought by the Church to be father) a salary that can sustain an entire family and, according to the social teachings of the Church, the mother and children can stay home and out of the efficiency-oriented pressures of market modernization. Carlson is sympathetic to this classical Catholic remedy; he agrees, for family cohesion and economic dependency, that women and children should for the most part be kept out of the marketplace. In his and the Church's view, this is not an act of discrimination; it is a means of protecting and liberating women and children from the family-decentering pressures of market-style modernity. But Carlson is not convinced that the Church's family-wage solution to the ravages of the market is radical enough. The real cure for him is the return to agrarian life and the economic dependencies of the farm. Carlson's critique of industrialization is, in effect, a critique of modern capitalism. In this, he is also in agreement, as we will see, with the analysis of the Religious Consultation on Population, Reproductive Health, and Ethics, even though its final definition of the problem and range of solutions are vastly different than those of the Howard Center.

Carlson makes some important points. He fails to understand, however, that there are at least two steps that can be taken before we fold up our factories and large corporations, move from our cities and suburbs, and return to the farm. One step, mentioned in Chapter One, is gradually to retool industry and corporations to conform to the rhythms of family

---

2. Allan Carlson, "'Be Fruitful and Multiply': Religious Pronatalism in a Depopulating America," *This World* 21 (Spring 1988): 18-30; "The Fertility Gap: The Need for a Pro-Family Agenda," *This World* 26 (Summer 1989): 35.

life — more sixty-hour combined work weeks for couples with children, more twenty- and thirty-hour positions with benefits, more onsite child care, and more mandated and compensated time off when the baby is born. In short, we should work toward a world reformation of the culture of employment so that it fits the scale of families with children. Isn't this an avenue to explore? Carlson ignores this possibility. He also ignores another fruitful direction: the worldwide growth in both religious and secular circles of marital preparation and education — early, deep, thorough, and as intentional as learning to read, write, calculate, analyze, and deliberate. I investigated this partial answer in Chapter Eight. Such a world emphasis on deep and extensive marital preparation would not only be important for the skills in intersubjective communication and conflict resolution that would be taught but also for the deep cultural commitment to the institution of marriage that its implementation would doubtless create. Carlson ignores this approach as well. Carlson is for the intentional use of government taxes to reward family formation. I have acknowledged that this too should be part of the mix — part of the total cultural work of renewing families. But Carlson includes a relatively small number of elements in his strategic package and overemphasizes the plausibility of the agrarian solution.

The World Council of Churches

The Howard Center questions the importance of controlling population growth as a condition for economic development. On the other hand, both the World Council of Churches and the United Nations have linked population control, economic development, and the rights of women and have made these the anchor of their worldwide strategies. This certainly can be seen in the work of the World Council of Churches (WCC), not so much in the pronouncements it has made but in the questions behind the numerous studies it has commissioned. Since the third assembly of the WCC in New Delhi (1961), the WWC has concentrated much of its energies on limiting population, encouraging economic growth, and enhancing the status of women.

Gradually a fourth set of concerns was included. These had to do with more supportive attitudes toward singles, lone parents and their children, homosexuals, and alternative family styles of various kinds.[3] There was

3. Birgitta Larson, "A Quest for Clarity: The World Council of Churches and Human

very little discussion of the growing rate of divorce and family disruption, nonmarital births, their contribution to world poverty, the declining well-being of many women and children affected by these trends, and the need to go beyond the mere rhetorical support of marriage to its profound reconstruction and revival. Furthermore, there was little attention to modernization and globalization themselves as abstract forces with the potential for family disruption. In its various studies and statements, the capitalist economic policies of first-world countries were often taken to task, but there was little interest in gaining a more comprehensive view of the modernizing process, one that takes into account not only market forms of modernization but state and bureaucratic expressions as well. In addition, there was little attention to how modernization has disrupted, atomized, and colonized local, communal, and family cohesion no matter what the specific policies and no matter from where they originated.

Finally, the need to support marriage was mentioned in reports from meetings of the WCC in Geneva in 1966, Nairobi in 1975, and Sheffield in 1981. But generally such affirmations were made in passing as reports moved toward the more imperative tasks of promoting contraception as a condition for responsible parenthood, sanctioning abortion, and suggesting that the nuclear family must not be seen as the only viable form for the Christian family. The 1974 West Berlin consultation on "Sexism in the 1970s" was particularly forthright in calling for the churches to minister to alternative marriage and sexual lifestyles by forgoing exclusive attention to programming for the "nuclear family lifestyle."[4]

But in its gesture toward inclusivity of family forms and its attention to population control, contraception, and the world legalization of abortion, the WCC was more or less oblivious to how modernization was undercutting the very conjugal core of families, whether or not this mother-father unit was located within the context of nuclear families, extended families, or joint families. Furthermore, it neglected how this phenomenon itself contributed to the growth of the poverty that the WCC so rightly and desperately wanted to reverse.

Sexuality," *The Ecumenical Review* (online: www.findarticles.com/m2065nl_v50/20344100/p1/article.jhtml).

4. "Sexism in the 1970s: Discrimination against Women," report of the Berlin consultation (Geneva: WCC, 1975), p. 103.

The United Nations

The direction of the World Council of Churches from the 1960s to the 1990s paralleled the trajectory of the United Nations. Women's issues and population concerns were at the forefront in both of these international organizations. Health and economic forms of analysis were at the center of both organizations' understanding of the worldwide problems of families and their respective vision of a cure for these troubles. In the WCC, concern for the health of women, the control of population explosion, and the overcoming of world poverty constituted the foundation of an emerging Christian humanism — a synthesis of the theological themes of creation and redemption with a concern for a fuller and more actualized life in this world. A concern with the "quality of life" emerged in the UN as well. We saw this in part when reviewing the work of Martha Nussbaum. We should be reminded that her theory of human capabilities and her argument that they should be used to measure the development goals of all societies, even poor societies, were elaborated in part under the auspices of conferences and research initiatives of the United Nations, especially at the World Institute for Development Economics Research (WIDER) in Helsinki, an institute of the United Nations University.[5] Her work, along with that of the Harvard economist Amartya Sen and others, helped move the UN from measuring development in terms of Gross National Product (GNP) to more humanistic measures such as Gender-Related Development Index (GDI) and Gender Empowerment Measure (GEM) that took the differential economic value of both women's work and men's work into account.[6]

The culmination of this kind of thinking can be seen in the Programme of Action issued by the International Conference on Population and Development convened by the United Nations in Cairo in 1994. Among its various guidelines were several on sexuality, reproductive health, and the family. Once again, the issue of marriage — its reconstruc-

---

5. Martha Nussbaum, *Women and Human Development* (Cambridge: Cambridge University Press, 2000), p. xv.

6. For Nussbaum's discussion of the similarities and differences between her approach to capability theory and that of Sen's, see her *Women and Human Development*, pp. 11-15. See Amartya Sen, *Inequality Reexamined* (Cambridge, Mass.: Harvard University Press, 1992). For a discussion of these broader measures of development from a theological perspective, see Mary Stewart van Leeuwen, "Family, Faith, and Feminism in an Age of Globalization," in *God and Globalization*, vol. 1, ed. Max Stackhouse and Peter Paris (Harrisburg, Pa.: Trinity Press, 2000), pp. 221-24.

tion and revival — was noticeably absent from its recommendations. Although this is lamentable from the perspective of this book, the points that the Cairo conference did make deserve attention. It asserted that "gender equality and equity and the empowerment of women, and the elimination of all kinds of violence against women, and ensuring women's ability to control their own fertility, are cornerstones of population and development-related programmes."[7] States should provide equal access to reproductive health care to both men and women. Without mention of marriage, it asserts that "All couples and individuals have the basic right to decide freely and responsibly the number and spacing of their children. . . ."[8] At one place marriage is mentioned, not with regard to its renewal and reconstruction but with regard to the need for states and societies to guarantee that it "be entered into with the free consent of the intending spouses."[9]

As is widely known, various objections were registered from some of the participants of the conference, notably the Holy See, representatives of Roman Catholic countries such as El Salvador and the Dominican Republic, and Islamic representatives from Kuwait. Although the Programme of Action never advocated abortion as an acceptable general state policy for family planning, it clearly hoped it would be widely and safely available when needed throughout the world. The Holy See and some Islamic representatives objected to even that. But more interesting from the concerns of this book were their respective objections to the report's implicit individualism and its occasional attribution of sexual and reproductive rights to individuals outside of recognized marital relationships. On this issue, the Vatican representative wrote,

> With reference to the term "couples and individuals," the Holy See reserves its position with the understanding that this term is to mean married couples and the individual man and woman who constitute the couple. The document, especially in its use of this term, remains marked by an individualistic understanding of sexuality which does not give due attention to the mutual love and decision making that characterize the conjugal relationship.[10]

7. *Report of the International Conference on Population and Development* (New York: United Nations, 1994), p. 12.

8. *Report of the International Conference on Population and Development*, p. 12.

9. *Report of the International Conference on Population and Development*, p. 13.

10. *Report of the International Conference on Population and Development*, p. 145.

Notice that the reservation of the Holy See used the phrase "conjugal relationship" rather than "nuclear family." It is safe to say that the Roman Catholic Church, powerful in many parts of the world where extended families are still prevalent and married couples are still often firmly attached to these larger units, has no particular investment in the highly differentiated, neo-local, nuclear family. But the Holy See appears fully aware that there are powerful forces undercutting the conjugal relation wherever it is located and that policy statements such as the Cairo Programme of Action may help set the cultural context for the further disruption, if not deinstitutionalization, of this conjugal core.

The UN has made momentous contributions to human rights and the rights of children.[11] This began in 1959 with its Declaration on the Rights of the Child and culminated with the Convention on the Rights of the Child accepted by the General Assembly in 1990.[12] This document is a significant contribution to the development of a world culture and legal polity friendly to the support and development of children. Its central ideas emphasize the dignity of each child, the moral significance of the "needs" of the child, and the way these needs constitute the ground of the child's "rights."[13] Once again, this is similar to the logic of Nussbaum's capabilities list; needs or capabilities, as the case may be, are goods that imply rights and must be enhanced and protected by fair legal, social, and cultural environments.

In this and other UN documents, religious and cultural traditions are respected, at least rhetorically, but they are never directly credited as being sources for defining and grounding human rights. Nonetheless, one detects throughout the Convention traces of the Roman Catholic principle of subsidiarity, i.e., the priority of parental and familial rights to raise and inculturate their children and guide their moral and spiritual development. Article 5 says, "States Parties shall respect the responsibilities, rights and duties of parents . . . to provide, in a manner consis-

---

11. The principal human rights documents are the Universal Declaration of Human Rights adopted by the United Nations on December 10, 1948, the European Convention of Human Rights (1950), the International Convention on the Elimination of All Forms of Racial Discrimination (1965), and, for our purposes, the Convention on Consent to Marriage, Minimum Age of Marriage, and Registration of Marriage (1964). These can be found at the University of Minnesota Human Rights Library at www1.umn.edu/humanrts/.

12. For a complete copy of the *Convention on the Rights of the Child*, see http://untreaty.un.org/English/TreatyEvent2001/pdf/03e.pdf.

13. "Children Rights: United Nations Background Note," www.un.org/rights/dpi1765e.htm.

tent with the evolving capacities of the child, appropriate direction and guidance in the exercise by the child of the rights recognized in the present Convention."[14] It also, as does subsidiarity theory, defines the role of the state as assisting, not replacing, the family: "States Parties shall render appropriate assistance to parents and legal guardians in the performance of their child-rearing responsibilities. . . ."[15] Although all of this can be affirmed as in keeping with my previous arguments, the Convention is also neglectful of the issue of marriage, its crisis, its dislocation by the forces of modernity and globalization, and how these trends themselves negatively affect the well-being of children. The United Nations is, on the whole, a pro-modernization international organization. It is also supportive of the market and market-oriented economic development. Because of this, it does not sufficiently submit these trends to careful analysis, especially in terms of how they affect intimate life. It is appropriately concerned with poverty, the ravages of war, the consequences of inadequate education, and the tragedy of poor health care for children and their mothers. But the Convention mentions not a word about the child's possible right to be reared by a committed and invested mother and father who also treat each other with love and respect. Hence, it fails to put the worldwide reality of marital disruption on the agenda. It does not acknowledge that education, health, income, and employment may not alone secure stable and loving environments for children and may not, in reality, be fully attainable if marriage itself is in disarray.

News reports coming from the 2002 General Assembly Special Session on Children indicated that the Bush administration was pressing for participating nations to emphasize the importance of marriage for the health and well-being of children. This strategy should be both welcomed and encouraged to mature. Promoting marriage without effecting marriage reform can be highly disadvantageous to women in some parts of the world.[16] Coerced marriage for a thirteen-year-old girl in India or Africa can end in early births, sickly babies, fistula, and other health problems for the young mother. The bolder move is to encourage both marriage *and* marriage reform, i.e., marriage that is voluntary, just, and appropriately timed, but that also permits the constrained and appropriate use of contraception and the limited use of abortion.

14. *Convention on the Rights of the Child*, Article 5.

15. *Convention on the Rights of the Child*, Article 18, 2.

16. For the report of the United Nations Special Session on Children, go to www.unicef.org.

The Roman Catholic Church

I covered the core ideas of the Roman Catholic Church in Chapter Six, especially its use of the Aristotelian ideas of kin altruism, the theory of subsidiarity, and the interpretation of both of these naturalistic ideas within the Christian doctrine of creation. But I did not fully develop how these ideas constitute the nucleus of an international strategy on families. Because Roman Catholicism believes that natural parents, i.e., the man and the woman who conceived the child, are on average more likely to be capable of long-term investment in the child than all possible alternatives, the Church is deeply committed as a world strategy to the protection and enhancement of the conjugal couple within the context of the committed, publicly recognized, and religiously blessed institution of marriage. The Church is committed to marriage, not just for its own faithful, but as part of its world mission — its social policy — for the good of nations, states, and people everywhere, Catholic and non-Catholic alike. It has a pro-marriage — a pro-conjugal couple — social philosophy for the entire globe.

Good marriages, according to Roman Catholicism, are part of what goes into the well-being of children, the well-being of women, the health of men and fathers, the good of societies, the good of industry, and the wealth and stability of nations all over the face of the earth. The Church's pro-marriage policy is part of its global vision; it is an expression of *cultural globalization*. What tennis shoes, jeans, Coca-Cola, Budweiser, McDonald's, and MTV are to the world of market globalization, marriage is to the moral and cultural globalizing strategy of this powerful and worldwide religious institution. Because the Catholic Church has a double language for speaking about marriage — both a personalistic and naturalistic philosophical language as well as a language based on revelation in creation and redemption — it can express its global vision for the fulfillment of all humans in the first language and use the second language (a confessional language) for its own members. All humans, Catholic or not, are from the Church's perspective children of God and deserving of a full, rich, and healthy life. Marriage makes a fundamental contribution to that fulfillment.

Because of this commitment to the centrality of the conjugal couple and marriage, the Roman Catholic Church has been skeptical of all forces that might disrupt this core value. As we have seen, since Leo XIII released *Rerum Novarum* in 1891, the Church has tried to curtail (not necessarily dismantle) the market forms of modernization (industrialization and urbanization) that could exploit working families. It has been just as alert to criticize the state when its zeal for bureaucratic control colonized and undermined the primary responsibilities of the family. It developed its doctrine of subsidiarity as a way of stating the priority of the rights and responsibilities of the conjugal couple with children; the task of states to support these parental couples without undermining them by taking over their responsibilities; and the duty of commerce and industry to provide a family wage for the primary breadwinner, basic standards of health at the workplace, and reasonable hours of employment.[17] Its doctrine of subsidiarity was a world strategy for families. Marriage was its vital heartbeat.

The Roman Catholic Church increasingly has seen its world strategy as pro-woman. This may be difficult to understand from the perspective of secular feminism, but here is how the reasoning goes. Women are made in the image of God, just as are men.[18] This is now stated emphatically in papal declarations and encyclicals, without the slightly Aristotelian qualification that lingered in the thought of Aquinas. Although the Church has supported the right of women to function in the workplace, when children are born, it has sought to promote the social conditions that make it possible for mothers to remain at home. This was the motivation behind the idea of the family wage.[19] From one perspective, its goals were laudable. Throughout this century, the Church has tried to protect mothers from the instrumentalizing pressures of an increasingly utilitarian wage economy just as it has tried to protect the birth process itself from the instrumentalizing and manipulating pressures of abortion, contraception, and certain forms of reproductive technology.[20]

Critics of the Catholic position have argued that abortion protects the health of the woman and makes her a person, an end in herself, by giving her the power of decision over her body. The Church has countered with the argument that when abortion is widely available and advocated, men pressure women all the more to have sex outside of the commitments of marriage and increasingly treat them as objects and means to be manipulated for their sexual gratification. Along with this has come the man's expectation that it is a woman's right and responsibility to abort

17. Pope Leo III, *Rerum Novarum*, in *Proclaiming Justice and Peace: Papal Documents from Rerum Novarum through Centesimus Annus*, ed. Michael Walsh and Brian Davies (Mystic, Conn.: Twenty-Third Publications).

18. Pope John Paul II, "Letter to Families," para. 6.

19. Pope John Paul II, *Familiaris Consortio*, para. 23.

20. Pope John Paul II, *Familiaris Consortio*, para. 28-30.

or, if she so chooses, to have the baby and raise it on her own, without the participation and responsibility of the father. The Church, with this analysis in mind, is not in the least surprised to see both the dramatic increase of abortions and the dramatic rise in the rates of out-of-wedlock births, not only in the U.S. and Europe, but throughout the world.

From the standpoint of the Church, its anti-abortion and anti-contraception stance is also pro-woman and anti-patriarchal. It protects women from instrumentalization, and it requires men to fine-tune their sexual needs to the constraints of marriage and the requirements of responsible procreation and parenthood. Even though the Church in this last century has now acknowledged the unitive power of sexual pleasure and intimacy and does not believe that sexual intercourse is solely for the procreation of children, it does teach that the bonding power of sex should be expressed within the rhythms of a woman's natural cycles of fertility, that men should be taught to empathize and respect these natural female patterns, and in the end express their sexual intimacies with a generalized openness to the new life that might spring forth from their sexual intimacies. Sexual pleasure, from the standpoint of the Church, should never be fully disconnected from procreation, birth, and the sacrality of the new life that might come forth.[21] It advocates a consistent ethic of life that shuns birth control, abortion, heroic forms of reproductive technology, assisted suicide, and the death penalty.[22] If the world could be taught to live up to this ethic, a higher level of human fulfillment might indeed be achieved, both in this life and the next. Rather than seeing this as an ethic of self-denial, sexual repression, and irrational renunciation, the Church's commitment to Christian humanism views this ethic and way of life as the path to authentic human self-actualization. This is the path for the integration of sexuality into the fullest possible range of other truly significant human goods such as health, an adequate standard of living, education, aesthetic enrichment, rest, and harmony.

I will not attempt a systematic comparison of these four different

---

21. For a little-noticed prediction abut the consequences of contraception (and by implication abortion), see this statement in *Humanae Vitae:* "Another effect that gives cause for alarm is that a man who grows accustomed to the use of contraceptive methods may forget the reverence due to a woman, and, disregarding her physical and emotional equilibrium, reduce her to being a mere instrument for the satisfaction of his own desires, no longer considering her as his partner whom he should surround with care and affection." In *The Papal Encyclicals* (McGrath, 1981), para. 17.

22. For Pope John Paul II's position on a consistent ethics of life, see his *The Gospel of Life* (New York: Random Hou..e, 1995).

strategies. My purpose instead is to show that such ambitious world family programs actually exist and that to enter into an inquiry about a global strategy for families is to venture into a territory that different intellectual and cultural armies are already competing to occupy. The most striking contrasts between the various positions, however, do merit notice. These have to do, first, with the role of religion as a resource for solving the world crisis of families and, second, the factor of marriage as a point of leverage. These two points can be formulated into questions. *Does a viable world strategy consist basically of economic, educational, and health interventions that only need to respect religious and cultural traditions without actively drawing on them as positive resources? And second, does a particular world strategy propose addressing, and in fact reconstructing, the institution of marriage, or can families be strengthened by various supports that merely treat marriage as a private issue not amenable to guidance by public policy whether influenced by states, religious bodies, or diffuse social movements?*

The Religious Consultation on
Population and Reproductive Ethics

I want to conclude this chapter with an analysis of another world strategy relevant to families. This is the program of the Religious Consultation on Population, Reproductive Health, and Ethics. Under the direction of the eminent Roman Catholic moral theologian Daniel Maguire of Marquette University, this project enjoys the funding of several leading foundations.

The project is unique in various ways, but especially from the perspective of the first of the two questions stated above, i.e., the one dealing with the role of religion as a positive resource for addressing the world family problematic. The Religious Consultation believes that the religions of the world *are positive resources,* especially when properly and fully interpreted. Its position on the role of the world religions in developing a public philosophy and policy for families is similar to one that Gloria Rodriguez and I advocated in our book *Reweaving the Social Tapestry: Toward a Public Philosophy and Policy for Families* (2002) written for the Uniting America series of the American Assembly of Columbia University.[23] We argued that a public philosophy and policy for families cannot be built just on the disciplines of sociology, the health sciences, and economics, as important as these may

23. Don Browning and Gloria Rodriguez, *Reweaving the Social Tapestry: Toward a Public Philosophy and Policy for Families* (New York: W. W. Norton, 2002).

be. The great religious traditions must also play a role — in fact, a leading role. To think that the societies of the world can develop their social philosophy for families by forgetting, repressing, or ignoring their religious heritages is an extreme expression of the arrogance of modernity. Yet many of the modern human sciences assume just that. In holding this view, they are an expression of what some philosophers call "foundationalism" — the belief that some extra-tradition starting point in neutral empirical fact or some philosophical *a priori* can provide an objective and irrefutable place from which to define law, social policy, and culture.[24]

The argument of this present book continues the same theme — that such pretentions are wrongheaded, alienating, and finally nihilistic. They imply the severing of culture from history, tradition, and the meanings that they bring to our social existence. My view in this book has been that history and religiocultural traditions are storehouses of classics, i.e., treasures of wisdom that need to be constantly interpreted and reinterpreted even though they also require criticism and revision. But one cannot criticize what one does not understand, and one cannot revise or reconstruct that which one has forgotten if not repressed. The world disruption of families requires, among other things, the memory, interpretation, and reconstruction of the world's religiocultural traditions. I have given special attention in this book to the resources of the Christian tradition on marriage and family, but always with an eye toward a developing dialogue with the other religions of the world.

In maintaining a positive attitude toward the great storehouse of wisdom about families contained in the world religions, I hold much in common with the agenda of the Religious Consultation on Population, Reproductive Health, and Ethics. The Religious Consultation believes, as did the great sociologist Max Weber, that religions are a major force in shaping cultures, societies, and even economic arrangements. It also believes that religions are ambivalent; they contain within their histories great resources for the human good, but they as well possess interpretations of life that can prove destructive of the human good.[25] Hence, the religions of the world must be properly interpreted so that their positive and life-fulfilling features can be brought forth. The Religious Consulta-

24. Richard Bernstein, *Beyond Objectivism and Relativism* (Philadelphia: University of Pennsylvania Press, 1983); Paul Ricoeur, *Hermeneutics and the Human Sciences* (Cambridge: Cambridge University Press, 1981); Richard Rorty, *Philosophy and the Mirror of Nature* (Princeton: Princeton University Press, 1979).

25. Howard Coward and Daniel Maguire, *Visions of a New Earth: Religious Perspectives on Population, Consumption, and Ecology* (Albany: State University of New York Press, 2000), p. 2.

tion agrees with philosophers such as Hans-Georg Gadamer and Paul Ricoeur — thinkers I have used throughout these pages — that religious traditions are a dialogue or conversation containing conflicting voices and themes. For this reason they must be interpreted — and indeed interpreted critically — with an eye toward discerning which insights within them are most abiding and central.[26] The Consultation also would agree with Ricoeur that understanding and interpreting a tradition entails criticizing its distortions in light of more fundamental, recurring, and philosophically testable themes that are also within the tradition. It seems to me that the philosophy of religion that undergirds the Religious Consultation is a synthesis of insights from both continental philosophical hermeneutics and American pragmatism. It follows the hermeneutic tradition in contending that genuine wisdom is gained by understanding the religiocultural classics of a tradition. It follows the pragmatic tradition in wanting to test these deep insights against the broad facts of experience.

But rather than attempting to deal with only one tradition such as Christianity or Judaism, *the Religious Consultation is seeking to ground modern wisdom pertaining to sexuality and family on the collective classics of the world religions.* They have done this by commissioning leading scholars, generally of liberal religious and political persuasion, to write scholarly articles about their respective traditions, discuss them at conferences, and determine whether these traditions contain progressive insights that are generally overlooked. Although Maguire and his colleagues never quite say so, their method is in part analogical, as is the comparative and critical method of this book. They are not claiming that the great religions say identical things about sex, family, and related topics. The claim is more that there are overlapping meanings and analogies between them — analogies strong enough to form the basis of a world culture and strategy.

But two warnings are in order. The disruption of families as seen in divorce, nonmarital births, father absence, and the emotional, economic, and social fallout of these phenomena, is not really the central concern of the Religious Consultation. Its main worry is overpopulation and its contribution to poverty and the contemporary ecological crisis.[27] Its central

26. Hans-Georg Gadamer, *Truth and Method* (New York: Crossroad, 1982); Ricoeur, *Hermeneutics and the Social Sciences* (Cambridge: Cambridge University Press, 1981).

27. That this is the central concern of the Religious Consultation can be seen in the lead article of its "Religious Consultation Report," 2, no. 1 (May 1998) when it announced its interfaith project. Its title was "Project on 'Right to Family Planning, Abortion, and Contraception' in Ten World Religions." The wider range of family issues is not the focus of the Consultation.

"precommitment," to use a term from Gadamer, is to find within the major religious traditions a sanction for the limited use of contraception and abortion as a way to address ecological and overpopulation issues. Nonetheless, in the process of pursuing its main agenda around population and reproductive issues, the project does discuss important matters relevant to the crisis of families — topics such as the possible basis of gender equality in the world religions and the obligations that men have to women. In short, it addresses the question of patriarchy, an issue crucial to the crisis of families. Are these religions incurably patriarchal, or is their involvement in patriarchy to be explained more by how cultural and political forces have time and again captured and exploited them for various androcentric agendas that in their essence they do not in fact support?

The Religious Consultation is not beyond criticism. Its retelling of the story of the world's great religions is somewhat stacked. The fact that it has enlisted primarily scholars with progressive religious and political commitments means that the results of their scholarship have not been tested by dissenting voices. In analyzing this project, I will not make either positive or negative judgments about the adequacy of the Consultation's historical scholarship. I leave that to others. I am primarily interested in its belief that a viable ethic of reproduction must take what Paul Ricoeur has called the "long detour"; a sustainable world ethic must go through, not around, the challenging task of interpreting and retrieving the great civilizational religions — their symbols, metaphors, and narratives.[28] *From a philosophical perspective, the Religious Consultation has repudiated a foundationalist approach to reproductive ethics; rather than going immediately and directly from the facts of overpopulation interpreted through the utilitarian or individualistic logics of the health sciences and economics, it proposes to examine the visions of life of the great religions and bring the motivating and orienting power of their respective ontologies (their views of the fundamental character of being) into the international discussion about sex, gender, and reproduction.* I propose that we learn from this methodology for what it might teach us about a closely related topic — the emerging world disruption of the very integrity and cohesion of families before the pressures of modernization and globalization.

I do have a more profound criticism of the Religious Consultation beyond its inclination to stack the deck in its search for a progressive religious perspective on reproductive ethics. This has to do with its neglect of marriage as either part of the problem or an aspect of the cure. The Con-

---

28. Paul Ricoeur, *Freud and Philosophy* (New Haven: Yale University Press, 1970).

sultation neglects the realities of divorce, nonmarital births, the deinsti-tutionalization of marriage, the increasing absence of fathers from their children, and what these trends themselves contribute to world poverty. The reality of too many people on the globe clearly contributes to poverty, but so does family disruption. This has been one of the major themes of this book and is, for the most part, sadly neglected by the Religious Con-sultation. Nor do the scholars associated with the Consultation investi-gate with care how the revival and reconstruction of marriage is a major part of any world strategy that will lower poverty, improve the lives of chil-dren and mothers, reintegrate fathers into the lives of their families, and possibly even help lower the population. There is a modest amount of evi-dence that family disruption is often associated with males throughout the world having more children than women do. They do this by having children with several women — a trend that doubtless contributes to both poverty and overpopulation.[29] Marriage must be part of both the analysis and the solution, even if the central issue is seen to be overpopulation rather than the disruption of families as such. This leads to the question, What is the Consultation's analysis of the world situation that has cre-ated the reproductive crisis? In short, what is its analysis of the world con-text of sex?

The Five Dimensions and Comparative Ethics

In analyzing the work of the Religious Consultation, I will employ my five dimensions of practical reason that I discussed in Chapter Seven on femi-nism and the family. I argued there that practical-theological ethics is complicated by the actual "thickness" of practical-moral reflection, i.e., the thickness of practical reason. The Religious Consultation is not ex-plicitly doing practical-theological ethics, although its inquiries into Prot-estantism, Catholicism, and Judaism are in many respects examples of practical-theological ethics. Taken as a whole, however, the Religious Con-sultation is certainly an exercise in a practical philosophy of religion. It is trying to unearth the enduring philosophical yield of the great religions in order to identify their practical implications for the fields of popula-tion and reproductive ethics. Whether one's task is a practical-theological ethics with special attention to Judaism and Christianity or a practical-

29. Aaron Sachs, "Men, Sex, and Parenthood," *World Watch* 7, no. 2 (March-April 1994): 13.

religious ethics with inclusive attention to all the major religions, I hold that the five dimensions of practical reason are helpful for analysis and essential for the development of constructive solutions.

The five dimensions of moral thinking or practical reason listed in Chapter Seven were, (1) a visional level conveyed by narratives and metaphors that characterize the ultimate context of experience, (2) an obligational dimension guided by some implicit or explicit moral principle, (3) assumptions about basic human needs and tendencies and how they should be morally organized, (4) assumptions or analyses about the social and environmental constraints of action, and (5) specifications about actual good practices that should follow the proper ordering of the above four dimensions. I want to review the comparative work of the Religious Consultation in light of these five dimensions. What follows is a modest exercise in comparative ethics.[30] I will ask, What is the Consultation learning about the deep visions of life and being in the world religions and what analogies and differences does it find between them? What is it discovering about how the visions, narratives, and metaphors of these religions shape their respective views of human obligation in the sexual field? How do these religions, as interpreted by the Consultation, identify the basic human tendencies brought to human sexuality and reproduction? Fourth, how does it interpret the pressures and constraints of our current social and ecological context with regard to sexual ethics? And finally, how does the Consultation define our present practices, and what does it advocate for their change? What do judgments at the other four levels mean for what we should concretely do?

---

30. The field of comparative religious ethics is relatively new. Its leading books are Ronald Green, *Religious Reason* (New York: Oxford University Press, 1978); Robin Lovin and Frank Reynolds, eds., *Cosmogony and Ethical Order* (Chicago: University of Chicago Press, 1985); David Little and Sumner Twiss, *Comparative Religious Ethics* (New York: Harper & Row, 1978). It is relatively easy to briefly position my view of comparative ethics with these three perspectives. Green concentrates primarily on my level two — theories of moral obligation with a definite commitment to seeing various forms of Rawls's neo-Kantian justice as fairness as implicit in the world religions. Lovin and Reynolds concentrate on a combination of my levels one and four, i.e., cosmogony (a way of speaking about religious visions) and various naturalistic assumptions found in ethics, something similar to my level three about assumed types of tendencies and needs. Little and Twiss concentrate on various moral logics and justifications without much attention to visions or tendencies and needs.

The Religious Consultation's Social Analysis

Let us begin with my dimension four — the question of the social and environmental contexts of families. The Religious Consultation is concerned with the dynamics of modernization and globalization, as I have been in this book. But it generally defines modernization as the global spread of capitalism. Capitalism is the new common social environment for the world. But it is also having devastating consequences for the natural environment, thus making it the new enemy. So too is the money economy that goes with it. In their introduction to the edited volume titled *What Men Owe to Women: Men's Voices from World Religions* (2001), John Raines and Daniel Maguire write, "Global capitalism, a set of economic and political institutions but also of pervasive cultural values, is everywhere more and more revolutionizing the on-the-ground conditions of human living."[31] But then they go on. The reliance on money as the central medium of exchange is the major problem. "Today the global market has drawn the everyday life of the poor into a worldwide money system."[32] Whereas once the poor could survive on subsistence farming, barter, and the exchange of goods, now they need cash. Consequently the poor people of the world must follow the cash. Whereas children once provided poor families with laborers for agriculture, fishing, and hunting, in the new cash economy children cost money yet provide neither helping hands nor dependable support in old age. But old habits and traditions die slowly; when poverty descends upon a people, both emotional and financial needs often drive them to have even more children as a source of security in old age. As countries grow poor and overpopulation sets in, global capitalism enters quickly to exploit their cheap labor, further deepening dependency on the cash economy. Under these conditions, poverty and social disruption grow even greater.

Upon several occasions, the editors and authors of the Religious Consultation follow a contributor to one of its books, *Visions of a New Earth* (2000).[33] David Loy, Professor of International Studies at Bunkyo University in Japan, argues that from a functional perspective, global capitalism works today as a religion. He goes on to say,

---

31. John C. Raines and Daniel C. Maguire, *What Men Owe to Women: Men's Voices from World Religions* (Albany: State University of New York Press, 2001), p. 2.

32. Raines and Maguire, *What Men Owe to Women,* p. 2.

33. David Loy, "The Religion of the Market," in Coward and Daniel Maguire, *Visions of a New Earth,* pp. 15-28.

The discipline of economics is less a science than the theology of that religion, and its god, the Market, has become a vicious circle of ever-increasing production and consumption by pretending to offer a secular salvation. The collapse of communism makes it more apparent that the Market is becoming the first truly world religion, binding all corners of the globe into a worldview and a set of values whose religious role we overlook only because we insist on seeing them as "secular."[34]

But according to Loy and many of the authors of the Religious Consultation, the religion of market capitalism is a failed religion; it promises wealth and a higher standard of living for all but actually divides the world into the powerful who control the economic engines and vast numbers of the poor who suffer its dislocations and become trapped in the spiral of overpopulation and economic marginalization. In the introduction to *Good Sex: Feminist Perspectives from the World's Religions,* its editors report that the eight women scholars who contributed to the volume also "came to see capitalism, a global economic system, as the functional equivalent of a world religion."[35]

This analysis of the world social environment and its implications for the organization of human sexuality has some similarities to the one advanced in this book. But whereas I have emphasized the spread of technical rationality, the Consultation limits its analysis to only one of its two major manifestations — market rationality. Whereas I followed Habermas and Wolfe in speaking about two forms of technical rationality — the market form and the bureaucratic form — the Religious Consultation is preoccupied with only the former, i.e., market rationality. The Consultation seems not to worry about the spreading power of states over the field of sexuality, family, and reproduction. Whereas the Roman Catholic Church, as we saw above, has expressed fear about the disruption to sexuality and family by both state and market, the Consultation seems worried only about the latter. With the demise of communism, the Religious Consultation's critique is aimed completely at the specter of the world domination by the capitalist machine.

But isn't its analysis overdone? Isn't the issue not so much how to break the power of a money economy but rather how to guide it so that

34. Loy, "The Religion of the Market," p. 15.

35. Patricia Beattie Jung, Mary E. Hunt, Radhika Balakrishnan, eds., *Good Sex: Feminist Perspectives from the World Religions* (New Brunswick, N.J.: Rutgers University Press, 2001), p. xiii.

the market can cooperate with government, civil society, and religion to enrich families without wrecking them? Isn't the task rather to perform a cultural work, of the kind advocated in this book, that must necessarily find a role for a more humane market and coordinate its possible fruits with a protective state and a reconstruction of the marriage and family traditions of our respective religious faiths?

The Consultation and the Visional Level of Practical Ethics

Although the Religious Consultation may overemphasize the sins of the new global market, it is correct to criticize it. In doing this, it agrees with the Roman Catholic Church and the conservative Howard Center. The market tends to unleash a systematic utilitarianism that can reduce all personal relations in families and face-to-face communities (Habermas's "lifeworld") to means that can be easily sacrificed to the utilities of market gain, indeed to market greed. The Consultation borrows much from Buddhism's analysis of human existence around "excessive and unrealistic desires," i.e., greed.[36] The Consultation claims that global capitalism, and its deleterious consequences, is fueled by desire and greed. These are the human qualities that fire the consumerism and the utilitarianism behind the capitalist hegemony.

Authentic religion, according to the Consultation, is the great antidote to this utilitarian and consumerist drive. And here the Religious Consultation contains an important insight, one that justifies its long detour back into the world religions rather than simply being content with the economic and health perspectives so dominant in the United Nations and many contemporary nongovernmental organizations. From the point of view of the Religious Consultation, one cannot defeat the utilitarianism of the market solely with the utilitarianism of the health sciences and economic development. *There must be, in the endless chain of means to various human satisfactions, some ground for appealing to intrinsic values — intrinsic goods that can resist being reduced to an unbroken series of utilities.* The Religious Consultation sees religion as the great counterbalance to the various utilitarian strands of modernity. David Loy indicts the current academic claims about the scientific and naturalistic basis of the fashionable rational-choice market theory:

36. Daniel Maguire, *Sacred Choices: The Right to Contraception and Abortion in Ten World Religions* (Minneapolis: Fortress Press, 2001), p. 58.

Yet there is nothing inevitable about our economic relationships. That misunderstanding is precisely what needs to be addressed — and this is also where religion comes in, since, with the increasing prostitution of the media and now universities to these same market forces, there seems to be no other moral perspective left from which to challenge them. Fortunately, the alternative worldviews that religions offer can still help us realize that the global victory of market capitalism is something other than the attainment of economic freedom: rather, it is the ascendancy of one particular way of understanding and valuing the world that need not be taken for granted.[37]

This claim is arresting and one consistent with a theme that has run throughout this book. As I pointed out in previous chapters, the Abrahamic religions (Judaism, Christianity, and Islam) have one highly important common element — *an ontology of the gift*. They share the idea that the ultimate power of the universe is generous and, prior to our own acquisitive efforts, gives good things, not the least of which is the gift of life. Human life, as a gift, is sacred and must be treated as an end in itself that resists all attempts to reduce it to a means. Furthermore, the fundamental mode of being-in-the-world for these religions is gratitude and thanksgiving, generally expressed through an attitude of prayer.

The ontology of the gift is a theme that runs throughout the Religious Consultation, sometimes so deeply as to nearly undercut its willingness to endorse a highly restrained use of abortion. To summarize the sense of the sacred that Maguire believes his colleagues have found in the world religions, he writes,

> We and the rest of nature form one fragile and precious community, perhaps the only one like it in all the folds of the universe. The life miracle happened here and possibly nowhere else. One thing all religions of the world agree on is that we should pause daily and be grateful for this privilege. We don't do that. We're not a grateful people.[38]

A view of life — a view of being — that sees gratitude as the primary response undergirding the religious way of being is what Maguire feels that the world religions have in common. Some religions believe in a god or

37. Loy, "The Religion of the Market," p. 17.
38. Maguire, *Sacred Choices*, pp. 12-13.

even many gods, but some such as Buddhism, Taoism, and Confucianism are "profound responses to the sacredness of life" even though they possess no concept of a divine being.

Nonetheless, the Consultation holds that all religions have their origin in a sense of the sacred, i.e., an "experience of awe, wonder, reverence, and appreciation of the gift of life. . . ."[39] One sees this in Hinduism in the concept of *Brahman* — "the life principle or spirit."[40] Even Buddhism's understanding of the Right View implicitly emphasizes the goodness of life through its teaching that "all things and all people are interdependent and linked" and for that reason must be respected and cherished.[41] Although there is no understanding of a transcendent divine in Confucianism, there is a view that "*peace and harmony* are the ultimate state of the whole universe and the ultimate goal of human life."[42]

The authors of the Consultation nearly lapse into what Max Weber would call "innerworldly mysticism" in their celebration of native American religions. The tones of gratitude for the gift of life and solidarity with the rest of nature seem most stunningly illustrated there. The sacredness of the Land — all of it, both rocks and birds, both waters and the living creatures within — is a widely shared feature of native American spirituality.[43] Some native American mythologies depicted all creatures as first humans and then only later did they differentiate into humans, animals, and other living creatures. In John Raines's summary of their discussions, "All animals are thought to be endowed with spiritual force and must be approached, therefore, with the kind of respect and care you would show a human brother or sister."[44] The taking of animal life was done by native

39. Maguire, *Sacred Choices,* p. 21.

40. Maguire, *Sacred Choices,* p. 50.

41. Maguire, *Sacred Choices,* p. 58. Buddhism, because of its emphasis on the suffering of this life and the need to escape to *nirvana,* may be the most challenging test of the Consultation's claim that the world religions share a vision or ontology of gratitude for the gift of life. But there are those views of Buddhism that see it has having continuity with Hinduism's unitary sense of the divine, albeit more likely in later forms of Mahayana and Hinayana Buddhism, which established this sense through the perpetual life-giving sacrifice of the Buddha himself as a soteriological figure. For a summary of this view, associated with the views of the French historian of religion Paul Mus (1902-1969), see Frank E. Reynolds, "Toward a History of Religions in South and Southeast Asia: Some Reflections on the Work of Paul Mus," *Religious Studies Review* 7, no. 3 (July 1981): 228-33.

42. Reynolds, "Toward a History of Religions in South and Southeast Asia," p. 75.

43. Reynolds, "Toward a History of Religions in South and Southeast Asia," p. 138.

44. John Raines, *The Justice Men Owe Women: Positive Resources from World Religions* (Minneapolis: Fortress Press, 2001), p. 90; see also Christopher Ronwanièn:te, "A Native North

Americans, we are told, with a mixture of gratitude, grief, mourning, and self-limitation.

There is little doubt that the Religious Consultation often romanticizes non-Western religions and tends to overlook the dialectical relation between God's transcendence over nature and immanence within nature in Judaism, Christianity, and Islam.[45] Nonetheless, it does have a point: the positivity and harmony of life is basic to the world religions, and this is quite different from the visions of negativity, agonistic strife, and manipulation that undergird the means-end, utilitarian logics of modernity. The gift of life and its interdependence — this is what the Consultation finds time and again at the foundations of the great world religions. The ontologies of these religions are not identical; that is not the claim. But neither are they categorically different. They have more in common with each other than they do with the power-oriented and commodifying ontologies of an economistic modernity and the disciplines that serve it. The vision of being of the great religions may still be the only remaining resource to break the hold of contemporary atomistic and agonistic ontologies that ignore the sacredness and interconnectedness of life and that relentlessly seek to bend other life to the will of separate individual satisfactions.

Ontology of Gift and Gender Equality

If the world religions in various ways see life as a gift — as something positive that we do not create but receive prior to our individual efforts — what difference does that make, according to the Consultation, to ethics? This, of course, is a question that spans both what I call the visional *and* the obligational levels of practical-moral thinking. Put simply, it is the question of the relation of religion and ethics. If most of the world's religions — and I think most clearly the Abrahamic religions — experience life as a gift deserving the response of gratitude, what does that mean for how other people and the rest of creation should be treated? More specifically, what does that mean for how men should treat women and women treat men?

American Perspective: To Protect the Ground We Walk On," in Raines and Maguire, *What Men Owe Women*, pp. 259-80.

45. For a systematic statement of the dialectical relation between God's immanence and transcendence in the Western religious tradition, see Charles Hartshorne, *Reality as Social Process* (Boston: Beacon Press, 1953).

In reviewing the religions of the world, the Consultation fully admits that for most of their histories and in most of their various cultural expressions, these religions — especially those associated with more complex civilizations — have been patriarchal. Gender differentiations were turned into disadvantages for women. But time and again, its authors argue that there are deeper visions — deeper ontologies — that can be uncovered and developed as grounds for more genuine mutuality between the sexes. In addition, these authors repeatedly tell a historical story that shows how self-serving cultural and political elements in the societies surrounding these religions time and again corrupted and obscured their more fundamental visions. There is doubtless some credibility to their various arguments. In earlier chapters, we saw how Azizah al-Hibri and Adbullahi An-Na'im named Islamic feudalism as the source of hard-core Islamic patriarchy. Asghar Ali Engineer tells us much the same thing. He argues that through later legal interpretations of the Qur'an that formed Shari'a, various cultural and political biases of the *ulama* and Caliphs created a "big gap between the scriptural, that is, the Qur'anic pronouncements, and Shari'ah formulations."[46]

But the authors of the Consultation also echo al-Hibri and An-Na'im in showing the deeper link between Allah the creator of a good creation and the fundamental equality of men and women. Engineer echoes these two writers when he translates verse 2:228 of the Qur'an to read "The rights of the wives (with regard to their husbands) are equal to (husbands') rights with regard to them."[47] He translates 4:1 to read "the Lord Who created you from a single being *(min nafsin wahidatin)* and created its mate of the same (kind) and spread from these two men and women. . . ."[48] Engineer holds tight to the logical relation between ontology and moral obligation in his interpretation of Islam; the "isness" of women's equality before Allah and the "ought" of historical circumstances where the sexes should indeed treat each other equally. He acknowledges that there has been slippage and accommodation to historical pressures, and he is critical of *hadith* and Shari'a when various interpretations that compromised women's equality were absolutized into divine law.[49]

Hinduism is more complex but has a similar story, according to the

46. Asghar Ali Engineer, "Islam, Women, and Gender Justice," in Raines and Maguire, *What Men Owe Women*, p. 114.

47. Engineer, "Islam, Women, and Gender Justice," p. 124.

48. Engineer, "Islam, Women, and Gender Justice," p. 124.

49. Engineer, "Islam, Women, and Gender Justice," p. 124.

Consultation. From one angle of vision, it has been perhaps the most oppressive of the world religions for the health, well-being, freedom, and dignity of women. Few religions appear to undermine the status of women more than these words from the Laws of Manu:

> By a girl, by a young woman, or even by an aged one, nothing must be done independently, even in her own house. In childhood, a female must be subject to her father, in youth to her husband, when her lord is dead to her sons; a woman must never be independent. Though destitute of virtue, or seeking pleasure elsewhere, or devoid of good qualities, yet a husband must be constantly worshipped as a god by a faithful wife.[50]

All this can be found in the ancient sacred texts of Hinduism, and they have become through history central to many of its daily practices. Indeed, as we saw in Chapter Three, the Hindu insistence on the dependence of women on male guidance had analogues in the honor-shame codes of the Mediterranean world surrounding early Christianity. But there is, according to the Consultation, another side of the Hindu story that has been ignored or repressed through the ages, but is there nonetheless.

For Hinduism, as we saw above, *Brahman* — the sacred force of the universe — is in everything. It is in the human self *(atman)*, either in a complete or qualified way depending on the view of particular schools of Indian thought. As the Bhagavadgîta puts it, "He who sees the Supreme Lord, existing alike in all being, not perishing when they perish, truly sees."[51] The Supreme Lord, we are told, is in women, too. The *Svetasvatara Upanisad* (circa fourth century B.C.E.) tells us that the divine is identified with women and girls as well as men and boys. Note the words, "You are a woman; you are a man; you are a boy or also a girl."[52] At this level of its analysis, the Consultation is working at the visional or ontological dimension of practical-moral thinking. But it is also saying, in effect, that religions do not always consistently relate their deep ontologies to the ob-

---

50. Maguire, *Sacred Choices*, pp. 44-45; a slightly different translation can be found in *The Laws of Manu*, trans. Wendy Doniger and Brian Smith (New York: Penguin, 1991): "Men must make their women dependent day and night, and keep under their control those who are attached to sensory objects. Her father guards her in childhood, her husband guards her in youth, and her sons guard her in old age. A woman is not fit for independence" (9.1-3).

51. As quoted by Anatanand Rambachan, "A Hindu Perspective," in Raines and Maguire, *What Men Owe Women*, p. 26.

52. As quoted by Raines, *The Justice Men Owe Women*, p. 7; as quoted by Rambachan, "A Hindu Perspective," in Raines and Maguire, *What Men Owe Women*, p. 27.

ligations of actual concrete practices. Hinduism had an ontology that mandated equality. But historical circumstances, pressures, and self-serving agendas prevented this ontology from working itself out in reality.

The Consultation, it appears, believes that more actual consistency existed between the deep ontology and concrete practices of certain native American traditions than in some of the other religions. Christopher Jocks, in analyzing the Mohawks of the Iroquois nation, shows the connection between gratitude and respect for women that existed in the longhouse tradition of the Mohawk tribe. Longhouse rituals began with the "Thanksgiving Address" for all things on earth and in the sky.[53] Jocks, a scholar and a Mohawk descendant himself, believes this attitude of gratitude for all of nature gave the men of this tribe a special tie with and respect for women. Women were seen to have a profound connection with nurturing and caring for life, and this was so whether they were actual mothers or not. He writes, "Women are respected because they nurture the spirit of the people and remind them of their responsibilities, their kinship with all life."[54]

One does not have to believe that the authors of the Religious Consultation are always correct in their historical and comparative judgments to acknowledge that they raise interesting hypotheses. The most central is the idea that the world's great religions contain variations of a vision of life that elicits gratitude for and connectedness with nature and other human beings, that holds this gratitude stems from a sense of the sacred value of both persons and the whole of nature, and that requires an ethic of respect and solidarity for and with all humans and all other living creatures. Beneath the distortions, the inequalities, and the oppressions of their actual historical development, these religions are ready to be reinterpreted and reconceived as vital inspirations for a more just relation between men and women.

Basic Human Tendencies and Their Environments

Much of this book has been dedicated to the argument that these same possibilities of reinterpretation can be found in Christianity. Christianity has an ontology and a vision that requires an ethic of equal regard be-

---

53. Ronwanièn:te, "A Native North American Perspective," in Raines and Maguire, *What Men Owe Women*, p. 262.

54. Ronwanièn:te, "A Native North American Perspective," p. 264.

tween the sexes. But I have pressed two other arguments that the Religious Consultation does not develop. One has to do with the centrality of reinterpreting and reviving marriage itself as the center of a new family ethic. Furthermore, I have contended that a careful analysis of the marriage symbolism of Christianity reveals its powerful capacity to compensate for certain natural reproductive asymmetries between men and women — asymmetries that human anxiety and sin exacerbate but do not necessarily create. These asymmetries are not in themselves either evil or sinful. In certain environments, they have been productive for human life and survival. Whether they are evil or sinful, i.e., whether they give rise to either premoral or moral evil, depends on additional circumstances, some of which arise from the misuse of human freedom and the additional pressures of social and historical circumstances. But a satisfying world ethic of sex, marriage, and family must take these fundamental natural inclinations into account.

I have no basic quarrel with the Consultation's program of uncovering a suppressed religious sanction for a healthy use of contraception and a use of abortion within carefully defined legal limits when the mother's health, mental or physical, is at stake. Its religious ethic defending the limited use of abortion makes sense theologically and ethically. The Consultation argues that life is sacred, but under certain circumstances the good of some life can conflict with the good of other life. This may happen when there is conflict between the sacred goodness of a fetus and the sacred goodness of the life and well-being of the mother. When this happens, without renouncing the sacrality of life on either side, more mature and stable forms of life must be affirmed at the possible cost of less mature and unstable forms.[55] I am prepared to accept the argument that the world religions are ambiguous on this point and that suppressed evidence showing their openness to abortion can be found. Furthermore, I am receptive to the Consultation's attempt to find a link between the principled use of contraception and abortion and its interest in ecology and the control of the world explosion in population.

But one senses that the Consultation at times lacks elements of realism, both about the nature of human sexuality and about its own complicity with the forces of modernization. In terms of my understanding of the five dimensions of practical-moral reason, the Religious Consultation may be weak in both its views of the basic tendencies and needs that shape human sexuality and in its theory of modern social environments.

55. Maguire, *Sacred Choices,* p. 28.

First, let's take a deeper look at its view of modern social environments. It is critical of market capitalism, although it never completely rejects it or argues for a socialist alternative. But its ready identification of modernity with capitalism and consumerism fails to see a deeper dynamic, i.e., the worldwide spread of technical rationality whether in its market or bureaucratic forms. If technical rationality is the dynamic to be contained and morally guided, rather than simply its market form, then the Consultation must face its own reliance on technology in the guise of contraception and abortion. The use of contraception and abortion as an expression of technological intervention needs containment and moral guidance as well, and the Consultation aspires to do this. But does it see the issues clearly enough with sufficient realism both about human reproductive processes and the nature of modern societies? I think that the Religious Consultation has room for improvement on both of these issues.

The Consultation would do well to develop a strong antidote or countermeasure to balance its reliance on the technologies of contraception and abortion. If religion is a counterbalance to utility maximization, there also needs to be a balance to the technologies of reproductive control. I support the proper use of contraception and the constrained use of abortion. But when contraception and abortion interact with the dynamics of an increasingly individualistic world culture hell-bent on enhancing short-term satisfactions with the powers of technical rationality, it is not clear whether a worldwide increase in the use of these two reproductive tools will actually result in lowering poverty, reversing the growth of the population, dampening the fires of consumption, and limiting destructive environmental consequences. Implementing a responsible ethic of contraception and abortion is more challenging than the Religious Consultation seems to think. Granted, it may help to retell the great religious stories of the world religions. It may be correct to uncover these religions' life-affirming ontologies and their promotion of prayerful gratitude as a fundamental way of being-in-the-world. It helps to show what this means for gender equality and more just relations between men and women. But religions are never simply abstract visions or airy stories; nor can they be reduced to their great narratives plus their general moral principles. In my terms, religions are never simply made up of the first two levels of practical-moral reason, i.e., the visional and the obligational. To be effective, to be real, to have a bite, to serve human needs, they must relate effectively to the remaining three dimensions as well. This means in part that they must find ways to embody their visions and abstract moral principles in powerful institutional expressions and complex, and at times messy, practical rules designed to order and ritualize the conflicting goods of everyday life.

The Religious Consultation does not get to this level of analysis and recommendation in a fully realistic way. Getting practical by advocating a more widespread use of contraception and abortion is not concrete enough. This initiative needs to be supplemented and balanced by a more robust discussion of marriage. Certainly the word "marriage" is mentioned occasionally in its literature. The view of marriage as historically found in a few religions is sometimes given attention.[56] Certainly the question of gender relations and the obligations of men and women are repeatedly brought up for review. And clearly, these emphases are relevant to the question of marriage. For the most part, however, marriage itself and its reformation is not part of the constructive agenda of the Religious Consultation. Furthermore, the link between justice in gender relations and the institution of marriage is seldom directly and forcefully stated in the literature of the Consultation. The lack of interest in this question is troubling.

The institution of marriage has had many purposes throughout history. I have tried to look at some of these purposes within Christian history. Interpersonal intimacy, mutual assistance and protection, the containment and direction of human sexuality into personally and socially productive purposes, the procreation of children, the reinforcement of the hard work of raising them with the rewards of sexual exchange and the approval of publicly and communally established institutions, and the protection of women from the asymmetries of male-female reproductive strategies and burdens. However, the liberal use of contraception and abortion outside of the institution of marriage may serve to dismantle the centrality of marriage in organizing the wide range of difficult-to-order goods that marriage has traditionally tried to organize. We may be seeing that happen today in the worldwide increase of nonmarital births, teen pregnancies, the impoverishment of women who have children without the supports and protections of marriage, and the associated increase of venereal diseases, i.e., both the growth of the number of people who have them and the actual appearance of new types of infection.

The Religious Consultation is rightly concerned with the poverty of

56. Historical discussions of the nature of marriage in some religions are occasionally provided by the Consultation, but generally without further commentary about its role today. See for instance the following: Raines, *The Justice Men Owe Women*, pp. 36-37, 51, 58-59; Raines and Maguire, *What Men Owe Women*, pp. 134-35, 218-20, 223-24.

women, but never discusses the link between poverty and the collapse of marriage, its failure to be reconstructed, and the need to place it on more authentic religious and cultural premises. Too many children, too little education for women — these are the main causes of poverty that the Consultation identifies. And its analysis is accurate, as far as it goes. But the fraying of the institution of marriage is a third, and quasi-independent, factor in poverty for women and children. Furthermore, the Consultation seldom discusses the world spread of venereal diseases, although it does occasionally address HIV and AIDS.[57] But contraceptive protection and education for women are thought to be the main cures; the revival and reconstruction of marriage as an additional factor is largely ignored.

The Religious Consultation is basically oblivious to the archaeology of male-female reproductive strategies. There is no discussion of the insights of the new evolutionary psychology and no awareness of how the world religions had dim awareness of these deep tendencies, as we saw was the case not only in Aristotle and Thomas Aquinas but in the Jewish thinkers Nachmanides and Rashi, the Islamic thinker al-Ghazali, and the Stoic thinker Musonius Rufus. Nor is there awareness in the Consultation of how religious symbols in these traditions recognized these tendencies in males and females, affirmed them as part of creation, but also compensated for them, balanced them, and guided them in their religious symbols and institutional arrangements. They did not always do this as justly and fairly as we would like today, but in their creative moments they nearly always took steps toward higher equality when compared to their social and cultural contexts. These religions frequently regressed, as we have seen time and again. But it is important to recognize that unimpeded and unguided by culture, religion, and institutional arrangements, males can procreate much more easily, are initially less involved in offspring, and have lower investment in children than females who carry infants to term and expend huge amounts of energy in giving them birth. This asymmetry is not necessarily a natural evil, but it can lead to gross injustices for women and children and indeed long-term but more subtle losses for males. These natural asymmetries are increasingly being cut loose from the guidance of culture and tradition and allowed to function in communities rendered less cohesive by the colonizations of modernity.

These differing male-female reproductive strategies are increasingly

57. Raines and Maguire, *What Men Owe Women,* pp. 3, 229, 233. See the special attention Thai Buddhism and African religions receive in connection with the spread of AIDS in Raines, *The Justice Men Owe Women,* chs. 5 and 6.

being guided only by the rational calculations of market and bureaucracy. Left by these inadequate teachers, they may unleash a whole range of family disruptions, if not outright pathologies. One does not have to be a naturalistic reductionist or dismiss the importance of cultural factors in shaping and directing these tendencies to acknowledge their influence on human life. They are tendencies — just that — and not inevitabilities. If I thought otherwise, I would not be arguing for the importance of marriage as a religiocultural work. Nonetheless, realism dictates that we be aware of these asymmetrical patterns and inclinations. To acknowledge them is not to conform to them. *Humanae Vitae,* the most decisive anti-contraception and anti-abortion document of the Roman Catholic Church, nonetheless made a point that must be taken seriously if the Religious Consultation is to realistically press its case for the cautious but free use of these methods of population control. It states,

> Another effect that gives cause for alarm is that a man who grows accustomed to the use of contraceptive methods may forget the reverence due to a woman, and, disregarding her physical and emotional equilibrium, reduce her to being a mere instrument for the satisfaction of his own desires, no longer considering her as his partner whom he should surround with care and affection.[58]

In others words, a world marked by the availability of contraception and abortion had better take the institution of marriage with even greater seriousness. Without this balancing factor, women may be further denigrated, children detached from fathers, and significant portions of society become more poor and unhealthy. Fatherlessness, as we have seen, is one of the key worldwide results of these trends. It is true that one can always entertain dreams that government supports, the education and employment of women, and the compensatory supports of informal communities can make up the difference, but such efforts are not likely to completely do the job if these trends grow at the rates of the recent past. In reality, all of these advances are needed — more education for everyone, including women; more and better jobs for everyone, including women; and reliable and effective contraception and other forms of health care. But also needed are better, more meaningful, more communicative, more adequately supported, and more equal forms of marriage.

The Religious Consultation must also acknowledge the recent, dra-

---

58. *Humanae Vitae,* in *The Papal Encyclicals,* para. 17.

matic, and unanticipated advances in population control. Much of this is a product of reflexive globalization. It has come from the grassroots by women — and perhaps men — through new information from the mass media seeping down to village, town, farm, and the teeming megacities of the world. There is much work still to be done, but it does suggest that population reduction should not be won at the risk of undermining basic institutions such as marriage, family, and religion. Hence, balance and nuance should characterize all proposals, even those of the Religious Consultation. Predictions that India would have a population of 2 billion souls by the end of the twentieth century appear now to be around 600 million too high. Its birthrate is now at 3.0 children per woman, but may be as low 1.85 by 2050. The predominantly Catholic Brazil's birthrate has declined from 6.15 to 2.27 in the last half century.[59] Indeed, as many observers, including the Howard Center, have predicted, within a few decades the world's major problem may be a peculiar form of under-population — two few young people to take care of the rapidly growing number of the aged.

Progress on all of these fronts at best will come slowly, and especially in some parts of the world. But it has been the purpose of this book to say that the revival and reformation of marriage is part of the mix. It cannot be ignored. And this project is the responsibility of all the sectors of society — civil society (including the religious institutions of all the major faiths), government, and the market. The renewal and reformation of marriage is, as I have argued throughout this book, *a complex cultural work*. Although all sectors should accept responsibility for this task, religious institutions should take the lead.

Christianity, as I have argued, has important contributions to make, especially in its profound understanding of the ontology of life as gift, its high valuation of children, its belief that childbirth participates in the divine creative process, its theological ground for the equality of husband and wife, and its powerful marriage symbolism that not only portrays marital commitment as a reflection of divine love but also builds on ambiguous male inclinations and redirects them toward higher degrees of responsibility and parental investment. But, as the Religious Consultation argues, many of the great religions of the world may contain similar insights. These religions have housed the great symbols of marriage in the past. And it is these symbols that require fresh interpretations for the fu-

---

59. Barbara Crossette, "Population Estimates Fall as Poor Women Assert Control," *The New York Times,* March 10, 2002, p. 5.

ture. This will entail a new interfaith conversation about a subject that has been neglected. It will require a new confidence about the role of religions to shape cultures and societies. And it will call for a new capacity on the part of these religions to find fruitful *analogies with one another* — analogies that themselves might increasingly form the sensitivities and working consensuses of the cultures that surround them.

Index of Subjects and Names

Index of Scripture References